T0328623

CREDIT DATA AND SCORING

The First Triumph of Big Data and Big Algorithms

CREDIT DATA AND SCORING

The First Triumph of Big Data and Big Algorithms

ERIC ROSENBLATT
George Washington University, Washington, DC, United States

Academic Press is an imprint of Elsevier
125 London Wall, London EC2Y 5AS, United Kingdom
525 B Street, Suite 1650, San Diego, CA 92101, United States
50 Hampshire Street, 5th Floor, Cambridge, MA 02139, United States
The Boulevard, Langford Lane, Kidlington, Oxford OX5 1GB, United Kingdom

Notices
Knowledge and best practice in this field are constantly changing. As new research and experience broaden our understanding, changes in research methods, professional practices, or medical treatment may become necessary.

Practitioners and researchers must always rely on their own experience and knowledge in evaluating and using any information, methods, compounds, or experiments described herein. In using such information or methods they should be mindful of their own safety and the safety of others, including parties for whom they have a professional responsibility.

To the fullest extent of the law, neither the Publisher nor the authors, contributors, or editors, assume any liability for any injury and/or damage to persons or property as a matter of products liability, negligence or otherwise, or from any use or operation of any methods, products, instructions, or ideas contained in the material herein.

Library of Congress Cataloging-in-Publication Data
A catalog record for this book is available from the Library of Congress

British Library Cataloguing-in-Publication Data
A catalogue record for this book is available from the British Library

ISBN: 978-0-12-818815-6

For information on all Academic Press publications visit our website at https://www.elsevier.com/books-and-journals

Publisher: Candice Janco
Acquisition Editor: Scott Bentley
Editorial Project Manager: Laura Okidi
Production Project Manager: Punithavathy Govindaradjane
Cover Designer: Christian Bilbow

Typeset by TNQ Technologies

Contents

Preface

Computers are presenting you with products to buy, political stories they want you to see, pictures and updates from friends, potential dates, and what diseases you should be worried about. You carry a computer in your pocket, stare at one at work, and consult it for weather, directions, messages, news, watch the stock market gyrate, and check your bank accounts. Passwords are now your most precious memories. In the early days of the Internet, people thought it would enhance individuality. People would talk to each other, privately, honestly. But it has not really turned out that way. If you are honest, you know that your autonomy slips away more every day and that you hang on to the Internet, cell phone, computer, social networking sites, entertainment networks, etc., as if you are a fish on a line. Information about you is held by all the companies you deal with via computer, and they use it to manipulate you every way to reel you in. Maybe, there is a you separate from these devices, and the decisions of these devices, but that separate you grows smaller each day.

Your connection to an outside world becomes ever more mechanized, more mediated, and colored by the medium, people appearing in staged photos, sometimes vanishing in a few seconds, emoji, and ring tones. Do you know those around you? Do they know you? You speak to robots, read digitized facts, obtain your money from screens not tellers, pay bills with plastic (which goes where? is tied to what?), buy plane tickets, find subway and bus times, and take scooters (owned by whom) to get to places on Google Maps. This is not a book trying to alarm you. If you would buy this book, a computer would have already ordered it up for you.

Are there historical events that explain it, or is it just progress as usual? This is a book that discusses a critical turning point, the first great, successful, meaning-altering data vacuuming of your personal data by Credit Reporting Agencies and how that data were scored and you were scored. Except for a short resistance, a few papers barely read, and the self-righteous speeches of a few regulators, this ran its course in the United States decades ago and is spreading to other countries, not quite like a wildfire, but inevitably. Your credit score has been accepted and internalized. It takes your human place in virtually every major financial transaction you enter into to. In the United States, it might as well be you in countless settings.

Credit scoring is the first large-scale example of an artificial intelligence (AI) assessment of each person, used to replace separate identity. It is not a book with villains, however. It is not even clear that the holding and scoring of credit data is bad. However, that it was hugely important to the history of AI seems to me undeniable. Furthermore, it is deeply unregulated and unregulatable, and captive of self-interest and money interest. Along the way, people only acted with ordinary selfishness, business-only pursued profits as capitalism allows, and your personal information was only stolen in law-abiding ways that was believed to improve our lives. Still, we shall see how and why the data and scoring have huge dollops of capriciousness, how wrong they can be, how wrong computers, big data, AI, and the future are likely to be, and how it is spreading throughout the world. And you probably cannot stop it. Even worse, you have nobody to complain to. Computers do not care what you think.

Anyway, here is how it happened.

CHAPTER ONE

I used to have a reputation. Now I have a score.

Abstract

Originally, credit decisions were made based on the three Cs: capacity, collateral, and character. Character was a subjective and reputational determination of the discipline and motivation of the borrower. It was replaced with a credit score by a company called FICO, which data-mines credit histories held by three national Credit Reporting Agencies Experian, Equifax, and TransUnion. This mathematization is supported by the Federal Government, particularly the Federal Credit Reporting Act, a law originally written almost 50 years ago. The CRAs collect our data for free from companies that loan money and then charge those same companies to have it returned, mixed with the data from other creditors, along with scores. Only creditors that want to reward or punish consumers contribute data, but anyone that risks money on a consumer, such as a landlord or employer, can obtain it.

In the middle to late decades of the last century, it was commonplace to say that credit risk depended on the three Cs: collateral, capacity, and character. When underwriting a mortgage the collateral is the home—and the more the buyer puts down on the house, the safer the loan. The borrower's capacity is his/her income relative to his/her monthly expenses, along with the savings to handle bumps in the road. A nice fact about these two Cs, or whatever the language of your country dictates, is that they are relatively easy to measure. Character, though, is a tough one. We never really know one another's character. We know only fragments about our neighbors and less about strangers. However, in the U.S. and in many countries, we came up with something that seemed fairer and more organized: we created the credit report and then the credit score.

The original idea for credit reports everywhere was to establish whether a person kept his/her financial obligations. Welshers would be publicly outed, so they could be prevented from doing it again. In the 1920s, a fifth of all department store purchases in the U.S. were made on credit, so this was a big deal. There were at that time over a 1000 U.S. credit agencies, but consolidation in the 1970s and 1980s would yield three winners: Equifax, TransUnion, and Experian (then called TRW). (Many readers around the

Credit Data and Scoring: The First Triumph of Big Data and Big Algorithms
ISBN: 978-0-12-818815-6
https://doi.org/10.1016/B978-0-12-818815-6.00001-7

world know these names as well.) Equifax was a little bit ahead of the others in terms of national aspirations and automation, and when they were about to computerize their operations, consumer suspicion (remember that quaint notion) prompted the U.S. Congress in 1970 to pass the Fair Credit Reporting Act (FCRA).[1] Despite regular amendments that give ever more attention to privacy and accessibility, as the information age and cyber-crime surge together, the FCRA retains much of its original flavor. We live in the shadow of decisions made 50 years ago. The FCRA was and is the national and comprehensive law on credit reporting.

While the FCRA, first passed in 1970, was the first major law to regulate big data, it was regulating data that was already out there, already being shared, just not generally on computers, and without rules or responsibilities. The law added rules but also enshrined the notion that this was a category of data that could be collected and passed about. Laws in the U.S. tend to freeze a perspective that might hold sway for an astonishingly long time. The FCRA, tent pole of a great and elaborate structure, ratified a number of remarkable positions that have taken on increased importance and dangers since the law was passed. Most importantly, it grant creditors the right to send voluminous records about the consumer to any Credit Reporting Agency (dominated by the big three) that agrees to follow the numerous rules about how to keep, report, and sell such information.

In this age of astounding hacks, public settlements of same, locks, freezes, monitoring, and constant anxiety over cyber-crime, it may come as a surprise to most consumers that they were informed that credit companies would be sending this data to CRAs, and agreed to it. They do this because section 632(a) (7) of the FCRA states the following:[2] "If any financial institution that extends credit and regularly and in the ordinary course of business furnishes information to a consumer reporting agency described in section 603(p) furnishes negative information to such an agency regarding credit extended to a customer, the financial institution shall provide a notice of such furnishing of negative information, in writing, to the customer."

As a consequence, the Federal Reserve created something called Model Notice B-1, which creditors typically bury in the blizzard of disclosures that each person agrees to when they get a loan. It says:

> *We may report information about your account to credit bureaus. Late payments, missed payments, or other defaults on your account may be reflected in your credit report.*[3]

Yeah, you got it when you accepted that credit card. Moreover, you signed it. Now the creditors send in your data where it can be hacked with everything else sent in by creditors. CRAs collect this consumer data from thousands of firms, organize it, and resell it to anyone who can show that they have a permissible purpose, which is almost anyone or any firm that has a financial relationship, in place or sought for, by the consumer. There is no opting out of this data sharing, and the FCRA specifically preempts state law in the key areas. This access to consumers' private affairs is nearly absolute. Even in privacy-focused Europe, access to information about how consumers pay their debts is widely shared—a growing fact of modern life.

Remarkably, suppliers of much of the data, called data furnishers, provide this data voluntarily in the U.S., and have always done this for free. This is not because of the law, but it is allowed by the law. Moreover, nothing is as cheap as free. It is understandable that the CRAs would cash in on this gift. But why do data furnishers (in the U.S.) provide this data? Well, as we shall see, not all of them do, and those that do often only provide part of it. Still, a lot of them furnish a great deal. When I started using the data in the 1990s, I thought the reason was that they had to do this in order to hear the experiences of the other creditors. Credit agencies had a strict give-to-get policy. But then the U.S. CRAs gradually eliminated their restriction about who could buy their data, yet the creditors kept contributing. Having asked several executives of CRAs why over the last couple years, I found their opinion to be that reporting adds to the limited enforcement power that creditors have over consumers, by punishing debtors who fail to pay them back. When borrowers do not pay back an uncollateralized loan, most lenders usually charge it off and sell it to collection companies for pennies on the dollar. As for collateralized loans, the collateral is usually worth less than the debt after expenses of collecting and selling. Hence, creditors want to incentivize anyone who can, to pay their bill—and what they can do easily is put a mark on a consumer's credit record if the payment is not made.

This is more or less affirmed by the CRAs' pitches for data furnishing. An example appears on the Equifax website.[4]

Furnishing Data to Equifax:

Get more out of your customer account data.

Become an Equifax data furnisher.

Your customer data is your most prized possession, and we understand. By furnishing your customer account data to Equifax for inclusion in our industry-leading credit file, your data can create big benefits to your business, your customers, and other credit-grantors.

Help your customers improve their credit.

By reporting your data to Equifax, you are uniquely able to reward your good-paying customers by further strengthening their credit file, and at the same time, motivate slow-paying customers to pay in a timely manner in order to protect or improve their current credit score.

Reduce the potential for overextending credit.

If other creditors are making lending decisions on your customers, the presence of your trade line on their credit report will ensure the lenders get an accurate assessment of your customer's current credit obligations and payment behavior, which can reduce the possible overextension of credit.

One problem with this as the basis for contributing data is that providers of what is called *service credit*, landlords, cell-phone companies, and so on that provide services and expect to be paid back afterward do not need "to reward ... good-paying customers by further strengthening their credit file, and at the same time, motivate slow-paying customers to pay in a timely manner in order to protect or improve their current credit score." Landlords almost never report because they can just evict non-payers.[5] For rent payers to have positive payments recorded, they need to sign up and pay for a rent-tracking company. Utility providers, internet, communications, and many other service providers are large enough to report but are (a) already anxious over public relations and legislative issues and (b) they do not see the benefit since they can simply withhold the heat, stop the internet service, etc. That is a loss for evaluation of those at the lower rungs of the economic ladder or, for reasons of youth or choice, who do not happen to have a history of non-service credit. Services create real obligations and the steadiness of paying on time for services, or having payments made automatically by bank or credit card, speaks volumes about the reliability of consumers. Service credits could well be part of the credit record and can be included in credit scoring, but the data is not forwarded.

Likewise, emergency lending, pawn-shop loans, pay-day loans, emergency personal loans, and so on—these are reported to their own CRAs but not to the national CRAs. It is understandable because such loans are typically collateralized by goods or the next paycheck. Yet the emergency loan companies, who charge astronomical rates (if figured annually), do obtain both standard and emergency credit data to inform who they should lend to. In addition, it goes without saying that all the things people buy with cash are likewise not being sent to CRAs. Of course, because there is usually some electronic trace of such payments, many consumer firms control this data, at least the fragment they see. But they probably do not share it (except with hackers).

Whether to hear about welshers before lending or to punish late-payers, both rationales explain a key fact that has profound implications: the great majority of data furnishers in the U.S. are companies that rent money to people as a business. Even among that group, those companies only report what they think is in their interest to report. For instance, these companies have lately mostly ceased reporting how much people pay of their credit card debt each month, though this would tell us something profoundly relevant to new applications for debt or services: are they falling behind, catching up, or just using their credit cards instead of currency? They stopped reporting the data to prevent competitors from finding out and making a play for their most profitable customers, but it makes the point that data moves from here to there to serve the goals of the agents who transmit it.

The sequential dates of the CRAs going national, the FCRA being passed, the Information Age developing, and credit scoring are the key to understanding how things came to their present state. The FCRA and the flow of voluntary data to credit agencies both happened before hyper-digitization made data ubiquitous and liquid. In the last two decades, privacy anxiety has skyrocketed as constant hacks and identity theft have revealed how easily privacy is forfeited now: data can be copied and passed on to anyone without cost. However, these dangers developed after the die was cast. The FCRA guaranteeing intrusion of consumers' privacy may run counter to the spirit of laws being made today (in the U.S. and Europe at least), whose goals at least appear to include protection of consumers' privacy. But do not expect it to change. The FCRA is baked into the U.S. financial system, and something like it in many national systems, and underpins the basic technological structure of commerce. Almost nobody even understands that it could be changed or that it innately threatens privacy. New laws give consumers the right to opt out of the system, but given how things have developed, that requires a sacrifice by consumers that, on balance, they are not willing to make. Consumers are required to provide credit data and scores to rent, work, get a cell phone, and borrow for a home; turning that off is tantamount to going off the grid. We are literally locked in place by technological traces of our behavior. For instance, most of us allow Google to know our whereabouts at all times. Without that, our maps will not work.

The reach of the Information Age is extended by artificial intelligence (AI) because computerization also made analytics of this data possible, hardly a news flash today. But credit scoring was revolutionary when Fair and Isaac started tinkering with credit scores in the 1950s, and ultimately resulted in a whole-sale reinterpretation of credit data in the 1980s when FICO scores became regularly sold by the CRAs to accompany credit reports. Credit scores started with a sensible idea that is still a sensible idea: all this data and the point of collecting it were not really to punish welshers but to make good loans or agreements going forward. Thus, FICO's models essentially data-mine 10 years or more of information from each credit report for anything that affects the possibility that a borrower will go late on a bill within 2 years, turning each credit report into a delinquency probability score between 300 and 850. FICO scores really do not care or even have views about character; they are computer models that support the decision-making process of whoever acquires the credit reports and credit scores. Credit scores were a new use of technology, turning our familiar and human understanding of people into something both alien and effective.

It turns out that the most important clues to future delinquency (and most financial breakdowns) are not missed bills, though that is still a bad signal, but indicators that a consumer has been living within their means for a long period. Whatever we thought character meant has morphed. The new thing, which might be called liquidity over time, is not identical to income, with which credit scores are only slightly correlated. It is a combination of age of credit accounts, limits on credit (particularly revolving cards which are moved up as customers demonstrate repayment habits), payment of balances, lack of credit searching, and a host of related details, which all in their way make a kind of sense but do not in most cases guarantee a failure of intent or moral lapse. Furthermore, it all comes together in a bundle which one would not arrive at through intuition. The truth is that credit scores work better predicting delinquency and car accidents than any effort to diagnose character and have long outrun in complexity the computer engineers (like me) who supposedly create them.

Credit scores have lasted because they work. They are loosely tied to character but they work well predicting how classes of new borrowers will behave in their credit practices.

Of course, they work whether FICO, their originator, makes the model or not. They are nothing but computer models that relate future repayment probability to past details contained in credit reports. Yet, in the U.S., credit scores are and remain largely the domain of the FICO company. This is because many creditors, particularly ones that securitize their receivables, have standardized on the use of FICO. They deem it too much trouble to change scoring models, since different models give slightly different answers. The CRAs each have a license to produce FICO out of their data, sharing the profits on credit scores with FICO. While FICO's lock on scoring annoys the CRAs no end, and the three have again and again unsuccessfully tried to challenge the FICO score with their own shared model called Vantage, the need for a credit score has nonetheless helped to make them a joint monopoly: it is too hard for a new entrant to collect enough data to run the FICO score. Moreover, no major creditor will act without one.

FICO scores are particularly interesting to me, and hopefully to you, because they were the first large-scale victory for AI and the Algocracy,[6] a term for how computer-supported algorithms, using digital recordings of people, have replaced human decisions. FICO scores control tens of millions of potential borrowers every year, using data collected by them as they go about their business largely unconscious of being tracked. FICO holds the first trophy in this war, but not the last. It is commonplace now to expect algorithmic interpretation of our facial features, voices, auto-traffic, dining experience, purchases, voting, recidivism, on and on, and it all started with credit scores. Even though credit scores are relatively simple, though, essentially nobody really knows why or what about them works or even what working means. This is even less true for scores and AI that have followed. They work because they work—usually—until some self-driving car kills someone. But then there are 40,000 or so vehicular deaths in the U.S. each year anyway. Are a handful of deaths by algorithms such a big deal?

These algorithms do not work perfectly, but they often work better than individuals using their judgment, and they will be everywhere we turn.

In the U.S., and now being copied throughout the world, the first large battle of computer and identity was credit scoring. (Won by computer.) If we were even going to put our foot down about data kept about us or about its use, it had to happen with that first law that enabled collection of so much information, the FCRA. But we did not. We have regulated it, which means we have accepted it. As we discuss this supposedly regulated industry that came early to computerization and was so key to commerce in this most commercial of nations, we will be mindful that we are describing the largely completed computer terraforming of a once very human matter: reputation—replaced by a score.

Endnotes

[1] The Federal Trade Commission makes a copy of the Fair Credit Reporting Act (FCRA), as amended over the years, available in PDF form at www.ftc.gov/system/files/545a_fair-credit-reporting-act-0918.pdf. I last reviewed this on July 13, 2019.

[2] Taken from the FTC copy of the FCRA, provided by PDF, at https://www.ftc.gov/system/files/545a_fair-credit-reporting-act-0918.pdf. I last reviewed this on August 15, 2019.

[3] The language from *Model Notice B-1* was taken from Cornell's *Legal Information* Institute at https://www.law.cornell.edu/cfr/text/12/appendix-B_to_part_222. I reviewed the site on August 15, 2019.

[4] The Equifax pitch to data furnishers, the list of creditors who can give them consumer data is at www.equifax.com/business/data-furnishers/. I last reviewed this material on July 10. 2019.

[5] An involved article about the lack of rent-reporting to CRAs and how consumers can mostly pay to have the data sent in is provided by *NerdWallet* at www.NerdWallet.com/blog/finance/credit-report-rent-payments-incorporated/. It was written by Ben O'Shea on June 18, 2019 and reviewed last by me on July 10, 2019.

[6] Regarding the Algocracy, it is orienting to watch a *YouTube Ted Talk* by Peter Hass published on December 15, 2017. I last watched the video on July 9, 2019, at www.youtube.com/watch?v=TRzBk_KuIaM.

CHAPTER TWO

The credit industry in the United States

Abstract

Although banks tend to be competitive, the three Credit Reporting Agencies Experian, Equifax, and TransUnion have dominated credit data collection and reporting in the U.S. for 30 years, though the three companies all started well before that and consolidated to their present national positions. Furthermore, the laws they live by have been relatively stable since the Federal Credit Reporting Act (FCRA) was passed in 1970. The FCRA has had two key regulators, the Federal Trade Commission and, since Dodd Frank passed, the Consumer Finance Protection Board, neither of which do much to reign in the CRAs. The CRAs share a lobbying group, which represents their common interests and publishes a manual of how creditors report to CRAs and handle credit disputes. Only money-renters contribute data to CRAs. Cell phone companies, cable companies, and landlords could report but generally they do not.

Banks in the United States are chartered and highly regulated. The largest U.S. banks, all household names, go way back: JPMorgan Chase (1914), Bank of America (1930 a key date), Wells Fargo (1852), Citigroup (1812), and Goldman Sachs (1869). Yes, there are some giants that seem to have lasted forever; but they compete vigorously, have broken up and reformed, have thousands of direct competitors, and until the financial crisis, new banks formed at a rate of 100 per year. Far more stable in the last 30 years or so, in this country, is the credit industry: there has been neither alteration of the major players (Equifax, TransUnion, and Experian) nor major change in the ways they do business in nearly 50 years, since the passage of the Fair Credit Reporting Act in 1970. In some other countries there are even fewer major credit reporting agencies: Germany, the world's fourth largest economy, has only one, called Shufa. Data organizations are famous in the Information Age for their tendency to monopoly. It is in many ways a stroke of luck that three different companies essentially went national in the 1980s, at the commercial beginning of the Information Age, and have sustained a continuous triopoly since.

Credit Data and Scoring: The First Triumph of Big Data and Big Algorithms
ISBN: 978-0-12-818815-6
https://doi.org/10.1016/B978-0-12-818815-6.00002-9

Equifax began in a Tennessee grocery store in 1898. The proprietor compiled a list of customers he considered to be credit-worthy and distributed that list to other business owners for a fee. The business grew and took the name Retail Credit, Inc. By 1920, the company had 37 branch offices throughout North America already on its way to being the national CRA we see today.[1] In 1974, it ceased allowing investigators to misrepresent themselves and their motives when out collecting information. In the early 1990s, Equifax (the name it took in 1979, derived from equitable factual information) stopped using credit data for direct marketing purposes or to categorize consumers based on their buying habits. By 1986, the company deployed data on 150 million consumers and by 1987 Equifax operated in all 50 states.

Experian[2] may go back nearly 200 years. According to a very colorful history available from the company. What I believe to be reliably true is that the company was established in the United States as TRW Information Systems and Services Inc., a subsidiary of TRW Inc., when it acquired a company called Credit Data in 1968. Credit Data was in the credit business but not a behemoth. By the mid-1980s, the consumer services part of TRW held the credit histories of 90 million American consumers. In November 1996, TRW sold the unit, as Experian, to two Boston private equity firms: Bain Capital and Thomas H. Lee Partner, who resold it a month later to The Great Universal Stores Limited in the UK, which seems to have had virtually no effect on the U.S. business but may have helped Experian take an international point of view.

TransUnion is the most recent national CRA. It was created in 1968 as the parent holding company of Union Tank Car Company, a railcar leasing operation. In 1969, it acquired the Credit Bureau of Cook County (CBCC), which maintained 3.6 million card files in 400 seven-drawer cabinets. Through constant and no-nonsense expansion of computerization and acquisitions, it assembled a national register of virtually all national consumers. By 1988, TransUnion maintained consumer credit data in all 50 states. When I hit my own stride in collecting credit data, in 1996, Trans Union was the Chicago CRA, indistinguishable from the other two, perhaps with a Midwest focus that my company did not really concern itself with. In 2005, the company was spun off from its parent, Marmon Group, and went public on the NYSE on June 25, 2015. Despite a list of activities on their website, in my U.S. experience, they are essentially unchanged from 1996 to the present, and probably they go back to 1988—so only 30 years for TU.

These three companies sell data to, and receive inquiries from, creditors all around the country. They have a file and sell a file on most Americans. The Bureaus (CRAs) are also keepers of history, even for creditors that go out of business. In addition, for both furnishers and buyers of data, they have the machinery to perform the legal duties of holding and selling all this information—for instance, they can show consumers what is available about them. Data from the major main stream is sent in regular cycles, usually monthly, to the national CRAs, according to directions from the Consumer Data Industry Association (CDIA), the trade association of the CRAs. The CDIA is an interesting organization. When I worked a regular day job, I would go to the CDIA when I wanted to negotiate with all three CRAs together. Here is text from their website: [3]

ROLES

Consumer Data Industry Association (CDIA)

An international trade association representing the consumer credit, mortgage reporting, employment and tenant screening, and collection service industries. Headquartered in Washington, DC, CDIA provides legislative assistance and a lobbying function to its members and works with the consumer reporting agencies to establish standards for the consumer reporting industry.

For more information about CDIA, visit their website at www.cdiaonline.org.

Consumer Reporting Agencies

Individual companies that collect, store, maintain, and distribute information on consumer credit history. For more information about the agencies, visit their websites at:

www.equifax.com

www.experian.com

www.innovis.com

www.transunion.com

Metro 2 Format Task Force

Despite the competitive and organizational barriers within the credit industry, the consumer reporting agencies continue to work together to develop, maintain, and enhance an industry-standard reporting format. The task force's mission is to provide a standardized method for the reporting of accurate, complete, and timely data. The Metro 2 Format Task Force comprises representatives from Equifax, Experian, Innovis, and TransUnion and is supported by the CDIA.

For information specific to data reporting, click on the Metro 2 option at www.cdiaonline.org.

One line of this is oddly defensive. "Despite the competitive and organizational barriers within the credit industry ..." I assume they are instinctively pushing back on the same notion that occurred to me, that there really is not all that much in the way of differences, or barriers, between these three companies. They are identical, and identical in their cooperation with FICO to vend credit scores based on whatever snapshot of data they provide. As we shall see, they act as one in accommodations made with governments and creditors.

For reasons I do not fully understand, and it may just be a kind of dust thrown up to obscure the seeming collusion between them, the communications of the CDIA regularly treat the three main CRAs as equivalent to a company called Innovis, which almost but never quite became a national CRA.[4] The plight of Innovis is interesting because it illustrates the virtually unassailable barrier to becoming a true national repository, which requires that the CRA achieves three critical milestones that most credit grantors or guarantors will need.

First, a new entrant needs to get the major creditors that report to the present CRAs to report to it. Innovis gets a lot but has some huge holes, for instance, American Express and many Visa and Master card accounts are missing. Next, the competitor would probably need to have at least 10 years of historic information from virtually all these creditors because that is the allowed amount of positive data. Consumers who do not see that will probably be angrier if credit is denied because of that. Therefore, even if Innovis could convince every creditor to report to them, those accounts would take 10 years to mature. Third, they need to have credit scores. Nearly all decision makers want a credit score to support their decision. FICO could perhaps take up their case with some sort of score, but they have not done this. My guess is that FICO thinks the gaps at Innovis are too large, including a complete lack of public record data (which Innovis has not acquired) and a dearth of inquiries (which they receive at vastly lower rates), both of which go into usual credit scores. Vantage could potentially make them a score with some degree of popularity, but Vantage, owned by the three national CRAs, probably would not move to bolster a possible competitor. (There are several chapters entirely devoted to credit scores, so I will say no more about that now.) The main point is that the only competitor on the horizon, Innovis, remains only on the horizon. Moreover, there is no one else even close.

Although there are only the three national collectors of data, there are several hundred firms in the country that can hold data on consumers and sell it, for instance, employment screening companies. They often repackage data from the three majors. Most firms not specifically making money in the U.S., however, steer clear of being defined as a CRA, in order to escape the legal burdens. In the FCRA, a Consumer Reporting Agency is defined as any person or firm "which, for monetary fees ... regularly engages in ... assembling or evaluating consumer credit information ... for the purpose of furnishing consumer reports to third parties. (15 USCS § 1681a)." CRAs have the greatest burdens under FCRA, though, partly through a fortuitous evolution in technology, the national CRAs have managed to keep those burdens low. For instance, they provide a free credit report to borrowers. This might have been exhausting, because it is paper intensive, if there were paper anymore. But now, it is just another website, and the free credit report is sent electronically, via PDF. The demand on CRAs to police requests for credit reports and scores and only respond to permissible ones, has become highly simplified. They need to see written permission by borrowers from small companies, but larger companies are presumed to get permission on a regular basis; their permissibility is assumed, subject to audits. Finally, disputes of data errors at the CRAs could hardly be done more on the cheap. We will give this its own chapter.

Regulators (the FTC and CFPB) tout the FCRA and the transparency and accuracy of credit data. The following appears on the FTC website.[5]

Your rights under the Fair Credit Reporting Act include:

- You have the right to receive a copy of your credit report. The copy of your report must contain all of the information in your file at the time of your request.
- If you contest the completeness or accuracy of information in your report, you may file a dispute with the CRA and with the company that furnished the information to the CRA. Generally, both the CRA and the furnisher of information are legally obligated to reinvestigate your dispute as long as it is not frivolous.
- CRAs must correct or remove inaccurate, incomplete, or unverifiable information in their files. CRAs must remove obsolete information from their files.
- If you are a victim of identity theft or are on active duty with the military, you have more rights under the FCRA.

- Only those with a permitted purpose or with your express permission may access your file.
- Generally, employers must have your express written permission to obtain your report.
- Any company that denies your application, or takes an adverse action against you, based on information obtained from a CRA, must inform you of the adverse action and must supply you with the name and address of the CRA they used.
- You have the right to have a free copy of your credit report in numerous instances including when your application for credit or employment is adversely affected because of information supplied by the CRA. You can get a free credit report each year in any case.
- You may opt-out of lists provided by the national credit bureaus that are based on your credit file.
- You may sue under the FCRA for violations of the Act.
- Credit scores are available to you on request from mortgage credit agencies and sometimes from mortgage lenders. There may be a fee for the score.

What is unmentioned by the regulators is that this 1970 law gave safe harbor to a system where almost any company that chooses to, and only companies that choose to, can send huge amounts of information about their customers to three CRAs which earn money turning that information over to almost anybody. I am sure that prison guards represent their job as keeping the peace and protecting prisoners (and if a few mishaps happen, it is not the guards' fault). Nevertheless, the idea of just letting the prisoners go is never discussed.

Anyway, we will see in coming chapters about *the completeness or accuracy of information in your report* and what happens if I *contest* it.

Endnotes

[1] The term CRA is often used in this book, standing for credit reporting agencies in most countries but standing for what is essentially the same thing, a credit reference agency, in many countries. It is a collector and disburser of consumer credit histories and related data. In the U.S., the major firms are Experian, Equifax, and TransUnion. CRA is also a common acronym that stands for the Community Reinvestment Act or Credit Rating Agency, both of which have something to do with credit but almost nothing to do with this book.

[2] A document named *A Brief History of Experian, Our Story*, by Nigel Watson, is given at www.experianplc.com/media/1323/8151-exp-experian-history-book_abridged_final.pdf. I last viewed it on July 10, 2019.

[3] The Metro 2 format for data furnishers to send information to CRAs is described at www.cdiaonline.org/resources/furnishers-of-data-overview/metro2-information/. I last reviewed it on July 10, 2019.

[4] While I verified this myself three years ago, looking at their data, it is echoed on in a blog titled *Who Is Innovis? Are They A Fourth Credit Bureau?* at a website called *Smart Credit*, by John Ulzheimer, written on June 20, 2011 and reviewed last by me on July 10, 2019. The URL is www.blog.smartcredit.com/2011/06/20/who-is-innovis-are-they-a-fourth-credit-bureau/.

[5] The *FTC Summary of Rights* can be read at www.consumer.ftc.gov/articles/pdf-0096-fair-credit-reporting-act.pdf. The CFPB's URL is www.consumerfinance.gov/learnmore/. I reviewed both URLs on July 10, 2019.

CHAPTER THREE

My credit report—some of it is right

Abstract

Data from tradelines (voluntary records from moneylenders), inquiries (requests to CRAs from creditors), and public record and collections (legal actions taken by creditors) are the foundation of the credit report and credit scores. I obtain my own credit report and display all this information (mostly its absence in my case), much in this chapter but all of it in the appendix. Accounts have been dropped, some of the data seems obscure, there is no record of bills paid except to moneylenders like credit card companies, and the fact that I pay my entire revolving balance each month is suppressed. Yet this is how I and everyone are judged financially. FICO, CRAs, and moneylenders appear well-served, while regulators appear hapless and consumers have little authority to control or expand their records.

WHAT IS IN A CREDIT REPORT

FROM myFICO[1].

Identifying information

Your name, address, social security number, date of birth, and employment information are used to identify you. These factors are not used in credit scoring. Updates to this information come from information you supply to lenders.

Trade lines

These are your credit accounts. Lenders report on each account you have established with them. They report the type of account (bankcard, auto loan, mortgage, etc.), the date you opened the account, your credit limit or loan amount, the account balance, and your payment history.

Credit Data and Scoring: The First Triumph of Big Data and Big Algorithms
ISBN: 978-0-12-818815-6
https://doi.org/10.1016/B978-0-12-818815-6.00003-0

Credit inquiries

When you apply for a loan, you authorize your lender to ask for a copy of your credit report. This is how inquiries appear on your credit report. The inquiries section contains a list of everyone who accessed your credit report within the last 2 years. The report you see lists both voluntary inquiries, spurred by your own requests for credit, and involuntary inquires, such as when lenders order your report so as to make you a pre-approved credit offer in the mail.

Public record and collections

Credit-reporting agencies (CRAs) also collect public record information from state and county courts, and information on overdue debt from collection agencies. Public record information includes bankruptcies, foreclosures, suits, wage garnishment, and liens.

myFICO can speak knowingly of credit reports because credit reports are the totality of inputs to FICO scores. But what is the input to the credit report? Of all these sections, all but public records come from creditors. Inquiries are records of creditors (and other contract providers) asking to see credit reports of applicants. For the rest, over 10,000 lenders voluntarily furnish monthly data on the credit activities of 235 million US consumers to just three national CRAs, Equifax, TransUnion, and Experian, companies that have controlled the collection and sale of this information for at least 40 years. On a very basic, nitty-gritty basis, what do those CRAs know about each one of us? As somewhat of an academic, I, Eric, knew it would be easy to sit in my ivory tower and read statistics about this—and I am doing plenty of that too—but I thought it would all be a lot realer to me and for readers, if I grabbed my own credit report and looked it over.

Each one of us is entitled to get one free copy annually from each repository by going to www.annualcreditreport.com. You might as well, because when you apply for a new credit card, a job, a cell phone, or any number of things, the person you hope is going to take a risk on you is probably going to do that: you might want to know what they are going to be seeing. Anyway, that is what I did. I signed on the website and answered a bunch of very particular questions to prove it was I that was asking. They were not easy questions, such as what account did I close

7 years ago, but I got lucky with my answer and was informed I could have a credit report from one of the three companies that have these reports for everybody: Equifax, Transunion, or Experian. I chose Equifax and now I have my downloaded Equifax report. It was only a mildly unpleasant dose of technology: young people should get through it in a breeze. In this chapter are parts of my credit report. My whole credit report, as delivered, is in the Appendix.

I had actually never gotten my credit report before. I had used and created credit scores out of variables derived from credit reports, and they had been strongly predictive. It all fit my mathematical intuitions and in a global way was satisfying and effective for my vocational purposes, at least until the foray into the trend data. But my credit report is about me, just as yours should be about you. I expected that it would feel like a record of *me*, someone who has been employed steadily for 40 years, who worked for a big firm for 25 years, was a vice president for nearly 20 of them, had two homes and several mortgages, and paid everything on time. That my excellent bona fides, my long record of using credit wisely, and my recent high income would tell the world I was someone to be trusted. That is not what I saw. It is long all right. My *Equifax Credit Report* is 37 pages long, which is pretty ponderous, but not because it needed to be. It is just bloated. But at the same time, it left so much out that I know about myself.

It does not know about my education. It does not know my salary. It does not know I have saved plenty for retirement, have life insurance, put my kids through college debt free and have helped them since. Okay—well credit reports do not pretend to be a full-fledged financial picture of a person. It is supposedly a picture of my credit. Of course, what is that, exactly? This report has just mortgages and credit cards. The mortgages are entirely detached from the homes bought, and they are not even all here. The credit cards are detached from how much I spent or repaid, do not make clear that I have only ever used credit as a convenience and a way to get airline miles and not money, that virtually all bills including credit are just swept from my bank automatically; in addition, to vent a minor complaint, older credit card accounts (no late payments even in those days) are missing. Then there are also things that I paid faithfully for many years that are not here at all, for example my rent obligations (for over a decade), phone bills, electricity, water, oil, phone, internet, cable bills, newspaper, trash—well, those I paid for decades. These are all types of trades that sometimes appear on a credit report, though rarely, and can be used in the credit decision, but they are not on mine. The message I want the reader to get here is that this report is about a fraction of my credits and a fraction of the information that could be known about my credits—and yours probably is too. It thus risks being like a blog or a gossip column—catching a slice of me maybe, when it feels like it. What saves it mathematically and globally is that people that pay their mortgage, credit cards, and car loans—the things that get reported on credit reports—also pay rent, cell phone bills, and so on. Correlation saves the day! However, it is just a fragment.

Section 1 is called a Summary and *is* a sort of summary of my report, though one even more arbitrary than the entirety of the report.

ERIC ROSENBLATT

Report Confirmation

7796594480

Summary

Review this summary for a quick view of key information contained in your Equifax Credit Report.

Report Date	Oct 23, 2017
Credit File Status	No fraud indicator on file
Alert Contacts	0 Records Found
Average Account Age	10 Years, 9 Months
Length of Credit History	17 Years
Accounts with Negative Information	0
Oldest Account	CITICARDS CBNA (Opened Oct 01, 2000)
Most Recent Account	BANK OF AMERICA (Opened Nov 15, 2014)

Credit Accounts

Your credit report includes information about activity on your credit accounts that may affect your credit score and rating.

Account Type	Open	With Balance	Total Balance	Available	Credit Limit	Debt-to-Credit	Payment
Revolving	2	1	$47	$36,953	$37,000	0.0%	$27
Mortgage	1	0	$0	$70,000	$70,000	0.0%	$0
Installment	0	0					
Other							
Total	3	1	$47	$106,953	$107,000	0.0%	$27

Summary Revolving Mortgage Installment Other Statements Personal Info Inquiries Public Records Collections

There is stuff here that seems pretty random. Does anyone care that my average account age is 10 years, 9 months; and my oldest account from Citicards CBNA was opened Oct 01, 2000? (Though to be fair, these facts could be used in the creation of a credit score.) Both happen to be false. I had credit before 2000. I bought a house and got a mortgage in 1985 when my first child was born. Why was it dropped? Not exactly clear. Not up to the consumer. The FCRA requires CRAs to drop negative information about me within 7 years, 10 years for bankruptcy and unpaid tax liens.[2] Now I have no negative information whatsoever and never have. However, the CRAs happened to decide (collectively) to drop positive information after 10 years (from the last update by a lender) as well. This means the data of first credit, which is part of the FICO score and probably all credit scores, is not what it says it is, nor is the oldest account on a credit report necessarily the oldest account. On the other hand, it again may not matter much. According to this credit report, I first got credit 17 years ago: our risk models, and presumably all models, show that short files are the risk.

The Summary section continues by saying that I have two revolving credit cards that are open and one open mortgage, which is oddly misrepresented. It says I have a credit limit of $70,000, all available, but this is flatly contradicted by something later in the report with more details on the mortgage (see appendix): it is a line of credit for a quarter million. In other words, the summary data has what seems to me an obvious error, though presumably this is because a line of credit is not classified as revolving credit. However, it revolves. In addition, it seems just weird when it says I have a total balance of $47. That happens to be an important variable in credit scores and credit evaluations, because it is part of the determination of utilization—how much of my available revolving credit do I use. Typically, I put 3000 to 5000 on my main credit card each month, and that would be my balance. I always pay it off automatically before I get the next bill, but possibly I had a momentary $47 balance for a given day because around about there I had a 3000 dollar return on something I unbought. In short, my Summary is at least accidental and possibly all bollixed up.

Section 2 covers revolving credit cards in seemingly loving depth. My Section 2 has four parts, two devoted to my two open accounts and two to my supposedly only two closed accounts. I had closed accounts earlier in my life, but there is no sign of them. Maybe they were too long ago to matter but my open accounts must surely matter. Therefore, I scoured the first open one in more detail than I would normally and compared it to the card it represented, which is in my wallet—and here is what I found: it is called a Chase Card on the Credit Report (which it is) but the card itself shows Southwest and Visa in big letters on the front. Neither of these organizations is noted on the credit report, nor is the fact that I use the card for the dominant purpose of getting miles on Southwest. Fortunately, it is easy for me to look up the card itself under my Chase account and compare it month by month to the information on my credit report.

The credit report purports to having a volume of information about my use of this card: "up to two years of monthly balance, available credit, scheduled payment, date of last payment, high credit, credit limit, amount past due, activity designator, and comments." It might be useful longitudinal information if it were complete and true. I notice that December 2015, November 2016, and April 2017 are blank in every one of those lists (monthly balance, available credit, etc.). Was this right? Did something happen to me and my credit card in those months? Well, I have at times lost and replaced my card, a matter that Chase easily kept track of, merging old and new Chase Southwest credit cards with charges in the same month. But, perhaps, it caused blanks in my credit report. Still, the blanks look wrong because they are wrong. My April Chase bill in fact was there: it was simply posted in March for some reason. Where was March? In February. Where was February? That was the one that was really missing.

Then things get really weird ...

All of the months have blank Available Credit and blank Actual Payments, though I paid every month. My high credit is always exactly $14,792 except for the three blanks. My scheduled payments are always under $100: the scheduled payment happens to be what a borrower must pay to avoid a late fee, usually the lesser of $25 or 2% of the amount owed. They wish I would only pay the scheduled fee because then they could collect large interest payments. Amount Past Due and Activity Designator are always blank in my credit report.

Below I have copied what is shown for my Chase card:

Revolving Accounts

Revolving accounts are those that generally include a credit limit and require a minimum monthly payment, such as credit cards.

2.1 CHASE CARD

Summary

Your debt-to-credit ratio represents the amount of credit you're using and generally makes up a percentage of your credit score. It's calculated by dividing an account's reported balance by its credit limit.

Account Number Reported Balance $0

Account Status PAYS_AS_AGREED **Debt-to-Credit Ratio** 0%

Available Credit $27,000

Account History
The tables below show up to 2 years of the monthly balance, available credit, scheduled payment, date of last payment, high credit, credit limit, amount past due, activity designator, and comments.

Balance

Year	Jan	Feb	Mar	Apr	May	Jun	July	Aug	Sep	Oct	Nov	Dec
2015										$3,985	$2,051	
2016	$4,074	$2,172	$3,614	$4,295	$4,449	$6,532	$1,441	$6,125	$329	$4,768		$610
2017	$2,837	$3,529	$3,025		$4,750	$1,890	$3,514	$4,769	$8,722			

Available Credit

Year	Jan	Feb	Mar	Apr	May	Jun	July	Aug	Sep	Oct	Nov	Dec
2015												
2016												
2017												

Scheduled Payment

Year	Jan	Feb	Mar	Apr	May	Jun	July	Aug	Sep	Oct	Nov	Dec
2015										$39	$25	
2016	$40	$25	$36	$42	$44	$65	$25	$61	$25	$47		$25
2017	$28	$35	$30		$47	$25	$35	$47	$87			

Actual Payment

Year	Jan	Feb	Mar	Apr	May	Jun	July	Aug	Sep	Oct	Nov	Dec
2015												
2016												
2017												

High Credit

Year	Jan	Feb	Mar	Apr	May	Jun	July	Aug	Sep	Oct	Nov	Dec
2015										14,792	14,792	
2016	14,792	14,792	14,792	14,792	14,792	14,792	14,792	14,792	14,792	14,792		14,792
2017	14,792	14,792	14,792		14,792	14,792	14,792	14,792	14,792			

Credit Limit

Year	Jan	Feb	Mar	Apr	May	Jun	July	Aug	Sep	Oct	Nov	Dec
2015										20,000	20,000	
2016	20,000	20,000	20,000	20,000	20,000	20,000	20,000	20,000	20,000	20,000		27,000
2017	27,000	27,000	27,000		27,000	27,000	27,000	27,000	27,000			

Amount Past Due

Year	Jan	Feb	Mar	Apr	May	Jun	July	Aug	Sep	Oct	Nov	Dec
2015												
2016												
2017												

Activity Designator

Year	Jan	Feb	Mar	Apr	May	Jun	July	Aug	Sep	Oct	Nov	Dec
2015												
2016												
2017												

Payment History

View up to 7 years of monthly payment history on this account. The numbers indicated in each month represent the number of days payment was past due; the letters indicate other account events, such as bankruptcy or collections.

√ Paid on Time **30** 30 Days Past Due **60** 60 Days Past Due **90** 90 Days Past Due **120** 120 Days Past Due **150** 150 Days Past Due **180** 180 Days Past Due **V** Voluntary Surrender **F** Foreclosure **C** Collection Account **CO** Charge-Off **B** Included in Bankruptcy **R** Repossession **TN** Too New to Rate No Data Available

Account Details

View detailed information about this account. Contact the creditor or lender if you have any questions about it.

High Credit $20,100 **Owner** INDIVIDUAL

Credit Limit $27,000 **Account Type** REVOLVING

Terms Frequency MONTHLY **Term Duration** 0

Balance $0 **Date Opened** Nov 18, 2011

Amount Past Due Date Reported Oct 18, 2017

Actual Payment Amount Date of Last Payment Oct 01, 2017
Date of Last Activity Scheduled Payment Amount

Months Reviewed 70 **Delinquency First Reported**

Activity Designator Creditor Classification UNKNOWN

Deferred Payment Start Date Charge Off Amount

Balloon Payment Date Balloon Payment Amount

Loan Type Flexible Spending Credit Card **Date Closed**

Date of First Delinquency

Comments Contact
CHASE CARD
PO Box 15298
Wilmington, DE 19850-5298
1-800-432-3117

Okay, reading the whole report over (I only show a fragment here), even I am bored. What I see is a lot of data and a lot of blanks. Why are Available Payment, Actual Payment, Amount Past Due, and Activity Designator always blanks? Why not zero, or n/a, or a number? The credit report seems to be mine but it often makes no sense. What credit report gets right is that my credit is pretty old, my use of credit is significant, and I have never been delinquent. Throughout the credit report, for any trade line where payments were due in the last 5 years, there were green checks showing that I paid on time. It does not explain *what* I paid on time. What I always paid on time is every cent of what I owed. What they mean is that I paid at least my very low scheduled fee on time, what was the minimum of $25 or 2%. The difference is not minor. But I never fell behind in my payments, and that is important. Basically, I am a *good* credit. Most people that no longer need credit are.

My entire credit report is shown in the Appendix.

Endnotes

1 The part of the *myFICO* site with *What's in my credit report?* can be found at www.myfico.com/crediteducation/in-your-credit-report.aspx. I last reviewed it on July 10, 2019.

2 An article titled *How Long Does Information Stay on My Credit Report?* can be found from Equifax at www.equifax.com/personal/education/credit/report/how-long-does-information-stay-on-credit-report/. I last reviewed it on July 10, 2019.

CHAPTER FOUR

Credit reporting agencies: playing the long game

Abstract

The leading edge of criticism taken seriously by CRAs comes from the state attorneys general, highly political and often governorship-seeking officials who know the public resents CRAs. The CRAs, being businesses, accommodate complaints jointly so long as it does not cost them money nor give one or another of the CRAs advantage over the others. Among these accommodations is the National Consumer Assistance Plan, announced as a generous settlement by all CRAs jointly, which amounts to erasing virtually all collection and lien data from the credit reports. Charts are provided to show how this data is being erased. Neither consumers nor accuracy-interested modelers have a say in these settlements.

Are there reasons why I see all these errors in my credit report? I think that many of them are not screw-ups, but features of a system where holes in data are tolerated to keep agents happy, so long as it does not reduce the income of the CRAs. In the U.S., a CRA is a business, plain and simple. It is not a part of government. It does not stand for fairness, inclusiveness, or regulate its product on behalf of the citizenry. As a matter of fact, it wants to ward off the costs of regulation or any constraints on profits. Its executives derive income and status from leading this business, identify with it to varying degrees, and want to enlarge it or at least extend it. Like most large businesses in the U.S., few are doing anything particularly devious, but the goal of a CRA is not data management, analytic accuracy, or consumer protection: the goal of CRAs, as with any business, is rewards over time for the executives.

CRAs have a special franchise in the U.S. and in many countries in that they are allowed to collect information on consumers, much given for free, and, presumably, these rights could be injured or removed by law. Their means of earning money does not incentivize them to prioritize keeping individual consumers happy, at least in the primary data collection and disbursement business, because consumers do not pay CRAs. Their means of earning money requires them to prioritize keeping regulators at bay and keeping credit-grantors, who pay the most to CRAs and provide data

Credit Data and Scoring: The First Triumph of Big Data and Big Algorithms
ISBN: 978-0-12-818815-6
https://doi.org/10.1016/B978-0-12-818815-6.00004-2

for free, happy. However, in democracies, consumers can express themselves through government representatives who may have the power to press legal change and damage the business model. Therefore, to keep the basic business going, they have to appease government officials and regulators. It is part of the cost of doing business.

How have the CRAs dodged the slings and arrows of public disapproval, and the government that represents them? The path of avoidance is *regulatory capture*, the way such things are handled in America. This is not a moral judgment. It is just how we handle things in America, a land where the business of the land is business. Businesses compromise in all sorts of ways with government and regulators, to keep the income flowing while making elected officials and regulators look like they are doing their job of keeping the businesses under control.

In some countries, China for instance, CRAs or their equivalents try to fulfill state interest directly. This reflects an entirely different and centralized culture, where direct control by authorities is much more normal. I would say, from an American's perspective, that China-type state control of data is in many ways more frightening to the average U.S. citizen. In the U.S., there is really little consumer anxiety for how the government might control CRA data. Rather, it is more typically believed that the government is protecting us from CRAs. However, the CRAs do not waste time bemoaning their fate as public whipping boys. They are businesses, eternal and fairly clear on their goals: more profits and long-term profits, to support rewards to executives. Thus, they *play the long game*, which no politician has time for in the U.S. So long as no other firms can get ahead of them and create a better legal and sellable product, the CRAs generally give in to the parties they need to, even when it damages their product (makes their product less useful for predicting credit events—the work that brings rewards to economists).

So, this is a chapter about how the CRAs accommodate power figures, particularly the state attorneys general, who are by far the most nimble, free, and interested representatives of consumers who can face off with the CRAs. Taking on CRAs allows them to be observed taking the side of citizens. Quoting a group called *Ballotpedia.Org*: "The primary job of a state attorney general is to serve as a chief legal adviser to the agencies and legislative organs that make up his or her state's government, in addition to the citizens residing within the state. It is this last common aspect of the role, regarding an attorney general's duty to serve the people, that gives it the name the 'People's Lawyer,' … 44 states publicly elect their attorneys general, reinforcing the office's relationship with, and direct accountability to, the people." Meaning, they do it, at least in part, to get elected—to this office or better. Five of the present governors (as I write these words) were former attorneys general of their state, including the governors of the three largest state (California, Texas, and New York). State attorneys general earn positive headlines and prepare the path to governorship, by putting pressure on corporations (and other villains like polluters) disliked by voters. CRAs, who have something on most of us and are paid to snitch, are easy to dislike when we are reminded of their omnipresence.

An example of state attorneys leaning on CRAs occurred in the early 2000s around the issues of data privacy and data theft, matters in the news even then. The FCRA has traditionally had sections allowing consumers to obtain *fraud alerts* on their credit when they thought "in good faith" that they were victims of identity theft, or expected to be, and *freezes* if they actually had been a victim. A freeze means that nobody can look at your credit records until you release the freeze.[1] Freezes in many states cost money until 2018, not much, but it was a consideration. The FRCA requirements for making these tools available seemed rather weak consumer rights stuff, so the state attorneys general jumped in to make consumer rights stronger, and they did this very publicly. Every state attorney general, starting with California in 2003, made a very public effort to liberalize freeze options for consumers beyond what the FCRA required.

How did the CRAs handle this attack? It is a fascinating case history of how regulated entities pretend to be pushed around by regulators, while changing almost nothing. They accommodated, and they did it together. In 2007, all three of the major credit bureaus (following TransUnion's lead) announced that they would let consumers freeze their credit reports, regardless of the state of residency. State laws still apply, however, in instances where the cost or other details of the freeze are more favorable than they are under the industry-sponsored alternative. Of course, the CRAs did not come up with this *solution* until the attorneys general got involved, but once they did, they made their concessions with publicity and self-congratulation. Their agreements on this matter have since been incorporated by the Federal law, the Economic Growth, Regulatory Relief, and Consumer Protection Act, passed in 2018.

Another round of brave energy from the state attorneys general was their hostility to the Equifax data breach. Every single state climbed on the bandwagon and sued Equifax. But the lawsuits appear to have run their course. Recently (as of this writing), a settlement was announced with the FTC, one of the regulators of credit data along with the now Consumer Finance Protection Board. In the settlement, discussed at more length in the Data Security chapter, Equifax is supposed to devote 31 million dollars to repaying consumers directly, a pittance given their billions in income, and most of 700 million in monitoring services, a new growth industry for CRAs, driven by consumers' fear of hacks like the Equifax one. Equifax has also agreed to set up a cybersecurity "fusion" center to achieve better and more coordinated responses to breaches in the future.

A third confrontation of state attorneys general and CRAs occurred with respect to judgment and lien data, public record information that never looks good and consumers (and voters) do not like. The way that the state attorneys general could take action by suing the CRAs on behalf of the aggrieved consumers. Consumers and all who make contracts with consumers, such as creditors, are surely affected by how credit data is gathered, maintained, and used. But it is hard to see that the CRAs have any standing at all. Rather the CRAs are information conduits to lenders and contract issuers. Should CRAs not be trying to accumulate all data that reflects on consumers' ability to pay? Yet they are commonly the defendant in state legal actions and have, as a consequence, taken on what seems to me a remarkable role: they have been *settling* lawsuits, as if, they are an actor whose interest must be consulted. One such settlement is the creation of what is called the National Consumer Assistance Plan, under cover of which the CRAs have removed some information of great consequence to prospective contract-makers: the liens and judgements against consumers.

Below is one version of the plan, as publicly announced by a state attorney general.

> A.G. Schneiderman Announces Groundbreaking Consumer Protection Settlement with The Three National Credit Reporting Agencies[2]
>
> *Experian, Equifax, And TransUnion, Which Maintain* Consumer *Credit Information On 200 Million Americans, Have Agreed to Increase Protections for Consumers Facing Credit Report Errors And Provide Second Free Annual Credit Report to Consumers*
>
> *Agreement Increases* Protections *for Consumers* with *Medical Debt; Reforms Process for Correcting Report Errors; And Improves Accuracy of Reports*

A.G. Schneiderman: This Agreement *Will Reform the Entire Industry and Provide Vital Protections for Millions of Consumers Across the Country*

NEW YORK—Attorney General Eric T. Schneiderman today announced a settlement with the nation's three leading national credit reporting agencies, Experian Information Solutions, Inc., ("Experian"), Equifax Information Services, LLC ("Equifax"), and TransUnion LLC ("TransUnion"). The agreement means the companies will improve credit report accuracy; increase the fairness and efficacy of the procedures for resolving consumer disputes of credit report errors; and protect consumers from unfair harm to their credit histories due to medical debt. All three credit reporting agencies worked cooperatively with the office to develop these critical reforms.

The action above was brought jointly by 30 other state attorneys general, many of whom also announced the settlement with great triumph. They have scored a victory over the "unfair" CRAs. Meanwhile, the CRAs announced the same settlement, through their common trade agency, the CDIA, with the happy sounding title of National Consumer Assistance Plan.[3] In their press release, they have spun the entire episode as an improvement over their usual fine service to Americans.

National consumer assistance plan: June 09, 2016

Equifax, Experian, and TransUnion today launched a new website, www.NationalConsumerAssistancePlan.com, to inform and update consumers about implementation of the National Consumer Assistance Plan, an initiative launched by the three companies in March 2015 to enhance their ability to make credit reports more accurate and easier for consumers to correct any errors on their credit reports.

Providing both consumers and businesses with accurate, transparent credit reports is our first priority," said Stuart Pratt, President and CEO of the Consumer Data Industry Association, the trade association representing the consumer data industry, including the three national credit reporting agencies. The nationwide consumer credit reporting companies are making important changes to their procedures that will improve their ability to collect accurate information, and we want to make sure consumers know about the new options available to them."

The National Consumer Assistance Plan is being implemented over three years, and the new website will serve as a vehicle for updating consumers about changes to their ability to interact with the nationwide consumer credit reporting companies.

Most of the details of the settlement sound reasonable. Medical debts are presumed to be partly a result of long periods before insurers pay. Thus, medical debt cannot be reported for 180 days after the CRAs hear about it. The CRAs must provide more publicity for the website that provides free credit reports. Regarding errors, someone with the discretion to make a change must review furnishers' denial of correction. Moreover, CRAs will mount a "media campaign" regarding "consumer rights." But the CRAs have gone further. It seems they have used the incident to get rid of something they perhaps think will be a sore spot later—public records data. The CRAs have pulled all judgements and tax lien data from the credit report. Here are what they call the highlights concerning Credit Report Accuracy at a site from all three CRAs called nationalconsumerassistance.com:

> *Enhancing Credit* Report *Accuracy,*
>
> *Establishing National* Credit *Reporting Working Group to review and identify best practices,*
>
> *Requiring all data* furnishers *to use the most current reporting format,*
>
> *Eliminating the* reporting *of debts that did not arise from a contract or agreement by the consumer to pay, such as traffic tickets or fines,*
>
> *Prohibiting medical* debts *from being reported on credit reports until after a 180-day waiting period to allow insurance payments to be applied,*
>
> *Removing from credit* reports *any previously reported medical collections that have been paid or are being paid by insurance,*
>
> *Requiring debt* collectors *to include original creditor information with each account being reported for collection,*
>
> *Requiring debt* collectors *to regularly update the status of unpaid debts and remove debts no longer being pursued for collection,*
>
> *Monitoring data* furnishers *for adherence to the announced reporting requirements, and taking corrective actions against data furnishers for noncompliance.*

This certainly sounds consumer-friendly, and side-steps the date cleaning or what might have necessitated it, but what really happened is civil judgements and liens have been removed. The Experian site admits this[4]

> Experian no longer shows judgment and tax lien information as part of a consumer's credit history. Bankruptcy is now the only public record information that is collected routinely by the national credit reporting companies, including Experian.

Separately, Experian writes[5]

Tax liens, or outstanding debt you owe to the IRS, no longer appear on your credit reports—and that means they cannot impact your credit scores.

Tax Liens Removed from Credit Reports:

Tax liens used to appear on your credit reports maintained by the three national credit bureaus (Experian, TransUnion, and Equifax). Even if you paid the lien, it stayed on your reports for up to seven years, while unpaid liens remained on your reports for up to 10 years.

In 2017, however, all three credit bureaus implemented changes to eliminate civil judgment records (notes that a consumer owes debt to a court because of a lawsuit result) and half of all tax lien data. By April 2018, all tax liens were removed from credit reports by the bureaus.

The updated rules are the result of a Consumer Financial Protection Bureau study that found issues with reporting such information correctly.

"A lot of judgments and liens were linked to the wrong people, so someone may share your first and last name, maybe living in a different part of the country, and might have a lien or judgment that might get linked to your file," said Ankush Tewari, senior director of credit risk assessment at data firm LexisNexis Risk Solutions, in American Banker.

How Will the Tax Lien Change Affect My Credit?

According to LexisNexis Risk Solutions, only about 11% of consumers will see a change to their credit reports as a result of this action, and scores could increase by as much as 30 points overall.

However, the Consumer Data Industry Association, which represents the three credit bureaus, said in a statement in 2017 that "analyses conducted by the credit reporting agencies and credit score developers FICO® and VantageScore show only modest credit scoring impacts."[6]

It is only 11% because judgements and liens are relatively rare. But they are important if they exist. It points to a politicization of data generally, a pretense of fairness that covers up the immense scattershot of data formation and collection and scoring generally. The critical reason to get credit data is to observe failures on the part of consumers to keep contracts in the past; it informs all models. Creditors have now been denied a key category of information that was *settled away* by CRAs who see little reason to fight to keep it. Here are some charts showing the credit data picture. It comes from credit data I was able to obtain on a couple hundred thousand borrowers from all three repositories.

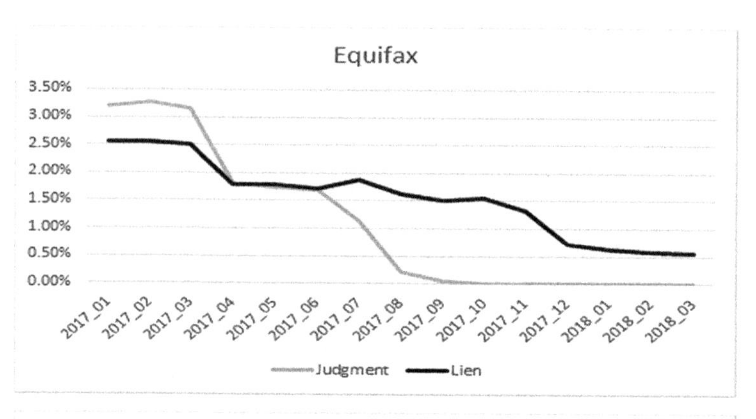
Equifax
3.50%
3.00%
2.50%
2.00%
1.50%
1.00%
0.50%
0.00%
2017_01
2017_02
2017_03
2017_04
2017_05
2017_06
2017_07
2017_08
2017_09
2017_10
2017_11
2017_12
2018_01
2018_02
2018_03
Judgment
Lien

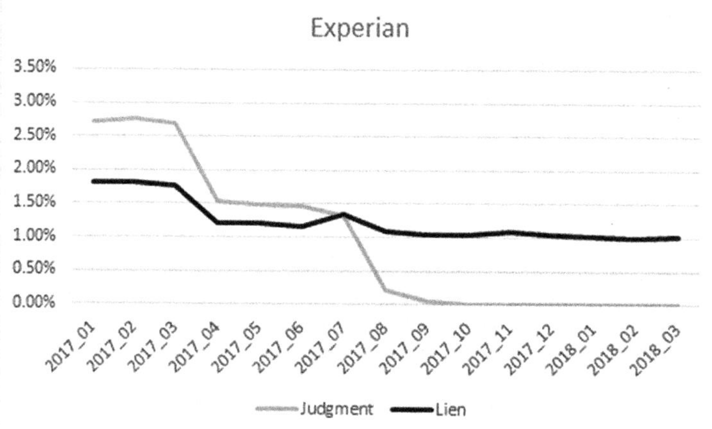
Experian
3.50%
3.00%
2.50%
2.00%
1.50%
1.00%
0.50%
0.00%
2017_01
2017_02
2017_03
2017_04
2017_05
2017_06
2017_07
2017_08
2017_09
2017_10
2017_11
2017_12
2018_01
2018_02
2018_03
Judgment
Lien

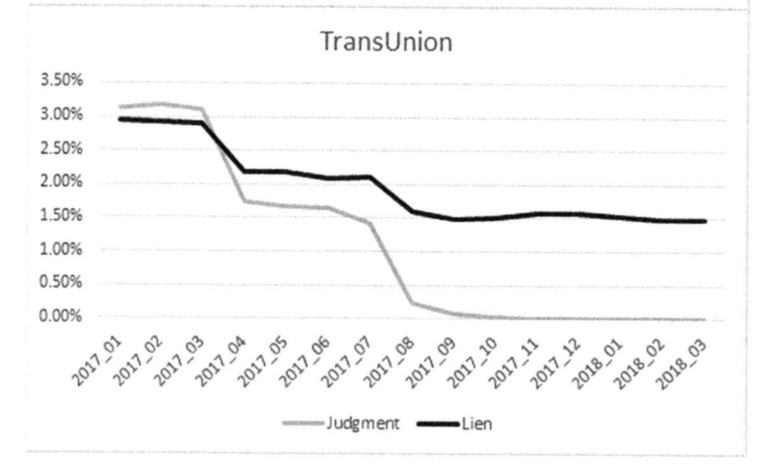
TransUnion
3.50%
3.00%
2.50%
2.00%
1.50%
1.00%
0.50%
0.00%
2017_01
2017_02
2017_03
2017_04
2017_05
2017_06
2017_07
2017_08
2017_09
2017_10
2017_11
2017_12
2018_01
2018_02
2018_03
Judgment
Lien

In addition, the rest of the liens are going as well, in short order. However, the data is only disappearing from the CRA data and thus the FICO score. It does still exist at LexisNexis, for example, for some extra cost. Now I do not know if the LexisNexis data is identical to what has been in credit reports. But here is part of the LexisNexis internet ad on this data.[7] It seems clear that they expect someone to turn to them now that the data is not available at CRAs.

LexisNexis risk solutions is the answer to the lien and civil judgment data gap

The LexisNexis RiskView Liens and Judgments Report delivers technology advancements that bolster the accuracy and currency of lien *and civil judgment content* ....

When access to most lien and judgment data is cut off later this year, it won't be business as usual

In 2017, the three Nationwide Credit Reporting Agencies eliminated most tax liens and civil judgments from their credit reports *as part of their National Consumer Assistance Plan. You have a lot to consider—especially since lien and judgment data has been a key piece of credit decisions for decades. Our offering can help you retain your competitive edge without the added expense of recalibrating your models ...*

Consumer Disclosure and Dispute Process: A transparent and robust dispute resolution process to help consumers report and correct inaccurate information ...

What does LexisNexis RiskView Liens and Judgments report offer?

- ***Broad Coverage**: The same nationwide coverage that has been included in credit reports historically*
- ***Actionable Details**: You have the flexibility to specify the type of judgment and lien content that you want to receive, and to select a variety of attributes and individual judgment and lien details ...*

Endnotes

[1] Credit Freezes are described in a *Wikipedia* entry from September 2017 entitled *Credit Freeze*. The URL www.en.Wikipedia.org/wiki/Credit_freeze was last reviewed by me on July 10, 2019.

[2] The press release from state attorney general Schneiderman of New York is available at www.ag.ny.gov/archive-press-releases last reviewed by me on July 10, 2019.The agreement signed by the state attorney general Schneiderman of New York and that of the three repositories jointly signed in March 2015 can be found at www.ag.ny.gov/pdfs/CRA%20Agreement%20Fully%20Executed%203.8.15.pdf, which I last reviewed on July 10, 2019.

[3] The quotation from *nationalassistanceplan.com* can be found at www.nationalconsumerassistanceplan.com/last reviewed by me on July 10, 2019.

[4] Experian's article *Judgments No Longer Included on a Credit Report* about judgements and liens are found at www.experian.com/blogs/ask-experian/judgments-no-longer-included-on-credit-report/written on June 15, 2018 by the Experian Team and last reviewed by me on July 10, 2019.

[5] The second Experian's article *Tax Liens Are No Longer a Part of Credit Reports* can be found at www.experian.com/blogs/ask-experian/tax-liens-are-no-longer-a-part-of-credit-reports/by Ismat Mangla on March 20, 2019 and last reviewed by me on July 10, 2019. These URLs seem to be in flux and have required me to update my references and quotes. However, the consequence for the data is the same.

[6] There are numerous relatively small differences between FICO scores and a scoring company owned by the three repositories called Vantage, differences outlined in many places, but one is a blog entitled *The Experian Credit Score* versus *FICO Score: Differences to Know* by Barry Paperno, published November 30, 2018, on the website *Credit.Com*, which can be found at www.blog.credit.com/2018/11/experian-credit-score-v-fico-64279/. The posting was last reviewed by me on July 13, 2019.

One difference between the scoring algorithms is that FICO, to create a score, "requires at least 6 months of credit history and at least one account reported to a credit bureau within the last 6 months. VantageScore only requires 1 month of history and one account reported within the past 2 years." This is in my view a very minor difference and reflects FICO's reluctance to score new borrowers with very low precision and VantageScore's interest in establishing a reputation for inclusiveness. FICO could easily provide a weaker model for the group covered by VantageScore and not FICO, but perhaps as a branding matter, or possibly on principle, refuses to do that.

[7] The URL www.risk.lexisnexis.com/products/riskview-liens-and-judgments-report has the ad for LexisNexus liens and judgements, reviewed by me on July 10, 2019.

CHAPTER FIVE

Data errors to keep money renters happy

Abstract

CRAs cannot require data from creditors and therefore accept data from whomever will provide it—mostly money renters controlling borrower behavior but afraid of losing customers who pay interest and late fees. Credit limits were held back for a time, but regulators stepped in after complaints from FICO and others, and limit data resumed.[5] There are two other issues that are not fixed. One is that borrowers who are 1–30 days late, despite paying delinquency and interest costs, are not labeled. Only borrowers who have been at least 30 days late are marked as delinquent. The second issue is that many data furnishers have stopped reporting the payment on revolving accounts. Now modelers cannot tell who uses credit as currency vs. who is living on it and becoming overextended.

Presumably, the U.S. CRAs play the long game with state attorneys general and any others who have government or regulatory power to avoid actions that could threaten the business model. However, the consequence is less data and weaker scoring models, and sometimes wildly wrong scores. Nevertheless, this is not where it stops. There are additional data-destroying accommodations to data furnishers—who supply CRAs with free raw materials and also are the paying customers of the CRAs. The CRAs could possibly stand up to the furnishers, but perhaps because the voluntary nature of data furnishing entitles them to some coaxing, the CRAs seem, in my experience, unwilling to do so.

Furnishers, naturally, share information with a goal in mind. They want to create consequences for non-payers, but they do not want to tell their competitors anything that will advantage their competitors, who are always trying to market new products and will poach a furnisher's customers if they can. How do they even know a rival's customers? They do not, really; but they are allowed by the FCRA to pay CRAs to look through their national data bases to gather names and addresses of borrowers who meet some set of criteria and send them letters from the furnisher with a "firm offer of risk." By looking at a national data base, the CRA is essentially looking at books of rivals. This is the source of all those credit offers that come in the mail.

Credit Data and Scoring: The First Triumph of Big Data and Big Algorithms
ISBN: 978-0-12-818815-6
https://doi.org/10.1016/B978-0-12-818815-6.00005-4

Therefore, if the characteristics are enticing, for instance the fact that an individual pays a lot of interest and fees, then a customer like that is going to get offers to switch credit cards, with come-ons like months of no interest. It is understandable that creditors would like to hide such valuable customers from each other. But can they under the FCRA? My reading of the first paragraph of the FCRA is that they cannot *legally* hold back such information:

> *The Fair Credit Reporting Act (FCRA) is designed to help ensure that CRAs (Consumer Reporting Agencies, including credit bureaus and credit reporting companies) furnish correct and* ***complete*** *[my bold] information to businesses to use when evaluating your application for credit, or insurance, or to employers or prospective employers.*

However, in practice, there seems to be no penalty for withholding data. I can think of three kinds of data that have been withheld over the years, without consequences—and those are from companies that *do* report. In the 1990s, furnishers began to hold back on the reporting of credit limits on revolving debt. Presumably, this limit gave a sense of the regard that the furnisher had for the consumer—a high limit meaning that they felt reasonably safe lending a large amount of money to that consumer. The percent of a limit that a consumer borrows is one of the biggest predictors in every credit model and score—a field called utilization. FICO and others complained publicly about this failure to reveal limit because credit balance divided by credit limit (utilization rate) is highly predictive of delinquency. In this case, the pressure worked. Credit limit was made a required field by "the federal banking agencies, the National Credit Union Administrate, and the FTC (the agencies)" who came together per the Accuracy and Integrity Rule of the Fact Act, quoted below, to require the limits on revolving accounts to be reported.[1]

> *ACCURACY AND INTEGRITY RULE: §222.42*
>
> *Section 222.42 requires furnishers to establish and implement reasonable written policies and procedures regarding the accuracy and integrity of the consumer information furnished to CRAs. The agencies carefully defined accuracy and integrity. "Accuracy" means that the information provided by a furnisher correctly: (1) identifies the appropriate consumer; (2) reflects the terms of and liability for the account; and (3) reflects the consumer's performance with respect to the account. "Integrity" means the information provided by a furnisher: (1) is substantiated by the furnisher's records; (2) is in a form designed to minimize the likelihood that the information may be incorrectly reflected in a consumer report; and (3) includes information in the furnisher's possession that the agency has determined would likely be materially misleading in evaluating a consumer's qualifications if absent. The credit limit, if any, is the one item of information the agencies have determined would likely be materially misleading if omitted.*

The agencies placed particular emphasis on the duties of furnishers to report credit limits. A credit limit typically applies only to open-end credit products, such as a credit card or home equity line of credit. The agencies explained that a key factor in evaluating the creditworthiness of an individual is credit utilization, for which the credit limit is necessary to calculate. Credit utilization measures the percentage of a credit line a consumer is currently using. For example, if a consumer has a credit card balance of $4,000 and the credit limit for the card is $10,000, the credit utilization rate is 40%. Credit scoring models treat high utilization rates as a negative factor and low utilization rates as a positive factor when computing a credit score.

Without the credit limit, credit evaluators must either ignore credit utilization data or resort to inferior proxies to estimate credit utilization, such as using the highest balance ever owed on the account as the credit limit. These substitute measures frequently overestimate the consumer's credit utilization, potentially resulting in higher perceived credit risk, worse credit terms for the consumer, and lower credit scores. Requiring furnishers to disclose the credit limit eliminates the need to rely on substitute measures, allowing credit evaluators to gain a more accurate picture of the consumer's creditworthiness. The regulation contains an exception to the disclosure requirement when the credit limit is not in the furnisher's possession and when it is not applicable, such as when a credit product does not have a credit limit.

As a modeler, I could not agree more with the sentiment. It has been largely followed since. However, the original non-contributors faced no penalties.

Two other omissions (that have occurred to me) remain, not covered by these agencies, who seem to act only when pushed hard by some law to do so:

One is payment amount for revolving accounts. This is simply what the consumer pays each month on this or that revolving trade line balance.[2] The balance owed is typically present but not how much of it is paid each month. We know it must be at least the minimum due, usually the lesser of 25 dollars or 2% of the balance, because paying less would create a missed payment and increase delinquency on the credit report. Being that we cannot see if what beyond 2% is paid, I have observed several models that demonstrate the predictive importance of knowing the payment each month, based on data that was available through 2013. *Transactors*, people that just use their cards as an alternative currency and pay off their balance every month, are better risks than *revolvers*, who do not pay the full balance and pay nearly usurious interest charges on what remains.

This was less telling in 1970 when the FCRA was passed, because credit cards were not considered by most as a preferred alternative to currency. In 1981, American Airlines became the first company to roll out the first rewards program card.[3] By the early 1990s, according to a white paper on *Credit Card Rewards* by Michael Turner,[4] the connection between credit cards and awards was well established. Fully two thirds of borrowers I see are transactors now, whether for rewards, safety, or to keep records of payments: but this absence of data keeps us from giving credit for it. This variable is not simply important because it is predictive. What is tantalizing about it, to those few of us who happen to have internalized the goal of making credit available more widely, is that it is a marker of risk, which *the borrower can quickly change*. Certainly, there are past delinquencies, inquiries, limits, and so on that affect the prediction of credit failure, but only time, often a long time, can reduce the modeled impact of these. However, borrowers, if they can change their life-style, can alter their transactor/revolver status immediately. If they cannot change their lifestyle to accomplish this, then their precariousness is genuine, and they are probably correctly categorized.

The evidence that this data has been deliberately withheld is that payment data was increasingly reported for credit cards in the period 2009 to February 2013, but then fell off suddenly as several large (well-known) credit companies suddenly withdrew the payment information. The charts below show this, based on millions of records. I do not have the data for Experian, and I have more months for Equifax than for TransUnion—but the story seems clear; payment date reporting grew from about three fifths to about four fifths from 2009 to 2013 and then dropped sharply to a little over a third.

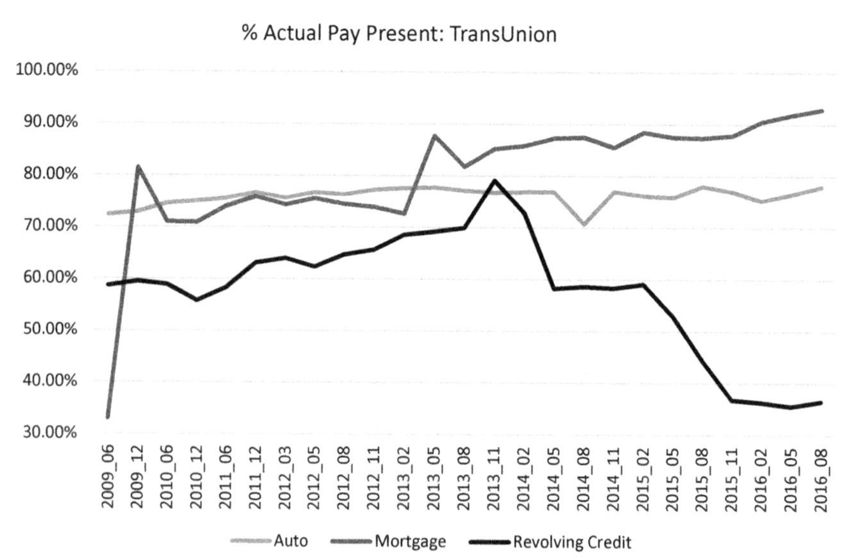

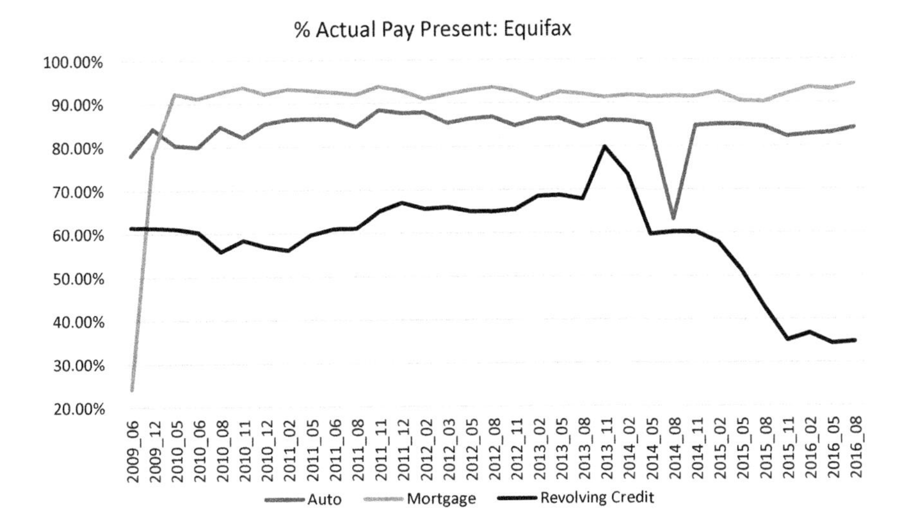

When I first noticed the drop-off, I discussed the problem with the CRAs. But they were very leery of tangling with their furnishers. I also discussed it internally, meeting the same anxieties. As the reader will see, I tried to have the data changed at least for myself personally, which was also futile. A last try is to obtain this data directly from the borrowers' bank account: this idea will be presented in a future chapter.

The last gap in furnisher data is any delinquency less than 30 days. Indeed, there is no space to enter it in data flows to the CRAs. We will go into the slightly technical details in the chapter Data Flows. However, a consumer's record shows current if the payment comes in less than 30 days after the due date. Being late, but late less than 30 days, does not prevent having to pay interest nor does it prevent having to pay late fees. Presumably, this means fewer consumers are upset by reading bad news about themselves in credit reports, and also this lessens the number of disputes because of late mail, or alleged late mail; but it also means that people who are not late at all miss out on the chance to demonstrate their far lower risk, and thus some of the less risky people fail to get mortgages or other credit, or get these at unnecessarily high rates.

Endnotes

[1] The Accuracy and Integrity Rule of the Fact Act can be found at the FTC site *Consumer Compliance Outlook* for the Third Quarter 2010. The URL is www.consumercomplianceoutlook.org/2010/third-quarter/furnisher-requirements and was last reviewed by me on July 12, 2019.

[2] Interest and penalties have never been reported, to my knowledge, but it would be possible to deduce these in many cases if the payment amount for each month were provided.

[3] *The History of Credit Cards*, an article written by Jay MacDonald and Taylor Tompkins on July 11, 2017 for *CreditCards.com*, discusses American Airlines' reward card. It can be found at www.creditcards.com/credit-card-news/history-of-credit-cards.php, reviewed by me on July 12, 2019.

[4] Opinions about the history of credit cards and rewards are informed by the White Paper titled *Credit Card Rewards: Context, History, and Value* by Michael A. Turner, Ph.D. for the August 2012 version of *PERC: Results and Solutions*. It can be found at www.perc.net/wp-content/uploads/2013/12/WP-2-Layout.pdf, reviewed by me on July 12, 2019.

[5] The reporting of credit limits by data furnishers was contentious issue for a while, until a law was passed, the FACT Act, which specifically requires U.S. data furnishers to send the information. The Federal Reserve's *Consumer Compliance Outlook* for the third quarter of 2010, authored by Kenneth J. Benton, Senior Consumer Regulations Specialist, and Michael F. Bolos, Research Assistant, Federal Reserve Bank of Philadelphia, explains that the FACT Act directs the federal banking agencies, the National Credit Union Administration, and the FTC (the agencies) to jointly write regulations establishing guidelines for furnishers to ensure the accuracy and integrity of information they furnish to consumer reporting agencies (CRAs), particularly credit limits. These regulations direct the credit industry to make sure certain data is collected called for by the Metro 2 at www.consumercomplianceoutlook.org/2010/third-quarter/furnisher-requirements/ and was last reviewed by me on July 14, 2019.

CHAPTER SIX

Historic complaints about credit accuracy

Abstract

Errors on credit reports were reported in two studies reviewed in this chapter, one by an organization called PERC in 2011, which carries out research in cooperation with the CRAs. The other is by a regulator, the Federal Trade Commission, in 2013. PERC found that only 0.9% of credit reports had errors that would change credit scores by as much as 25 points. The FTC found numerous small problems but only 2% of credit reports with errors that would cause a 25-point swing in the credit score. The method for identifying errors was to enlist individuals who would review their credit reports and object if they detected an error. A third paper is also reviewed, which points out the vast economic world not reported to CRAs, a matter never mentioned by any of the individuals recruited for the first two studies.

So far, we have a sample of one credit report (mine) at one repository (Equifax), in which trade lines are missing and there is dubious data where trade lines exist. However, I am not the only one who has found errors in their credit report. Errors in data collection have been reported and investigated for years. Because in any large body of data there are going to be at least a few minor odd details, the question of materiality is relevant. Is it only the errors that significantly change credit scores that even matter, as most future agreements will be based on the credit score? Moreover, do we count it an error when something is missing that is almost always missing: such as rent, utilities, or the payment amount on a credit card: in short do we get to judge the practices of the bureaus? The CRAs claim they have a low error rate, but what they mean is only that they are not altering the data that has been sent to them by furnishers. I found all sorts of errors on my credit report but I have little doubt that Equifax is correctly reflecting what was sent to them.

It is costly to study errors in credit reports. Consumers need to be recruited to review their credit reports and say if they believe them to be wrong. Two relatively recent papers that do this are *U.S. Consumer Credit Reports: Measuring Accuracy and Dispute Impacts* from PERC (Policy and Economic Research Council)—May 2011,[1] and *Report to Congress Under Section*

Credit Data and Scoring: The First Triumph of Big Data and Big Algorithms
ISBN: 978-0-12-818815-6
https://doi.org/10.1016/B978-0-12-818815-6.00006-6

310 of the Fair and Accurate Credit Transactions Act of 2003 from the Federal Trade Commission—December 2012.[2] The time frame would seem to protect us against the opinion I have often heard that CRAs were once regional and have grown more alike and more complete. The two reports sound like they are done similarly and should get about the same answers, but the FTC report finds about twice as many errors as the PERC report.

The PERC paper "reviews the accuracy of data in consumer credit reports from the three major nationwide consumer reporting agencies (CRAs)". It also measures the credit market impact upon consumers with modifications to their credit reports. Generally, the PERC paper paints a pretty rosy picture of credit report accuracy, but can PERC be trusted? The way the paper is funded worries me. For this paper, PERC was "retained by the CDIA to conduct ... [this] study given its expertise with credit information ..." The CDIA, standing for Consumer Data Industry Association is, per their website, "an international trade association representing over 100 corporate members that play a critical role in making today's economy work, including the nation's largest credit bureaus ..." But the big three of those 100 members are the three national CRAs, and it is their product whose accuracy this paper is testing. It does not seem too harsh to wonder if the PERC study, paid for mostly by the three major bureaus, is not doing all it can to find that those bureaus have a clean product. That does not mean the PERC study is necessarily wrong: but it is something like the cigarette companies paying for research into the dangers of nicotine addiction.

Credit scores play a large role in both studies. Errors only really matter much if they change the credit scores of the borrowers, because approval and pricing of credit will generally depend on the score. The credit score that PERC uses is the Vantage score, a scoring model owned by the CRAs, and a competitor to FICO. This score choice is problematic, as FICO is by far the more commonly used credit scoring company, and the only one used in the mortgage industry. The FTC study uses the FICO score. Why does PERC use the number two score? Perhaps because the CDIA can get Vantage scores for free, but it is also one more way the study stays close to the interest groups that presumably want to find a low error rate. As I have mentioned, Vantage and FICO are not very different though the public argument between the two, fought out through regulators and legislators, accentuates the slight distinction. FICO requires at least 6 months of credit history and at least one account reported to a CRA within the last

6 months. Vantage claims to be vastly more expansive because they only require 1 month of history and one account reported within the past 2 years. Other than this point, the two scores are scaled the same, built in the same way, and predict about the same.

Despite my skepticism, the PERC study sounds scientific. PERC worked with a consumer-recruiting company Synovate to collect 2338 seemingly unbiased individuals to review their credit reports and look for errors in them. The 2338 were paid a very slight amount, about a dollar, to make this effort, so the thought is that the people that agreed to do this were interested in the project or in getting their credit reports right. By various statistics, like income, the group seemed more or less representative of consumers in America generally. If the consumers identified an error—they were then offered another five dollars by Synovate (approximately—the money is paid in a funny way) to file what is called a dispute. That is, they could go through some bureaucracy to complain about the error and hopefully get it fixed. Of the total participants, 1461 reviewed one credit report and 877 reviewed all three. The people who looked at all three did not find more errors than the ones who looked at one, according to PERC. Of the total 3876 reports reviewed, consumers only thought 19.2% of reports had at least one error. Moreover, many of these errors were just header data like employer address and thus meaningless to risk judgments. Only 12.1% of credit reports seemed to their owners to have errors that could potentially matter.

The participants that complained generally got something changed. That differs enormously from my single personal experience. Perhaps the complaints were treated differently because of the study, but complaining often worked for the PERC consumers. When people did dispute something, they mostly got it fixed or erased; however, maybe half the time the dispute decision is made in the individual's favor because the credit reporter (the credit card company, for instance) did not get back to the bureau in 30 days. But, was that a change that affected them? Not usually. The reason is credit scores. Rarely is a credit report read trade line by trade line, month by month. Just because something in the credit report changes does not mean that the overall credit score is affected much. As PERC writes: "The main focus of this study is on the direct negative impact of credit report errors in the credit standing of consumers. That is, we examine credit score changes and credit score tier changes."

According to the study: "Of all credit reports examined, 0.93% had one or more disputes that resulted in a credit score increase of 25 points or greater; 1.16% had one or more disputes that resulted in a credit score increase of 20 points or greater; and 1.78% had one or more disputes that resulted in a credit score increase of 10 points or greater." That sounds like a mostly clean bill of health.

The second study, from the FTC study, is independent of the CRAs, their trade union, and the CRAs' credit score, Vantage. To quote the study: "The study design called for consumers to be randomly selected from the population of interest (consumers with credit histories at the three national CRAs). Ultimately, 1001 study participants reviewed 2968 credit reports (roughly three per participant) with a study associate who helped them identify potential errors. Study participants were encouraged to use the Fair Credit Reporting Act ("FCRA") dispute process to challenge potential errors that might have a material effect on the participant's credit standing (i.e., potentially change the credit score associated with that credit report). When a consumer identified and disputed an error on a credit report, the study associate informed FICO of the disputed items, and FICO generated a provisional FICO score for the report under the assumption that all consumer allegations were correct. After the completion of the FCRA dispute process, study participants were provided with new credit reports and credit scores. Using the provisional FICO score, the new credit reports and credit scores, and the original credit reports and credit scores, we are able to determine the impact on the consumer's credit score from both potential and confirmed material errors."

The authors synopsize their results this way: "Overall, we find that 26% of the 1001 participants in the study identified at least one potentially material error on at least one of their three credit reports. Although 206 consumers (21% of the participants) had a modification to a least one of their credit reports after the dispute process, only 129 consumers (13% of participants) experienced a change in their credit score as a result of these modifications. Each affected participant may have as many as three score changes. Of the 129 consumers with any score change, the maximum changes in score for over half of the consumers were less than 20 points. For 5.2% of the consumers, the resulting increase in score was such that their credit risk tier decreased and thus the consumer may be more likely to be offered a lower auto loan interest rate."

In both studies, the errors found are reviewed through the regular dispute process (only in the FTC study, hired help takes the trouble of filing the dispute from the participants). If the complaint is upheld through the dispute process, then credit score is respun (FICO for FTC, Vantage for

PERC). The final story is that score impacts of errors are double for the FTC what they were for the PERC.

	PERC	FTC
Percentage of reports that resulted in a score increase	3.1%	6.6%
Percentage with score increase ≥25 points	0.9%	2.0%
Percentage moving to a lower credit risk classification	0.5%	2.2%

Without a lot of probably fruitless digging, let us take these as the bounds of error impacts in the world of credit that typically is captured—at least as found in these papers and these techniques. It does not address the large categories of bill-paying that are invisible and so play essentially no role in any model. These gaps are not errors, according to the definitions of the studies. However, according to these studies, it takes bad luck (but not a miracle) to get materially hurt by the active and conspicuous errors that can be observed. Furthermore, even if you went to the trouble of obtaining a credit report, finding a problem, and complaining: it is impossible to say if that would help and how much—because the weight given that issue by the scoring algorithms is rarely estimable.

To my surprise, a paper that recognizes the impact that invisible data might be making was published by the same group PERC that I suggested might have been partial to the credit repositories in the paper just reviewed. PERC published a paper in June of 2012, titled *A New Pathway to Financial Inclusion: Alternative Data, Credit Building, and Responsible Lending in the Wake of the Great Recession* (Michael Turner, Patrick Walker, Sukanya Chaudhuri, and Robin Varghese) that had a very different take on the issue. According to the introduction: "Currently, most non-financial services, such as energy utilities and telecommunication services, only report negative data, such as very late payments, charge-offs, and collections, to Consumer Reporting Agencies (CRAs), also known as credit bureaus. This occurs either directly or indirectly through collection agencies. On the other hand, *fully* reported accounts are those in which positive data, such as on-time payments, mildly late payments, and balances, are also reported. This report assesses the impacts of including fully reported non-financial payment data—specifically energy utility and telephone payment data—in consumer credit files. These non-financial payment data are referred to as *alternative data* because they are not typically *fully* reported to CRAs. This report uses data obtained during and after the Great Recession and compares results to a similar analysis using data from 2005 to 2006, prior to the economic downturn.

Key findings from this research include:

Massive Material Impacts for the Financially Excluded: Among the so-called "thin-file population," including fully reported alternative payment data dramatically increases credit standings. In this group, 25% experienced an upward score tier migration (moved from a higher risk tier to a lower risk tier) as a direct consequence of fully reported alternative data being in their credit file. By contrast, 6% of the thin-file population experienced a downward score tier migration (from a lower risk tier to a higher risk tier). Including in this group those who become scoreable when alternative data is added, assuming that not having a score is viewed as very high risk, then 64% experience a score tier rise and 1% experience a score tier fall.

Credit Underserved Primary Beneficiaries of Alternative Data: As was the case when PERC examined credit reports from 2005, the largest net beneficiaries in terms of improved credit access are lower income Americans, members of minority communities, and younger and elderly Americans. For instance, those earning less than $20k annually saw a 21% increase in acceptance rates, those earning between $20k and $30k saw a 14% increase, and those earning between $30k and $50k saw a 10% increase. The rate of increase was 14% for Blacks; 15% for those 18—25 years of age; and 11% for those above 66 years of age. We also see dramatic differences between renters and homeowners, with renters experiencing a 17% increase in credit access when alternative data are fully reported versus just a 7% increase for homeowners.

Those with past Serious Delinquencies Benefit from Alternative Data: Consumers with a public record, including a bankruptcy and/or very late payments (90+ days late) among the traditional accounts reported to CRAs, witnessed more score increases than decreases (55% vs. 30%) when alternative data were included in their credit files. This suggests that those with blemished credit files also benefit from the addition of alternative data. This may be particularly useful because those with blemished credit may otherwise find it difficult to access mainstream credit to improve their credit standing.

The big movement, "massive," was for thin files, those with less than three trade lines, constituting 6.4% of the sample. It is not surprising to me that service credits make a huge and mostly positive difference for those who have done little money-renting. What this means is that voluntary contribution to credit information is insufficient for those, mostly young, who are not borrowing money from voluntary contributors. However, creditors could collect this information for themselves, but then they would find it difficult to integrate the new information into the credit scores they have been relying on. This is the danger of artificial intelligence: it is almost impossible to correct.

Endnotes

[1] The paper *U.S. Consumer Credit Reports: Measuring Accuracy and Dispute Impacts*, authored by Michael A. Turner, Ph.D., Patrick Walker, M.A., and Robin Varghese, Ph.D., was published on May 2011. It can be found at www.perc.net/publications/u-s-consumer-credit-reports-measuring-accuracy-dispute-impacts/ and was last reviewed by me on July 13, 2019.

[2] The paper titled Section 319 of the Fair and Accurate Credit Transactions Act of 2003: Fifth Interim Federal Trade Commission Report to Congress Concerning the Accuracy of Information in Credit Reports, prepared by Beth A. Freeborn, Loren Smith, and Peter Vander Nat. Paul Rothstein, can be found at www.ftc.gov/reports/section-319-fair-accurate-credit-transactions-act-2003-fifth-interim-federal-trade. I last reviewed it on July 13, 2019.

CHAPTER SEVEN

Differences in data between credit reporting agencies

Abstract

One way to study the effect of errors in credit reports is to have individuals review them and report what they think are inaccuracies. In this chapter, we simply compare data of the same individuals, at the same moment, at different CRAs. If there are differences in the data, at least one is either wrong or incomplete. This is a data-dependent task, but, given that the data is available, neither time-consuming nor reliant on personal memory. It turns out that the data varies substantially: trade line counts, delinquency counts, the number of hard inquiries in the last year, and in what the CRAs have determined about people by going online or in person to courthouses. Credit score differences as a result are discussed in a later chapter.

The manner in which errors have been studied in the previous papers was costly because it required that people represented by the credit reports individually review them. I believe there is an easier way, for those who can obtain the right data. It is not costly to study *differences* in credit reports from one national CRA to another. If two pieces of information about a person *disagree*, then at least one of them is wrong. A computer can run this test, at little cost, and the work done by a single programmer. The CRAs cannot get such data, because no CRA can review another CRA's data. A few institutions, however, collect data on the same people at the same time from all three CRAs.

Recall what *my*FICO described as the contents of a credit report[1]

- Identifying Information.

  Your name, address, Social Security number, date of birth, and employment information are used to identify you. These factors are not used in credit scoring. Updates to this information come from information you supply to lenders.

- Trade Lines.

  These are your credit accounts. Lenders report on each account you have established with them. They report the type of account (bankcard, auto loan, mortgage, etc.), the date you opened the account, your credit limit or loan amount, the account balance, and your payment history.

Credit Data and Scoring: The First Triumph of Big Data and Big Algorithms
ISBN: 978-0-12-818815-6
https://doi.org/10.1016/B978-0-12-818815-6.00007-8

- Credit Inquiries.

  When you apply for a loan, you authorize your lender to ask for a copy of your credit report. This is how inquiries appear on your credit report. The inquiries section contains a list of everyone who accessed your credit report within the last two years. The report you see lists both "voluntary" inquiries, spurred by your own requests for credit, and "involuntary" inquires, such as when lenders order your report so as to make you a pre-approved credit offer in the mail.

- Public Record and Collections.

  Credit reporting agencies also collect public record information from state and county courts and information on overdue debt from collection agencies. Public record information includes bankruptcies, foreclosures, suits, wage garnishment, and liens.

Let us go over these one by one, starting with the trade lines because the identifying information does not get used in the evaluation of credit history. I will start with some statistics so that readers can first get a sense of how the reports on trade lines are distributed. These records cover millions of borrowers,[2] going back more than ten years. I believe it is fairly representative of the American market but I am not offering a formal proof of that. It is the same millions of borrowers from three different repositories, obtained at the same moment from each one.

In all graphs, the precise names of the CRAs are masked to CRA 1, 2, and 3. CRA1 is a particular CRA, and this is carried forward in every graph. The same, of course, for CRA2 and CRA3. For a reader to pierce this veil, he or she would need to have access to substantial common data from all repositories, and then they would not need this evidence. I want to make my point, but not given away any private secrets, or to imply there is a better or worse CRA. The point of this chapter is not to point fingers at one or the other, just to make the point that there are differences between them.

We start with trade lines. These are contracts, nearly always debt contracts, which are reported by creditors to the CRAs. These are the main stuff of credit reports. Here is a graph.

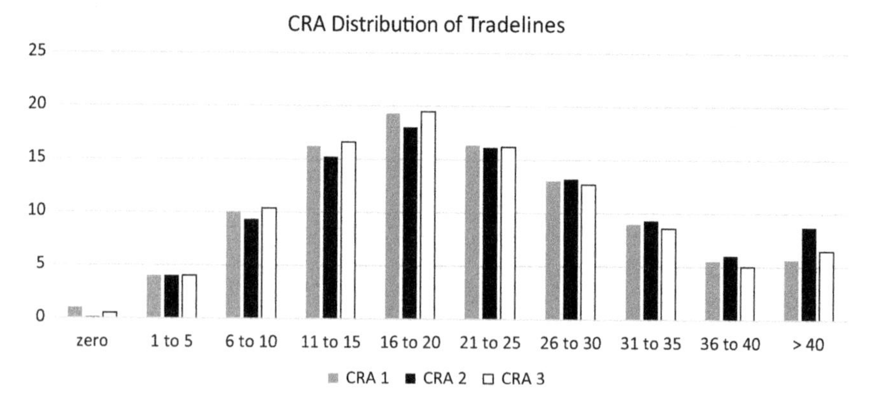

There are three CRAs here, CRA1, CRA2, and CRA3, blue (gray in print version), orange (black in print version), and green (white in print version) bars. Of course, these correspond to three particular credit bureaus in the U.S., but it is not important which is which. Across the chart horizontally, the X-axis in other words, are sets of bins each with three colors, starting on the left with a bin of people with no trade lines on their credit report, then moving one to the right to a bin of people with one to five trade lines on their credit report, then 6—10 trade lines, then 11—15 trade lines, and then the bin with the highest bars, 16—20 trade lines. There are blue orange and gray bars in each bin because the height of the bars is not perfectly equal but depends slightly on which CRA the data comes from. The height shows the percent of the CRA represented by the bin. The percent can be told by comparing the height of the bars to the vertical line on the left, the so-called Y-axis. Therefore, in the center bin, the gray bar is about 19%, while the orange bar is a percent or two below. That means the CRAs do not have quite the same percentage of borrows in that bin.

These are both open and closed trade lines, the ones that have not been purged. I was struck by how many trade lines there are, more than I have. More than 10 percent of people have more than 35 trades, counting both open and closed. Half have 11—25 trade lines. Of course, there are many that do not really represent efforts to borrow money, like my wife, who has a J Jill card, a Macy's card, etc. She gets these to receive coupons, or get an occasional discount, but it really means nothing more than that she shops there.

Therefore, in short, what I get from this chart is that Americans have a lot of reported trade lines, and that there are some differences in the average collection rate by a CRA. The differences at the individual level are more important and surprisingly large. The median difference is three trade lines between the highest count at a repository and the lowest count. The average difference is 3.6. It is possible that one of the numbers is right, but they cannot both be right. Is one an error? Would it be noticed by the reviewers used in the first two papers discussed in the last chapter? It does not seem so because the median is certainly not zero, and much less than half of the reviewers complained.

To bypass the relative irrelevance of closed trade lines here are the same charts for open trades only.

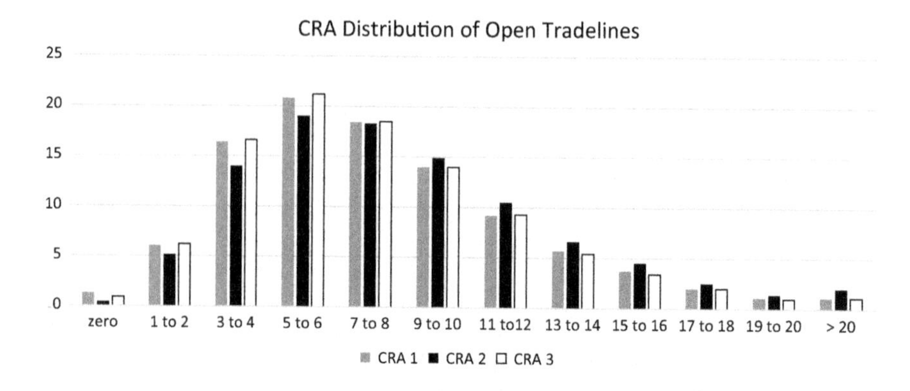

About half have between three and eight *open* trades, about a third the number of total trades (open plus closed). The differences in count at the individual level do shrink a lot. Individuals have a median difference of one open trade, the highest CRA count minus the lowest. On average, the difference is 1.3.

There is not a large difference, but most often, there *is* a difference, even for open trade lines.

Trades that are late do a lot of damage to credit scores and are frequently the most important cause of credit score drops. Here are charts that focus on that. Not surprisingly, there are differences in these as well.

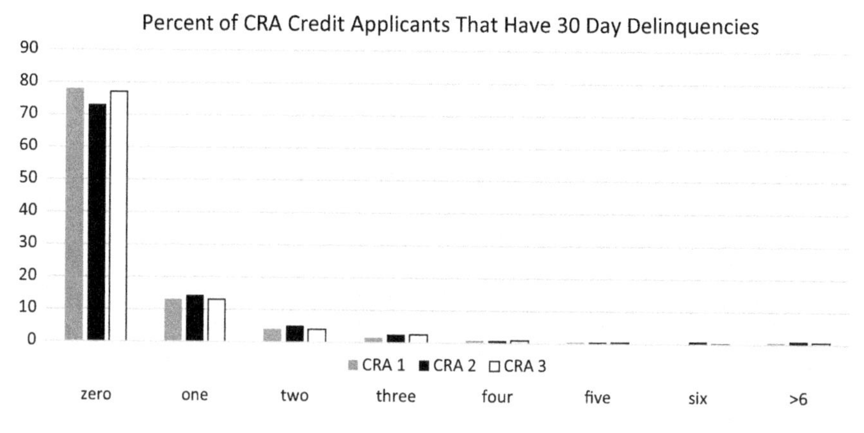

Next, let us look at inquiries. Only hard inquiries count in credit scores, that is, inquiries made by creditors who are deciding to lend money or services (cell phone, rent, etc.) after being asked for it by the consumer. Inquiry counts and types differ by nature from one CRA to another, as creditors (except for mortgage providers) typically go to one CRA or another with their inquiry: they would not usually bear the expense of going to all three. So, these can be expected to differ, even though they affect the credit score, not as much as trade lines or public records, but tangibly. Typically, an inquiry leads to a loss of some points, 5 or 10, from a credit score. These can happen fairly routinely and often mean nothing, but presumably some of those seeking this or that are in trouble and have worse performance on debts in the future. Hard credit inquiries stay on the credit report for a maximum of 2 years, but as per FICO, they are not used for scoring after 1 year, and only a little after 6 months. While the limit of 2 years for a hard inquiry to come off the credit report is widely acknowledged, in numerous websites and by the CRAs, it does not appear to be a legal requirement. FICO also makes an effort to dedupe inquiries that seem to be focused on the same goal, say, a mortgage. This, again, is a decision they make in their modeling efforts: it is not required by law. Some other party developing a score could choose not to dedupe.

Reviewing all hard inquiries that appear on credit reports, the difference in the number of inquiries between CRA records of the same person, at the same time, is only rarely zero, as shown in the following chart. Of course, these would be expected to vary a great deal; as creditors usually check only one repository. Different creditors, or different parts of the same creditor, will usually contract with one or another of the repositories (but often just one) to do these searches.

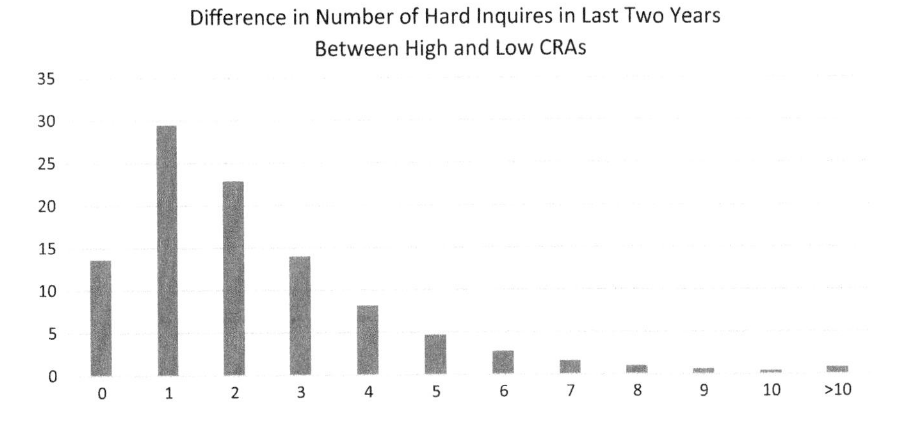

The most common difference is found in one, followed by two, and three. No difference (that is, 0) is fourth most common. About seven in eight consumers show a difference in number of hard inquiries over the last 2 years.

To summarize, there are many differences between what a CRA contains on the same consumer, differences in inquiries, public records, and trade lines, though public records are being erased at such a high rate that it seems pointless to chart the past. Differences do not exactly imply errors. For instance, our photos are all honest enough, though in one we are smiling, in another frowning, in one wearing a brown suit, and in another khaki shorts. In some sense, it would make a bit of a mockery of there being three credit companies if the same exact contents were available at each. However, this is supposed to be a public record of each one of us, *the* public record. If there are so many differences, it does not seem as if one or the other could be providing a final justice, that is, a true version without error.

Endnotes

[1] The myFICO site www.myfico.com/ is certainly a way to learn what FICO thinks about FICO. What I quote in this chapter is from that site at www.myfico.com/CreditEducation/In-Your-Credit-Report.aspx. I last reviewed both URLs on July 13, 2019.

[2] The data underlying these charts is anonymized. The scores are different not just because of data differences but because FICO models are created on the data slice of a single repository at a particular span in time.

CHAPTER EIGHT

Can credit errors be fixed? Probably not

Abstract

Data errors in credit reports are essentially unfixable. An individual does not pay the CRAs for collecting his/her data, nor is there an incentive for making the data correct. In 2003, Leonard Bennett testified before the House Subcommittee on Financial Institutions about the e-OSCAR process, which pretends to correct errors in credit reports but rarely does. This is a process that converts all arguments and evidence into a two-digit code, which is sent to creditors, who typically have software respond that there is no problem. While regulations pay lip service to the notion that credit reports should be accurate and complete, mine is not, and I attempted to file a dispute to have Chase report the monthly payments on my credit card. In the chapter, I discuss the many hours of effort I put in, leading to various bewildering software failures and no progress toward my goal.

An individual does not pay the CRAs a cent for collecting his/her data, nor receive a cent when it is sold. The individual can, however, pay for locks, patrols, watches, monitoring, and scans, all available because the CRA has gathered a chunk of that individual's data. Nevertheless, filing disputes are one thing the individual can do for free and supposedly the FCRA requires each CRA to pay attention. This chapter is about how well that works for the individual, which in my view is not well.

In 2003, Leonard Bennett testified before the House Subcommittee on Financial Institutions and Consumer Credit on behalf of the National Association of Consumer Advocates.[1] As a lawyer who frequently sued CRAs, he shared some of his stories as he attempted to piece together just how these companies conducted the investigations of disputes required by the FCRA.[2] Most of his clients had inaccuracies in their credit file—often due to identity theft or the peculiar tendency of furnishers to confuse two people with very similar names—but the basic method he describes in 2003 continued to be used at least as far forward as 2011 and, so far as my experience proves, to the present day.

As a preliminary matter, Bennett said that contacting a furnisher directly was pointless—they are largely immune under the FCRA, unless contacted

Credit Data and Scoring: The First Triumph of Big Data and Big Algorithms
ISBN: 978-0-12-818815-6
https://doi.org/10.1016/B978-0-12-818815-6.00008-X

by a CRA. Fine, let's assume the creditor knows enough to start their dispute with the CRA—what happens next? In a familiar display of cooperation, the three CRAs created a system called e-OSCAR, which exists to automate and streamline the dispute resolution process. With an estimated 20,000 disputes per day across the three CRA, it would take a veritable army of investigators to perform a reasonable review of all the supporting documents. What e-OSCAR does is take the written dispute letter and all supporting documentation and translate it into a 2-digit numeric code that is then sent to the furnisher.

The CRAs have nearly identical processes: low-paid, often foreign-outsourced employees sit in a room translating each dispute into a 2-digit code, according to Bennett. Even if given the lofty title of "investigators," as Bennett testifies, their sole job responsibility is data entry. The employees work from a quota system, expected to process each dispute in 4 min or less, translating to 15/h × 8 = 120 disputes investigated per day. They work from a limited number of 2-digit codes, and the assigned code generally has little to do with the underlying dispute. The furnisher never sees the documents sent in by the consumer to the CRA. For instance, two clients furnished handwriting samples and documentation around someone forging their signature. These disputes were reduced to a code meaning "Not his/hers."

The investigator at the furnisher only ever sees the two-digit code and never, according to the deposition of a furnisher's own employee, contacts the consumer for more details. He or she never contacts the CRA for more details either, not only due to the tight quota system, but also due to established policy at all three CRAs that Bennett likens to a shell game. The CRA pretends to satisfy its responsibility by sending the 2-digit code to the furnisher and asking if the furnisher can verify that it still wants the disputed item on the consumer credit report. If the furnisher replies that it does, as is overwhelmingly the case, the CRA rules against the consumer. The TransUnion deposition states that the CRA never acts on any information provided by any potential third parties (such as a government institution or a neutral witness) because such third party is "not the furnisher of information."

What about the furnisher's own investigation? In Bennett's words:

"Nearly every major furnisher who has been deposed has confessed to a policy of automated investigations in which the consumer has almost no hope of obtaining relief. The furnishers merely proofread the form from the CRA and match it to the data within their computer's account screen. There is no other means by which to verify and correct a credit-reporting dispute once the error has worked its way into the furnisher's computer account record. None of the major furnishers of which I am aware reviews original documents or paper records. In a May 21, 2003 deposition, Capital One's representative confirmed this fact for her employer." Remember that the consumer's data in the furnisher's system was the subject of dispute. Because they were not provided with any means to verify items in their own system, they responded to the CRA that they had 'verified' that their system contained the original derogatory item! In other words, their sole 'verification' was a form of proofreading—making sure their system in fact said what they originally reported to the CRA!

Bennett's testimony helped bring about a legislative change touted as a sweeping reform—but this reform appears meaningless to me. All the legislative changes that occurred were the allowance of consumers to more easily freeze their credit reports, matters which fix nothing and simply limit their participation in the credit world. I (Eric) decided to experience the error correct effort for myself and to see what a private citizen might do about the missing pay data. This certainly seemed to me to fit the criterion for incompleteness, seemingly the very thing which the FCRA intended to correct. There is that paragraph requiring data to be "correct and complete" from the FTC which I have already quoted, but the CFPB (the present regulator of financial credit), in their short summary of the FCRA, points out that an absence in completeness is grounds for dispute:[3]

- If you contest the **completeness** or accuracy of information in your report, you may file a dispute with the CRA and with the company that furnished the information to the CRA. Generally, both the CRA and the furnisher of information are legally obligated to reinvestigate your dispute as long as it is not frivolous.

The same point is made (about this field in fact) at a different FTC site, FTC.gov:[4]

Disputes to furnishers

You must investigate a consumer's dispute if it relates to:

- *the consumer's performance or other conduct concerning an account or other relationship with you. For example, disputes relating to the current payment status, high balance, date a payment was made,* ***amount of a payment made****, or date an account was opened or closed.*

So, I thought why do I not dispute this and learn about the dispute process first hand. I began by starting an on-line dispute with Equifax, because everyone does everything on-line.[5] What a nightmare it turned out to be! Nevertheless, it began sweetly enough, like a good horror movie.

The first page I saw had numerous tabs, some to put me at ease I guess, answer my questions, including HOW DOES IT WORK, WHAT SHOULD I LOOK FOR, WHAT DO I NEED TO START, and WHAT SHOULD I EXPECT. Then there were tabs under HOW DOES THE DISPUTE PROCESS WORK? These included: CHECK YOUR CREDIT REPORT, FILE A DISPUTE FOR FREE, and other comforting thoughts.

It was just introductory material. There was a picture of sympathetic looking woman, leading to a video. I listened to the compassionate feminine voice and proceeded to file the dispute. I faced a form with numerous questions about me and answered as best I could. I seemed to do it right—they found my file!—and so got a more difficult test of my identity (and memory!).

Question 1: "Your credit file indicates you may have a bank card, opened in or around August 2014. Who is the credit provider for this account?" Now I had my credit report. There were a lot of tempting answers, accounts I had, might have had. However, my credit report—and how often would someone have this—did not match date and account for any of them. I answered NONE OF THE ABOVE.

Question 2: "Your credit file indicates you may have an auto loan-lease. Who is the credit provider for this account?" Now this is a bit of a trick question. I have had auto leases but paid them off. The question is in the present tense.

Question 3: Your credit file indicates you may have a mortgage loan, opened in or around, August 2014. Who is the credit provider for this account? Well I had paid off all my first mortgages. Did this perhaps pertain to my Home Equity Line of Credit? Is there even a right answer?

Yet, somehow, I got all four questions right, with a lot of sweating, luck, and work. I was still in the game!

The next page asked me to upload any proofs I wanted to bring to my issue. I could upload in formats JPG, JPEG, TIFF, TIF, PING, GIF, and PDF. (Moreover, maybe if I were a millennial or younger, that one of these would have been possible!) I just ignored that, but had to pick what I wanted to dispute: PERSONAL INFORMATION, ACCOUNTS, NEGATIVE INFORMATION, and INQUIRIES. It seems to me there could be a lot of overlap in those words. I picked accounts, though I was already being dragged away from what I wanted to complain about.

I was given a bunch of buttons and picked among them, then months and values, triaged off into one little part of the universe, though I really want to write about a topic, about a general beef of non-reporting that covered multiple accounts, and every month on the account. But this type of complaint was not available to me, so I dutifully picked the one. I plowed on, finally receiving a page of facts about my Chase account, and my closest choice was "VERIFY HISTORICAL ACCOUNT INFORMATION". I then got a window full of things to dispute. One was "ACTUAL PAYMENT AMOUNT". It was always blank. It was never zero, or more, or less. I wrote in the balance in every box. I had paid the balance, exactly, every month! It was done by computer transfer, of course. The credit card company swept money from my account every month. And I also wrote this in a free-form box where I was allowed to express myself.

I thought I was doing pretty well. It had taken me an hour or so, but I was bowling all strikes. Then BOING! I was told there was some sort of error and it all disappeared. So, I did it all again, only a half hour gone this time, submitted the dispute again, and got the error *again*. After that, things got worse. I could not even get past the identity check. The above was as close as I was going to get to submitting this on-line. I tried a third time, and a fourth, and a fifth, and a sixth, and in each case, I saw the deadly message as below.

We are currently unable to process your request

I really have no explanation why I got through twice but could not submit, then never got through the ID part again. Because I was given the choice for "Web Email" vs. just "Close," I went for the Web Email route. This was in a confusing format, but I doubt it mattered. I was allowed to submit a written complaint but got no case file or record. I had nothing that I was aware of that I could use to see if they ever received it. When I tried to look up what I had done via the key on the credit report I had received, I got no response at all.

Then I did what many older people (in the U.S at least) do: I found a number to phone for Equifax disputes and phoned it. The man I spoke to was a pleasant fellow talking to me from the Philippines named Kevin. He began with an evident resistance to taking my dispute. He was, first of all, I think, honestly mystified that I was bothering to complain when my credit score was apparently high and my credit report did not show anything really bad ("adverse"); however, he eventually accepted that it was my business if I wanted to care about data regardless of harm. He was more resistant to the actual matter, not believing that it was even disputable. He plainly said that payments were just something Chase did not send. So, he knew. He said the job of Equifax was to "compile," and I should "call Chase." He said this a couple of times, in a couple different ways. I was not to be put off. I said that I knew that Chase knew what I paid, because it was on my statement, but I was holding Equifax responsible for FCRA requirements to get my data factual and complete.

With that, he dropped his objection and tried a different tactic to put me off: he pointed out that the record said I was born in 1956, not 1953, so I would have to send in my evidence of my birth data to file a dispute. I told him that the birth problem was nothing I cared to worry about: I just wanted to dispute the lack of payment. I made that argument almost word for word the same twice. After saying it twice, he suddenly dropped all objections and took my dispute, without excitement or encouragement, but he was obliging. He gave me a case number (8268060918), but by his tone of voice and former points, I did not expect much. Within 2 days, on a Saturday, I received the following email:

Dear Eric Rosenblatt

Equifax has completed your dispute for Confirmation Number 8268060918

VIEW NOW!

Etc. Etc.

Thanks for giving Equifax the Opportunity to Serve You

I guess I had an answer! Eagerly, I tried to get in by clicking the website on the notice (which will not copy), where I was presented with a number of identifying questions, but once again, I could not get in because the plain facts about who I was were rejected by the system. I tried to phone Equifax but was told that it was closed and unavailable to me. On Monday, I tried again. I spoke to someone in India, who had me wait on the phone to speak to someone else in India, who told me the system was down and to call back in an hour. I called back in an hour and was told the following, which I realize I have heard every time: "I am so sorry for your inconvenience," from a woman in Central America, who told me (as I always hear when I ask where someone is) "Equifax is a worldwide organization. She switched me to "Customer Service," where a computer explained they were having "unusual wait times." I was offered the chance to be called back and I took it. Of course, I was numb at this point.

About 10 min later, I was indeed called back and explained to by a nice woman with a new accent that the dispute response was that "I had never been late." I said that was not even my dispute and she sort of understood but, upon questioning, explained that all disputes were turned into computer codes and sent to the furnisher to check, and my problem was simply not one in the computer code. (This sounds like Bennett's testimony many years ago!) Maybe Chase saw my comments, maybe not—I never found out. But the response was I have never been late: end of story. In short, I simply could not dispute the issue bugging me. I have no rights without starting a court case and even then, probably not.

Basic impression that I formed: there is no real dispute process.

I would like to add a last comment on the almost humorous point that Equifax has my wrong birthdate. I had honestly never noticed that, even though it is right here in this book. Yes, looking at the version in the Appendix, it does say that I was born in 1956, making me 3 years younger than I really am. This is not used in credit score modeling, but it is, apparently, used to identify me and could be used by employers, insurance companies, etc. for the same purpose. It has perhaps caused me some trouble somewhere already, without my understanding why someone did not know who I was, and possibly (probably?) why I could not get back into my credit complaint, though it makes no sense that I could get in twice. (By the way, I later tried to get through to the on-line system with 1956 as my birth year: no luck.) It is just dramatic, if minor, additional evidence that credit reports have a degree of fiction in them.

Endnotes

1 The testimony on June 4, 2003 of Leonard Bennett to the Subcommittee on Financial Institutions and Consumer Credit regarding the *Fair Credit Reporting Act: How it Functions for Consumers and the Economy* is available at www.creditcourt.com/BennettFCRATestimony.html#page/. I last reviewed the URL on July 13, 2019.

2 The Federal Trade Commission makes a copy of the Fair Credit Reporting Act (FCRA), as amended over the years, available in PDF form at www.ftc.gov/system/files/545a_fair-credit-reporting-act-0918.pdf. I last reviewed this on July 13, 2019.

3 The Consumer Finance Protection Board summarizes their view of the FCRA October 13, 2018 under the title *CFPB Releases New Version of Model FCRA Summary of Rights* at www.mayerbrown.com/en/perspectives-events/publications/2018/10/cfpb-releases-new-version-of-model-fcra-summary-of, last reviewed by me on July 13, 2019.

4 In October of 2016, the Federal Trade Commission created a PDF entitled *CONSUMER REPORTS: WHAT INFORMATION FURNISHERS NEED TO KNOW*, accessible at www.ftc.gov/system/files/documents/plain-language/pdf-0118_consumer-reports-what-information-furnishers-need-to-know_2018.pdf. This document requires complete data from furnishers. I last reviewed this site on July 13, 2019.

5 *The Equifax On-Line Dispute Process* is at www.equifax.com/personal/disputes/. I last reviewed the site on July 13, 2019.

CHAPTER NINE

The mystery of credit scores

Abstract

As limited as are the data in credit reports, there are still hundreds if not thousands of variables in every credit report, and no human agreement about what is most important. Thus, they are data mined in models that predict delinquency or default, and the probability is called a credit score. FICO, by being first with such a score, and the cleverness to put it in a relative score from 300 to 850, has become a standard in many US markets. The score, created by computers, is immune to explanations of what this or that was done or happened, or even to pointing out errors in the data. To both give enough information about the score to avoid anger but still sell their proprietary model, FICO publishes hints, but not explanations, about what makes their scores work.

You may still remember that there were some odd blanks in my credit report, some missing old cards and mortgages, and some oddball numbers. But despite that, my credit report was all positive and my credit score is high. I have many years of credit with no late payments. But would I get the lowest possible rate on a mortgage, if I wanted one on, say, a second home? Will I get that two-percent-back credit card? That is a practical worry that I might give an hour to, if I knew what to do. For someone with less history or income than I have, or with a burgeoning family, or some big educational or medical expenses coming up, the question is not casual. My daughter worries about her credit score all the time, and with good reason. She has many bills ahead of her, expects to borrow, and knows that her credit score will drive her costs and may even prevent her from doing what she is trying to do. Though my daughter has an excellent score now, she never does anything financial without some anxiety about whether the consequence might be to lower it. The problem is that neither she nor I know exactly what raises or lowers it, despite both of us being students of credit scoring. Should we raise our limit, pay off a card, reduce our mortgage? The effect might be up tomorrow and then, later, down. Or visa versa.

The difficulty answering such questions is that in virtually all cases the contents of the credit report will go through a mysterious algorithm to become a credit score, run by the CRAs on every fresh new batch of credit for which the score is request. They will then get a single number between

Credit Data and Scoring: The First Triumph of Big Data and Big Algorithms
ISBN: 978-0-12-818815-6
https://doi.org/10.1016/B978-0-12-818815-6.00009-1

300 and 850 (in the United States) that represents the consumer's credit worthiness and general reliability. It seems to be in our nature to believe that the mystery adds to the meaning and wisdom of the result rather than just adding randomness and confusion. My observation is that this interpretation goes far further than my family. Now it is quite possible that I steer people to the subject of credit much more than the average conversationalist, but I cannot tell you how often that people crow to me with great pride that they have an 800-credit score (or higher). The only item I hear more readily is that someone went to Harvard: that seems an impossible secret to keep. The humor in this for me is that the person usually does not know much about how they got that score, apart from the fact that they are simply a superior being. What people see is the final answer and not how the answer was achieved. Do you know which questions you got right or wrong that led to your SAT score? But you remember your whole life what that SAT score was, long after you forgot the phone number you had at the time. For those overly proud of their 800 score, let me just point out that 21.7% of borrowers have a score of 800 or better in the most recent version of FICO. By the way, mine is 834—just saying.

Credit scoring was invented (according to *Wikipedia* but of course history is written by the winners) by FICO,[1] originally founded in 1956 as Fair, Isaac, and Company by engineer William Fair and mathematician Earl Isaac. The two met while working at the Stanford Research Institute in Menlo Park and tried to sell a credit scoring system to American lenders 2 years later. But the score did not really take at the time. Computers were still too scarce and credit reports were not widely computerized yet anyway. But somehow these guys, or the company, muddled along for a couple decades, not dying out but not picking up a lot of traction either. Oddly, there is little about them in these years to be found on the Internet, including the FICO website. Earl Isaac died in 1983, according to *Wikipedia*; and there is no entry for Bill Fair at all that I could find (though his obituary is on the Internet). But let us date the modern method of scoring, probably without involvement by Isaac or Fair, as 1981, with the introduction of the FICO score by Fair, Isaac, and Company. In 1991, the FICO score was made available at all three repositories. It gained users rapidly and experienced a major milestone when in 1995 most mortgage companies adopted credit scores. Maybe it took a while, but FICO happened. Credit scoring happened.

According to *Wikipedia*, FICO has approximately 60 variations of its predictive model. Part of the reason there are so many is that most score versions are estimated three times: one at each national CRA. FICO has both what are called "generic" versions, which predict the general riskiness of people regarding everything, and industry-specific models, which are slightly more predictive for the "bankcard, personal finance, mortgage, installment loan, and auto loan" industries. Each different version, including the industry-specific versions, does something ever so slightly different. For instance, Classic FICO predicts the probability that a borrower will fall 3 months behind on *any one* credit trade line. NextGen predicts the chance that a borrower will be 3 months late on an average trade line. FICO 9 is different in several small details that are used to form the prediction. For instance, it will use a rental trade line if this is reported by a landlord (though rent is rarely included in the credit report). Each new score costs a little extra.

Vantage, a score owned jointly by the three national CRAs, is FICO's key corporate competitor. Vantage is trying to get traction for Vantage 4.0 now, following three previous Vantage versions. (It is probably pushing an even later version as you read this.) Vantage, owned jointly by all the repositories, has the same weights and variables at all three national CRAs; but because there are usually slight differences in data at the CRAs, most borrowers have three different scores, such as FICO, depending on the Bureau. That means 12 Vantage scores. Per the Experian website: "The first two versions of the VantageScore ranged from 501 to 990, but the latest VantageScore 3.0 and 4.0 use the same 300-to-850 range as base FICO scores."[2] Vantage now uses the same 300—850 scale as FICO and tries to make each value on that scale mean the same thing as FICO means. FICO tried to prevent Vantage from contesting the credit score space in the courts but lost.[3] Vantage then moved to copy the FICO score range, which, so far as I can tell, was never separately fought in legal forums.

Vantage's goal in using the 300—850 scale is to erase an important barrier to entry: familiarity. They are in the classic position of trying to disrupt a market dominated by one large company (think Google and Facebook). Markets believe they understand the FICO score, trust the FICO brand, and most market users would just as soon not have to deal with new scores. Additionally, most risk-taking companies already have contracts to get FICO scores, and inertia is a powerful force. In the mortgage world, mortgages are typically priced with the FICO Classic scores, which borrowers and lenders can obtain along with the credit reports for a few bucks. Mortgage insurers who co-insure most loans with over 80 loan to value ratio (examples being MGIC, Genworth, and Radian) use and trust the Classic

FICO score. Mortgage-backed security buyers create their prepay models on loans using FICO scores (though they may well have models using other scores as well).

It is not that these entities love FICO and would never consider another score, but there is a lot of inertia in the complex interweave of lenders, securitizers, and investors and nobody really wants to go through the trouble of getting new contracts, reevaluating their models, explaining the changes to investors, unless there is an obvious payoff for them. Of course, Vantage and other competitors that will come forth in the future believe there is a payoff. Recently, a bill passed, the Economic Growth, Regulatory Relief and Consumer Protection Act, which will require competition in credit scoring for mortgages.[4] However, this was then followed by some policy zigzags by the mortgage regulator. After years of meetings on the topic, the Federal Housing Finance Administration (FHFA) told the major mortgage securitizers, which they regulate, not to use Vantage, because it was owned by the CRAs.[5] But then just a few days ago (dated from my writing this line), FHFA, now under a new Director, appointed by Trump, reversed that thought. In that appendix the FHFA instructs the regulated Enterprises, who bear most of the credit risk in the United States, to undertake a review of credit scores with the notion of potential replacing FICO, or perhaps doing without FICO. The key limitation, as I understand it, is that "Each application must demonstrate use of the credit score by creditors to make a decision whether to extend credit to a prospective borrower. An Enterprise may address criteria for such demonstration in the Credit Score Solicitation. An Enterprise may permit such demonstration of use to include submission of testimonials by creditors (mortgage or non-mortgage) who use the applicant's credit score when making a determination to approve the extension of credit." I think this means that upstarts cannot produce a score. So far as I know, only FICO and VantageScore are embedded enough to deliver testimonials of use. This seems to open the door to Vantage and to modestly encourage the mortgage industry to move away from FICO—but this will be slow and policy may be reversed again. The announcement is shown in Appendix 2 for junkies of credit scoring, like myself.

Given this see-saw in one major credit sector, it is frankly hard to see how FICO preserves its US market power in the long run—its stock dropped 5% just after the announcement—but then it has been hard to see how it has preserved its market power this long. Market power, all power, is always surprising, in lasting until there is belief in its permanence and then in dissolving. Vantage is trying to represent itself as David taking on Goliath, though it is hard to see a firm owned by the national CRAs that have been around unchanged for decades as the plucky outsider. Note that it is only in the United States where FICO has this dominance. In other countries, scores come from all sorts of companies, often the CRAs themselves, individually, whichever one or ones is in place in that country. Indeed, in the United States all the CRAs have their own scores, and some companies do as well—they just do not have the market share of FICO.

A score is just a model on some scale, requiring regressions and the data to run them on. The main point is that nobody knows except very generally how their financial choices flow through to their credit scores. This profusion of scores just confuses the issue more. Some particular difference could raise one credit score and lower another. Why is the consumer so unable to figure out where and why they come out and where they do on this or that model? Unfortunately, transparency flies in the face of the natural capitalist wish to monetize information, which means not sharing it. Facebook does not give away all its data lest another networking company make a play for its customers. Likewise, FICO is coy on specifics because if they allowed themselves to be copied perfectly, they would be copied perfectly, and then they could no longer charge for what they do. Their models are "proprietary," allowing them to charge for them because nobody can simply copy it. But FICO does not own either the data or the tools of regression. They do own a brand, however, and they need the aura of mystery to keep their brand earning rents.

Here is material from the MyFICO website of the FICO score[6]:

> *FICO Scores are calculated from many different pieces of credit data in your credit report. This data is grouped into five categories as outlined below. The percentages in the chart reflect how important each of the categories is in determining how your FICO Scores are calculated.*

A picture follows that for copyright purposes I do not copy. But the picture is an attractive disk divided colorfully to show that the score is as follows:

30% Amounts Owed
35% Payment History
15% Length of Credit History
10% Mix of Credit
10% New Credit
Followed by quite a bit of prevarication

These percentages are based on the importance of the five categories for the general population. For particular groups—for example, people who have not been using credit long—the relative importance of these categories may be different.

The importance of any one factor in your credit score calculation depends on the overall information in your credit report....

Your FICO Scores consider both positive and negative information in your credit report. Late payments will lower your FICO Scores, but establishing or re-establishing a good track record of making payments on time will raise your score.

The importance of any one factor in your credit score calculation depends on the overall information in your credit report....

Frankly, the final story is pretty vague. "For some people, one factor may have a larger impact that it would for someone with a much different credit history." Well what factor is that? Am I someone strongly affected by that factor? Why does the consumer not deserve to know what is causing them money or time? I thought it might be possible to get more precision by clicking on the line above "How to Improve My Credit Score."

I thought I would hit the button and see what popped up. A lot did!

It's important to note that repairing bad credit is a bit like losing weight: It takes time and there is no quick way to fix a credit score....

Three Important Things You Can Do Right Now

1. Check Your Credit Report – Credit score repair begins with your credit report. If you haven't already, request a free copy of your credit report and check it for errors. Your credit report contains the data used to calculate your credit score and it may contain errors....
2. Setup Payment Reminders – Making your credit payments on time is one of the biggest contributing factors to your credit scores....
3. Reduce the Amount of Debt You Owe – This is easier said than done....
   - Don't open a number of new credit cards that you don't need, just to increase your available credit.

This approach could backfire and actually lower your credit scores.

- Have credit cards – but manage them responsibly.

To summarize, "fixing" a credit score is more about fixing errors in your credit history (if they exist) and then following the guidelines above to maintain consistent, good credit history. Raising your scores after a poor mark on your report or building credit for the first time will take patience and discipline.

Along with all that (and much more which I did not copy) was a lovely graphic of a cheerful woman by a colorful chart that is labeled "Credit Report." I am not sure what all that clarified. They are going to score you as they see fit, and you really cannot wriggle out of it, even if you know for sure you intend to repay whatever you charge. They make the true point that generally the FICO score follows common sense and the person who has for years paid all their debts and exhibits few signs of financial desperation will look good. But they ignore the fact that there are also irrelevant accidents going into scores. What if I sold my home and took a trip around the world using my credit card? I happen to know that would drive my utilization way up on the credit report. The fact that I have ample 401K to do this and would only be using my credit card for convenience and miles would not matter. For a time, I would fall in the utilization group of people draining their credit card limit just before collapsing financially.

Recently, perhaps because of the FICO/Vantage competition, I have started to see FICO and Vantage information appearing on credit card websites.[7] I have a Chase credit card. When I go to my account, I see a highly colored diagram, with a green circle around my score: 824. There are five bands of increasing score: red, orange, yellow, light green, and dark green. I am in the highest band, yes, which is a vivid, dark green. It goes from 74 percentile to 100 percent, covering the score 781 to 850. I want to be a one percenter, dammit!

My current credit balance shows 6096. But I have no *credit* balance. I would never borrow on my credit cards! I pay them off every month. But I suppose that is what I need to move from my bank account to my Chase credit account as of today.

I have 0 late payments, 0 inquiries, 2% utilization (which must mean they include my HELOC; no other limits could be anywhere near 50 times my balance), and then available credit of $280,094. For sure, that includes my HELOC.

Then there is a bunch of text.

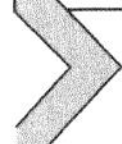

Positive score factors

Few or no installment accts with delinquent or derogatory payment status

An installment account is one with a fixed monthly payment for the life of the loan. Auto loans and student loans are common examples of installment loans. Paying your bills on time improves your score. You have paid all your installment loans on time or no more than 30 days late.

What You Can Do

Keep paying bills on time every month since it is important to maintaining a good credit score. If you remain behind with any payments, bring them current as soon as possible, and then make future payments on time.

Balances on bankcard or revolving accts not too high compared to limits

Bankcard accounts include credit cards and charge cards from a bank and are frequently revolving accounts. Revolving accounts allow you to carry a balance and your monthly payment will vary, based on the amount of your balance. Your balances on bankcard or revolving accounts are not too high compared to the credit limit amounts, which causes your score to improve.

What You Can Do

Keep low balances on your accounts; this will benefit your score.

Negative score factors

Your largest credit limit on open bankcard or revolving accounts is too low

Bankcard accounts include credit cards and charge cards from a bank and are frequently revolving accounts. Revolving accounts allow you to carry a balance and your monthly payment will vary, based on the amount of your balance. The largest credit limit among all the open bankcard or revolving accounts in your credit file is low. Having higher limits gives you access to credit without seeking new loans or becoming overextended which are triggers for higher risk

What You Can Do

Use credit responsibly and always make payments on time with your existing accounts. After a period of successfully managing your accounts, you can seek increases to your credit limit.

The date that you opened your oldest account is too recent

Your oldest account is still too recent. A credit file containing older accounts will have a positive impact on your credit score because it demonstrates that you are experienced managing credit.

What You Can Do

Don't open more accounts than you actually need. Research shows that new accounts indicate greater risk. Your score will benefit as your accounts get older.

Total of all balances on bankcard or revolving accounts is too high

Bankcard accounts include credit cards and charge cards from a bank and are frequently revolving accounts. Revolving accounts allow you to carry a balance and your monthly payment will vary, based on the amount of your balance. The total combined amount you owe on all of your bankcards and revolving accounts is high, a sign of increased risk. People who carry balances on multiple bankcards or other revolving accounts have reduced available credit to use if needed, creating a greater chance of becoming overextended.

What You Can Do

Pay down the balances on your accounts. Ideally, the balance on any revolving account should be 30% or less of the total credit limit on that account.

The balances on your accounts are too high compared to loan amounts

The balances on your accounts are high compared to the original loan amounts, lowering your score.

What You Can Do

Paying down the balances on your accounts will benefit your score.

The four points offered do not seem useful or desirable to me (not to mention there is no practical benefit to be trying to get higher than 824.)

"Your largest credit limit on open bankcard or revolving accounts is too low." I suppose I could call up Chase and have them make it larger than the $26,000 allowed now, but I have so far never used that much in a month and always pay it automatically out of my account. I presume this is here because a correlation that has been picked up between extremely high limits and very low delinquency rates and that is part of why I do not have an 850-credit score.

"The date you opened your oldest account is too recent." This one is sort of humorous, since I opened accounts decades ago that have been dropped from my credit report according to their rule of deleting data that has not been updated in 10 years. This message and my score are thus to some extent just artifacts of their process decisions, and having nothing to do with me. That is always true of credit scores: accidents with no bearing on credit risk get swept up into the credit score.

A next section is a what-if calculator that seems to promise specificity about what different things I might do and how they would change my credit score. But, the selection of what-ifs does not pass the useful and sensible test. For instance, I could see what the effect on my score would be if I had a "Public Record Child Support" on my credit score; but as my youngest is 25, that seems an unlikely event. I have an option in the what-if calculator to cancel my oldest card, but really my oldest card is not even here. Frankly, this is not the application I would envision to teach consumers about credit scores or give them advice.

The application I envision, and which could be made available to consumers relatively easily, will try to explain the credit score by allowing the consumer to change things that are on the credit report and see how that percolates through to the credit score. In other words, I would offer consumers the practical information they are probably seeking: what do they need to do to raise their credit score? I am not worried about being gamed, because I believe that people that can and do take these steps are demonstrating a control and motivation about credit that is normally a positive and unavailable signal all by itself. I would show the summary of the credit report. Here is mine again:

Report Date	Oct 23, 2017
Credit File Status	No fraud indicator on file
Alert Contacts	0 Records Found
Average Account Age	10 Years, 9 Months
Length of Credit History	17 Years
Accounts with Negative Information	0
Oldest Account	CITICARDS CBNA (Opened Oct 01, 2000)
Most Recent Account	BANK OF AMERICA (Opened Nov 15, 2014)

The words in values in red are presumably reflecting choices I had made in my life. The reader could change these in any way at all and see the effect on her credit score. Of course, much of that is done and past. The only value in changing it is to give the reader cause to see what she has ever done to raise or lower her credit score. At any time, the borrower could bring the credit report back to its original state. In that case (starting over) the app would not show a New Credit Score.

Now the above is a summary of individual trade lines that appear below. The app must say clearly that the borrower can either allow the summary to change and cease to sync up with the individual trade lines or she can change the individual trade lines. This is just because most people would probably like to just change the summary and do not want to have to alter details to engineer a particular summary. The truth is that you have to test-drive an application to see if people understand how to use it.

I would then present key additional parts of the credit report, particularly trade lines that have a negative payment history. Here I dummy mine to have some problems. Again, what is in red can be changed by the borrower, who can see what the impact would be on his credit score. In that case the summary would change and the credit score would change.

Account Type	Open	With Balance	Total Balance	Available	Credit Limit	Debt-to-Credit	Payment
Revolving	2	1	$47	$36,953	$37,000	0.0%	$27
Mortgage	1	0	$0	$70,000	$70,000	0.0%	$0
Installment	0	0					
Other							
Total	3	1	$47	$106,953	$107,000	0.0%	$27

The challenge of this application is to be simple and clear to the borrower, showing what data changes a credit score and making it possible for a borrower to make those changes and to unwind changes and try new variations. The reader might think me absurd for imagining computer applications, particularly as I seem so annoyed and lame in these technologies. In my defense, it was my job for many years to both think up and direct the creation of such applications. I claim no particular brilliance here, but it is on my resume. Awkwardness is also not necessarily the worst starting point. One way to create technology (or a book) is to start from confusion and imagine how to get out of it.

Endnotes

1 Seemingly unbiased references to FICO history can be found at www.en.Wikipedia.org/wiki/FICO, which I last reviewed on July 14, 2019.

2 From *The Difference Between VantageScore Scores and FICO Scores* by Louis DeNicola, published May 15, 2019 at www.experian.com/blogs/ask-experian/the-difference-between-vantage-scores-and-fico-scores/and reviewed by me on August 13, 2019.

3 See *FICO Lawsuit Against Experian and TransUnion to Proceed to Trial.* From May 29, 2009 by John S Kiernan, Senior Writer and Editor at *WalletHub* at website https://wallethub.com/edu/cs/fico-lawsuit-experian-transunion/25669/. I last reviewed the site on August 13, 2019.

4 The bill is described in *THE SCORE* from Vantage company, with an article entitled *The Economic Growth, Regulatory Relief and Consumer Protection Act* at the website https://thescore.vantagescore.com/article/398/signed-economic-growth-regulatory-relief-and-consumer-protec. I reviewed this website on August 13, 2019.

5 Per *FHFA issues new rule effectively prohibiting Fannie and Freddie from using VantageScore* from *HousingWire* written by Ben Lane on December 14, 2018 at the website https://www.housingwire.com/articles/47708-fhfa-issues-new-rule-effectively-prohibiting-fannie-and-freddie-from-using-vantagescore, reviewed by me on August 13, 2019.

6 Biased but more complete references to FICO history can be found on the FICO website: www.fico.com/en/abo ut-us#our_history. It was reviewed by me on July 14, 2019.

7 A *Wikipedia* site that discusses the variety of FICO and other credit scores is www.en.Wikipedia.org/wiki/Credit_score_in_the_United_States. It was last reviewed by me on July 14, 2019.

CHAPTER TEN

Making a credit score: it starts with data

Abstract

While credit scores are simply scaled probabilities of delinquency, based on regressions that related data in the credit report to performance on this or that debt, they play a starring role in the dehumanization of commerce. Thus, what is in the credit report (or not in the credit report) is critical. This chapter tries to explain what creditors (data furnishers in this context) say about people by looking at the data available in the TransUnion credit report. I review TransUnion data because I cannot directly obtain what comes from creditors, but the format they use is in what is called the Metro 2 published the trade association of the CRAs. Because the TransUnion format names are close to those of the Metro 2, I used this chapter to infer what is provided by the furnishers and explain it to the reader. A lot of data provided by furnishers is nonsense.

Credit scores are not conceptually complicated: they are tools to make predictions. The problem is that their precision is way oversold, the outcome is personalized far too much, the whole apparatus behind them has darkened our privacy, and they have played a starring role in the dehumanization of commerce. Ignoring those downers, predictions are a necessary and often fun part of life. Television and radio are full of people predicting who will win the Super Bowl or some election. They often do so from their guts, but even then, there is a perhaps unconscious sort-of-mathematical model of behavior that they have formed from watching numerous contests. For instance, a commentator rarely predicts that a team that loses a lot of games will beat a team that has won a lot of games. And sometimes, with saber metrics and so on, there is a specific statistical model, worked out like a credit score, that predicts outcome winners, pennant winners, etc.

Credit scores are models like sports forecasting models, except that they have a particular data source, which is the credit report, and they typically (but do not have to) predict a credit event, often that a borrower will become 90 days late on some trade line over the next 2 years. Credit scores data mine credit reports to get these predictions, meaning they do almost whatever works to improve the prediction. The Equal Credit Opportunity Act prohibits the use of race, sex, and age in models, but mostly

Credit Data and Scoring: The First Triumph of Big Data and Big Algorithms
ISBN: 978-0-12-818815-6
https://doi.org/10.1016/B978-0-12-818815-6.00010-8

(if they beware ECOA rules) the modelers can do as they please. Because one can only predict things in the future, credit modelers take credit reports from the past and predict something that happened between the date of the credit report and *now*, often predicting something that can be discovered by also buying a later credit report (just not later than now, since that has not happened yet). They assume that the predictive model will continue to work into the future and start using or selling this model for new business.

In this chapter, I focus on the particulars of the data in the U.S. that modelers mine for credit scores. It is messy stuff, but the details are important for practitioners and (I hate to admit I believe this) fascinating. However, they are probably only important and fascinating if you have to work with this stuff. However, this is the data out of which you, the reader, are described and represented to the world. You could just browse it to get a feeling for what we deal with. I have complained about messy and incomplete and will do so again; but, to be fair, there are few models that do not start with messy data. Messiness is part of modeling. I do not have an issue with the messiness per se, but with the trust given a score whose source has so many errors, and the inability of consumers either to correct this in the repository or demonstrate to creditors that their credit score or underlying data misrepresents them.

Most data (in pure count of lines of data) comes from credit companies. The credit companies which furnish data do so in a common format to all three CRAs, the Metro 2 format, described in the 2017 Credit Reporting Resource Guide. It is prepared by the Consumer Data Information Association, the trade association of the CRAs that they seem to turn to whenever they want to act jointly. Now here is the rub: most people, including me throughout my career, can see the guide but cannot actually see what furnishers give the CRAs. The CRAs all get identical stuff from data furnishers but add in their own inquiries, public records they get separately from court houses and other public place, and whatever else they can vacuum up, and then issue branded and corporately differentiated version, to companies like the one I worked for.[1] I expect each CRA would have all sorts of reasons why they need to change the furnisher data a little, but in the end they could just pass on what the furnishers provide, and they could also unify their work with public records and inquiries—but then there would be but one company, instead of three. Their stockholders would not like it.

Therefore, even institutional modelers have to infer what is in the Metro 2 data. I doubt it is altered all that much by the CRA but they do mess with it a bit, though it seems only in fields that are pretty inconsistent across furnishers already. It is from a particular version of the TransUnion credit report, which struck me as the simplest of the CRA versions, that I infer what furnishers have and can say about consumers. The TransUnion Guide for this version has 674 pages, that is, it is so long that only a careerist would possibly invest the time to follow it. It is divided into "segments," which I suppose are something like small chapters.

The TR01 segment (of the TransUnion record) is where all the trade line data is, namely that is where we get what the data furnishers sent in on the Metro 2. (There is some sense here.) In this chapter, I will lay out some of this data to give the reader (and myself) a flavor for the key fields available generally, therefore available for making a credit score. This is what is known about you. It happens here. It may be dull to you, but then have you ever seen your colon? You trust your care to a gastroenterologist and hope that is enough. When it matters enough, you learn something about it.

There are lots of other facts and segment names, which I put in an earlier version of this book, but now realize are painfully dull—so they are gone. Actual modelers of credit data, a relatively small group, should know all the details though many do not. They leave it to the programmer to make variables they can use in their regressions. The reader might browse enough to get angry at how disorganized it all is. If it were really your colon, you would be dead by now.

Anyway, I am going to stick to words that seem close to making sense. I am also going to take these fields in order, but not every single one, from the Metro 2 format list. I just want to give the difficult flavor of the data, as any credit score modeler sees it.

Portfolio Type: This is the first field based on the Metro 2 list. I think the reader will agree that it is a word combination that could mean almost anything. However, what it actually means can be more or less told from the possible values. The variables allowed by the Metro 2 format for Portfolio Type are: C = Line of Credit, I = Installment, M = Mortgage, O = Open, and R = Revolving. Portfolio Type appears in the TransUnion data as well, with exactly the same possible entries. It is what kind of debt we are talking about. This is a critical field in models, as installment debts and Revolving debts are quite different beasts and say very different things about consumer's behavior. However, lots of accounts have aspects of at least two categories, for instance, my HELOC, which is a sort of mortgage, and a sort of Revolving credit card. I could think of it as either. In the making of a credit score, I just try to use it every which way and see what does the best job predicting delinquency for the most people. A few choices are just too ugly to describe, so they are not considered. But the truth is that trial and error is the main stuff of scores and AI generally: that is how the sausage is made!

Based on what we see on the TransUnion data report (and the other two), "Open" trade line does not mean what the word usually indicates, that the trade line has not been closed. They include cards like American Express where the amount borrowed can vary, with no specified limit; however, the consumer is expected to pay back the entire debt each month. As such, these accounts are quite close to Revolving accounts in their impacts. Annoyingly, Open also includes trade lines that have been opened by Collection Companies. This means for the modelers that they have to also try to check for company name or prior delinquency to try to make that important distinction. Sausage!

Account Type—The term account type (which comes second after portfolio type) is like that first field Portfolio Type in that it relies on a word "Account" that means all sorts of things to all sorts of groups. Here are the first 10 entries mentioned by the Metro 2:

Auto
Unsecured
Secured
Partially Secured
Home Improvement
FHA Home Improvement
Installment Sales Contract
Charge Account
Real Estate, specific type unknown
Business Loan

The overlap and ambiguity are painful. TransUnion also has a field called Account Type Code, which is similar but not identical to this list. In models I have supervised in the past, where we were trying to distinguish first from second home mortgages, which played a role in scorecards, we used both. Account Type and Portfolio to make that distinction as well as we could. Note that we tried to be right but had no way or even way to know if we were always right. We could only test if, in the end, the field as the modelers interpret it, predicted the delinquency of future mortgages well based on the scorecard that was developed. Sausage! But I will not put down any more fields that make no sense, though there are others.

Date Opened—Thankfully, this is an organized, mostly unambiguous field. Scorecards look for the oldest date when a trade line was opened, because an earlier date is correlated with safety in the coming loan. Is this because it means the borrower is genuinely learning more about credit obligations, or is it true because the borrower is older, or are costs just going down for that borrower? (Age is highly correlated to age of earliest trade.) Being older is never mentioned as a reason, of course, bypassing the whole age issue.

Scorecards also look for recent trade lines opened, or average of trade lines opened, as new credit is usually correlated with problems to come. In addition, a spate of recent trade line openings is a negative. Perhaps this shows some desperation for credit, or some increase in indebtedness that is new to the borrower. Perhaps some or most of the time, but what about people who might have moved or had some other life event and have far more innocent reasons for getting new credit? Nevertheless, in scorecards, new credit indicates higher risk, on average, and everyone that engages in it loses some points. TransUnion calls this Open Date, reversing the words for whatever reason.

Credit Limit—This is a hugely useful field for credit scores. The limit usually shows what creditors have been willing to allow consumers to borrow, and thus gives us their votes about credit-worthiness. The credit limit of each trade, and the sum of all credit limits, tells us what borrowers have in the credit bank, and the difference between the total of limits and the total balance of debts owed is a very strong field for credit scores. It is specifically required in the Metro 2 formatting by regulators. TransUnion has the same field.

Highest Credit or Original Loan—This is sometimes used in credit scores instead of credit limit (when that is blank for some reason), though the great bulk of Revolving accounts will say what the credit limit is. High credit can also be used directly for scorecards: well, anything can. For loans that are borrowed then paid off, like mortgage, it is just the amount originally borrowed. It is most telling for Line of Credit, Open, and Revolving cards, where it tells us something about the consumer's credit liquidity (my term for unborrowed and available funds). TransUnion passes it on under the title High Credit Amount.

Terms Duration—This is how long the loan or agreement is intended to last, for instance, 30 years for most mortgage. It can be useful in scorecards for lines of credit, mortgages, and installment loans. TransUnion calls it "Term: Payment Schedule Month Count."

Scheduled Monthly Payment Amount—There are really two kinds of values here. For Installment, Mortgage, and Open debts, the amount due is set by the original terms of the contract. What is interesting here is that for Revolving cards and Lines of Credit, the amount due—the minimum—is tiny, usually the minimum of 2% or $25. I just noticed that is is only one percent for one of my cards. If the consumer pays the minimum but not all due, she owes interest but no penalty and is not delinquent. That is, the consumer is extending the loan, or perhaps adding to the loan. With interest averaging over 16% a year, this is a terrible financial choice for consumers that could pay the whole balance. Modelers (at least this is how I felt) would love to know if the consumer is making that poor choice, but because most of the time the payment is missing, we have to guess at the answer.

TransUnion uses the same variable name.

Actual Payment Amount: The Metro 2 documentation says: "Report the dollar amount of the monthly payment actually received for this reporting period in whole dollars only. If multiple payments are made during the reporting period, the total amount should be reported." This field basically allows us to determine whether the consumer is paying off Revolving debt and avoiding high interest on such debt. Another way to view this is that someone is living within their means, paying their bills as they come due, and not living on credit. TransUnion uses the same name. As we have shown, this is filled in for much less than half the revolving lines presently, though much more than that a few years ago, because most of the largest firms in the business decided to stop reporting it.

Account Status—This tells how many days past due the account is, or whether there was a charge-off, surrender of account, foreclosure, etc. It is astonishing that up to 29 days past due, the account status is current. It is not as if the borrower escapes penalties and interest for 29 days—or even that the lending company does not withdraw offers when this happens: the fact is simply not available to external parties to consider if the consumer wants more debt. Although many people think any holding-back of negative information is good, modelers certainly do not. A lack of negative information just means the credit score is weaker, and we see more averaged scores for everybody. If we really thought this were the right way to go about things, then why not just ignore credit data entirely? The values are provided in the next field, Payment Rating.

TransUnion puts this data in the MOP (Manner of Payment) grids. The fields are called the "Payment Pattern Account Codes." All the CRAs show this field for 7 years, for each account Open that long. I would say that mastering the MOP grid is the start of becoming a useful modeler of credit scores.

Current Balance—The Current Balance is supposed to contain the principal balance including Balloon Payment Amounts (when applicable), as well as applicable interest, late charges, fees, insurance payments, and escrow that are due during the current reporting period. The Current Balance may exceed the Highest Credit, Original Loan Amount, or Credit Limit. The balance divided by the limit is the very important variable "utilization." Often, a scorecard will use something like total utilization of all Revolving debt.

The field in TransUnion is called Current Balance Amount.

Amount Past Due—The data furnisher is supposed to report the total amount of payments that are 30 days or more past due in whole dollars only. This field should include late charges and fees, if applicable. Obviously, this could be big, though it is often crowded out by delinquency data from the MOP grid.

This is called Past Due Amount by TransUnion.

Date Closed—The date the account was closed to further purchases, paid in full or sold. For Line of Credit, Open, or Revolving accounts, there may be a balance due. Closed credit trade lines do not usually matter as much as trades still used.

Called Closed Date by TransUnion.

ECOA Code—Defines the relationship of the consumer to the account:

1 Individual—This consumer has contractual responsibility for this account and is primarily responsible for its payment.

2 Joint Contractual Liability—This consumer has contractual responsibility for this joint account.

3 Authorized User—This consumer is an authorized user of this account; another consumer has contractual responsibility.

5 Co-maker or Guarantor—This consumer is the co-maker or guarantor for this account, who becomes liable if the maker defaults.

7 Maker—This consumer is the maker who is liable for the account, but a co-maker or guarantor is liable if the maker defaults.

T Terminated—Association with account has been terminated by consumer.

X Deceased—[upon receipt of] "a legally sufficient ..." death certificate.
Z Delete Consumer—delete this consumer from the account.

TransUnion's name for this field is Equal Credit Opportunity Act Designator.

This completes the list of fields from the Metro 2 that I will describe. Some entries, like Industry Code and Account Code, have never worked in models I worked on and make little organized sense to me. Beyond the furnisher data, the CRAs of course add some other data that enters credit score models. For instance, they provide inquiry information from companies and people that have asked them for data about the consumer. The inquiries at TransUnion are in a record called IN01, which come with a date and an industry code. In practice, it seems that the date of the inquiry and the industry code of the inquiry are relevant to prediction. The dates tell us if the borrower has been searching for debt recently, a negative signal statistically. It may seem hard-hearted to rate people lower because of this evidence, but it is a time-honored practice for us, FICO, and presumably all credit cards. The explanation for this is desperation for cash, and it is probably often true; but a lot of these explanations are just narratives applied ex post and would often not be predictive of future delinquency, if the real reason for debt searching were known. For a mixture of statistical and public relation reasons, modelers often dedupe bursts of inquiries that could indicate not searches for cash per se, but cash to buy something large that the consumer wants. So, auto industry and mortgage industry inquiries completed in a relatively short period (a month or thereabouts) are often deduped to a single inquiry for the modeling.

Public records do not come from furnishers either. The field name at TransUnion is PR01. It has figured in many, maybe all, credit scores. Tax liens and any court decisions that a debt is owed appear here. Having them was a bad sign. Yet they are being eliminated, as I mentioned in a prior chapter: they will usually not appear on credit reports anymore.

Another record of special importance is labeled at TransUnion as AH11—trended history. This is data that has come in via previous month's Metro 2 and was retained by the CRAs in their data bases. The CRAs now sell 36-month snapshots on various variables. An important value of this record, at least a few years ago, is that it allows modelers to match the credit card balance in month N with the payment made in month N + 1 (that is, the payment is made the next month.) People that have payments that match the balance (that is, they paid their whole bill off) are transactors. People that pay less than the balance are revolvers, who are willing to pay high interest costs to husband their cash. Additionally, it would be possible to tell if borrowers are late with a minimum payment but not 30 days late. It would be an extremely useful part of the puzzle if furnishers had not largely stopped reporting payments.

Therefore, while that was somewhat laborious, my key point is that all sorts of data are missing or confusing. What is left is a lot, but what is not shown, because of political or corporate decisions, is a lot too.

Endnote

[1] The format names of the credit reports that were available to me are Total View from Equifax, ARF 7 from Experian, and T.U. 4.0 from TransUnion.

CHAPTER ELEVEN

Picking the Y variable, picking the X variables

Abstract

This chapter provides examples of how credit data is turning into variables that together predict very generally whether people will pay back the loans they take on. The most useful variable is one that shows how much money the borrower can still get from revolving credit cards. This variable shows the degree credit card companies have come to trust a person, growing larger as the consumer ages or if his or her wealth or income is higher. However, this is a data-mining exercise, not a meaning exercise. Other variables of importance are recency of delinquency, depth of delinquency, and number of recent tries for debt. I show some common graphical techniques and how to calculate them, including the Lorenz charts and information value chart.

Despite the data issues, credit scoring is a profitable enterprise and for modelers, it is their job. When something happens in regular and predictable ways, we claim to understand it and we feel comfortable with the flow of events. When things are not predictable, we feel anxious and confused. Let me momentarily divide science into hard science (with everything known) and social science, about people. In hard science, we want to predict things with certainty. When we look up the time the sun is going to set here in Frankfort Michigan, we expect to get an answer that is not vague. Water freezes at 0°C and boils at 100°C. Hard science is an encyclopedia of (pretty) sure things. If hard science predicts something and it does not happen, that is a problem.

Social Science, including credit score modeling, is much looser. Indicators like inexperience with credit, maxing out credit cards, or multiple attempts to get new credit: those are correlated with delinquency, not because the connection is intuitive (though it often is), but because, in some actual large amount of data, loans with credit report data like that went bad more often in all years. However, correlation is far different from certainty on a person-by-person basis. Loans do not always go bad

Credit Data and Scoring: The First Triumph of Big Data and Big Algorithms
ISBN: 978-0-12-818815-6
https://doi.org/10.1016/B978-0-12-818815-6.00011-X

when someone is maxed-out on their cards—indeed, less than a 10th of maxed-out borrowers fail—it is just that borrowers who max-out on cards failed more often.

FICO started the meme of giving credit probability scores a number between 300 and 850. This number is a marketing device: it sounds better than a straight probability, but the numbers map to the actual probabilities of delinquencies for the population they were built on. A score of 500 might have corresponded to a class of loans that became 90 days delinquent 10% of the time. A score of 700 might have corresponded to a class of loans that became 90 days delinquent 1% of the time. For loans with a score of 750, that probability might have been a third of a percent. If the economy and people's attitudes were stable, I think those probabilities would be stable. However, economic conditions are not stable. Home prices in the United States and many other countries charged up in the first half of the first decade and then crashed down in the second, retarding mortgage delinquency in the run-up and propelling it in the run-down. A lot happens that is not measured with credit scores. But the relative meaning of the scores—that 500s had problems 30 times as often as 750s—well, these ratios were a little squeezed but keep their place in line behind 700s and 750s.

When FICO makes a credit score, it is all with purchased credit reports. They have no loans and no data of their own. They purchase what are called archived credit reports, captured over 2 years ago, from reports stored by the credit-reporting agencies (CRAs) at the end of each month, and then FICO purchases the credit reports of the same borrowers from an archive 2 years later. They make their model predicting the delinquencies of the later reports from the condition of the first reports. All of the data is anonymized by the CRAs before it is given to FICO, so FICO does not know the individuals whose accounts they have, though typically they will know quite a bit, including when and pretty close to where, so they can try to account for economic conditions.

When FICO or anyone else creates a model, they need to define what they are predicting. This thing, this very specific and definable outcome, is often called the Y variable, or dependent variable. Everything predicted is a Y. In most cases of credit, we care whether someone will have a problem paying back a loan. In mortgages, there are delinquencies of different lengths one might worry about, 1 month, 3 months, 6 months, and final default.

There are also prepayment models, which focus on when loans are paid back. We may care for the life of the loan, or for 2 or 5 years. If we care about a long period, we may jump to a different sort of prediction, a hazard model prediction, that attempts to describe at any point in time, what is the chance of this or that happening.

The most common credit scores are the generic versions, which depend only on information in the credit report and predict the performance of the average loan, regardless of what it is for or what industry it is in (e.g., car, mortgage, etc.). FICO generic scores take snapshots of data at least 2 years back and use it to predict something that happens within 2 years of the snapshot.

X variables

These are the variables, often called attributes, all known at the time of origination, that are used to predict what will happen to a loan in the years to come. You saw my credit report. It is full of information, but that information is not yet turned into explanatory variables. The credit data that comes in for the purpose of making variables, in fairly similar structures from each of the three official credit repositories (Equifax, TransUnion, and Experian), is the same stuff as on my written report. There is a lot of information. It is overwhelming and chaotic, organized to the eye but hard to describe or compare to other credit reports. We, or anyone deciding to make a credit model, have to start by creating variables, or (synonymously) attributes. A variable might be the number of accounts, the average age of accounts, the number of months since I was last late.

What is the difference between stuff and variables? Stuff is a cacophony of material, unique to each person, what happened in a format meant for one reader just considering his own experience. Variables are commonalities that occur for a lot of people at once and allow for specific comparisons that draw specific distinctions. We can say that this group of people have such and such a variable (say it is no delinquencies in the last 5 years) and that having that variable indicates they are less likely to have a mortgage delinquency in the next 2 years. Turning stuff into variables is a time-consuming step because there are so many that seem like they might be associated with better or worse future performance, but each one is just a hunch at first.

Let me provide some examples of what I mean. Let us pretend that it is now January 2019 and we have the credit report of a person with two credit cards that had the payment pattern below in 2018. Moreover, at this point we do not have January 2019—so 2018 is the current month that we know about.

Our notation is:

0—borrower paid minimum required within 30 days of due date,

1—borrower paid minimum due 30–59 days late,

2—60–89 days late, and

3—90 or more days late

Month	J	F	M	A	M	J	J	A	S	O	N	D
Card1	0	1	2	3	2	0	0	0	0	0	0	0
Card2	0	0	0	0	0	0	0	0	0	0	0	1

For Card1, the borrower was late starting with the February payment and did not get back in the groove until June. For Card2, that same borrower paid all months in 2018 within 30 days of on-time, except that in December, the borrower was at least 31 days late. This particular borrower has two credit cards, but usually the attributes we are talking about apply to the borrower, so either card or both could contribute to the attribute. Credit score attributes that might be worth trying out (because they are not particular to this person but may be variables shared by a lot people) include:

Number of months since last 30 (or greater) day late: 0 for this borrower

Number of months since last 60 (or greater) day late: 8 for this borrower

Worst delinquency in the last 3 months: 1 month late for this borrower

Worst delinquency in the last year: 3 months late for this borrower

Percent of cards without 60+ in the last year: 50% for this borrower

Total number of open credit cards: 2 for this borrower

Every single credit person will have some value for every single attribute, even if they are missing the data to create that attribute, because then we can just classify their value as *missing*. So long as the missing by itself is predictive, or else the categories created for the non-missing are predictive, that is fine and, in fact, common. Let us think about one simple attribute for the moment: the number of months since a borrower was last 30 days delinquent on any card. I have just made up some data on that one, and here it is:

	Months since 30 days DLQ	No of borrows	No. defaults in 2 years	% Bad
0	Late now	100	12	12.00%
1	Month ago	200	17	8.50%
2	Months ago	300	22	7.33%
3	Months ago	500	27	5.40%
4	Months ago	900	27	3.00%
5	Months ago	1400	29	2.07%
6	Months ago	1600	29	1.81%
7	Months ago	2000	34	1.70%
8	Months ago	3000	46	1.53%
9	Months ago	4000	58	1.45%
10	Months ago	5000	70	1.40%
11	Months ago	6000	82	1.37%
12	Months ago	7000	94	1.34%
13	Months ago	8000	106	1.33%
14	Months ago	9000	118	1.31%
15	Months ago	10,000	130	1.30%
16	Months ago	11,000	142	1.29%
17	Months ago	12,000	154	1.28%
18	Months ago	13,000	166	1.28%
19	Months ago	14,000	178	1.27%
20	Months ago	15,000	190	1.27%
21	Months ago	16,000	202	1.26%
22	Months ago	17,000	214	1.26%
23	Months ago	18,000	226	1.26%
24	Months ago	19,000	238	1.25%
Leaving out 25 to 84				
	Never late	1,000,000	3000	0.30%

This is directionally plausible, though too smooth of course. There are fewer bads—and bad is just our customary term for a loan that goes delinquent—for the categories of recently delinquent on some other loan. This is realistic however. People having problems paying back one sort of debt at the moment are shakier bets when applying for yet more debt. In the FICO and Vantage model worlds, where the data is drawn from all credit users and predicts any or shares of all delinquencies that occur to all credit users, the numbers of people delinquent today or very recently will be much greater. Still, because they are delinquent today, they will take different actions than people not delinquent today; so, there will be biases: what happens will not be purely a result of current delinquency unalloyed. For mortgage applicants, the effect is clear and huge; people with current or recent delinquencies are vastly underrepresented. Nevertheless, some do apply and receive mortgages with current delinquency, that when it does happen, the *rate* of those recently delinquent going bad on their mortgage is usually higher.

In this made-up data, it seems as if every little bit longer that goes by since the last time the borrower was late means a lower delinquency rate. If only things were really that neat! If they were, then the way this attribute (or call it a variable or co-variate if you prefer) would end up in a model is as some sort of continuous variable. Month to last time late might enter the model straight up, or the modeler might take the log of months to last late or throw in months squared since last time late. It is not as if we can make arithmetic transformations willy-nilly. One or the other of the transformations will be the one which makes the prediction sharper—but all these are examples of using the time in a continuous sense: getting a little bigger or smaller always means something. Real data is usually lumpier, so let just invent some slightly more real looking data for the moment:

Here is a new chart for the first 6 months:

	Months since 30 days DLQ	No of borrowers	No. defaults in 2 years	% bad
0	Late now	100	12	12.00%
1	Month ago	90	7	7.78%
2	Months ago	110	8	7.27%
3	Months ago	100	12	12.00%
4	Months ago	200	10	5.00%
5	Months ago	300	14	4.67%
6	Months ago	500	19	3.80%

In this little bit of made-up data, things do not continuously get better as the time since being delinquent gets longer. Having a last delinquency 3 months ago looks as bad as having one now—12% of borrowers became delinquent in each case. There could be all sorts of reasons for that (if it were true). Certainly, one big point is that the samples are small, so results will be volatile. But besides that, there could be *sample bias*, a rather important topic when modeling generally and a particularly important topic when decisions important to people will be made based on those models. Sample bias just means that any sample, any bunch of data, has some accidental tilt that has something to do with how that sample was created or selected. A common sort of sample selection occurs with election polls that use landline telephones. Only certain sorts of people even have a landline any more, or publish their number, or pick up the phone. All sorts of tilts go into the sample creation. It is a rare sample that does not have a severe bias. The likely bias in this case that would drive this is that very few will apply for a mortgage with a current delinquency, or that few lenders will encourage it. Still, a few will be undeterred for whatever reasons, and they might be people that are genuinely financially strong, perhaps because they plan to put down a large down payment. Maybe without these psychological distortions, the real rate of mortgage failure would be much greater than 12% for people delinquent right now. Along with this, there might also be some few that believe that 3 months is the right time to wait after a delinquency, so that a batch of weak borrowers comes in exactly 3 months after a delinquency. There are forces that shape data, and the data shapes the models, and the models shape those forces again by turning down people with recent delinquencies and thus causing them to wait.

To make cleaner or smoother models and when facing small numbers generally, it is common to *bin* attributes. That simply means putting things together, not always going for the smallest slice of data that can be defined. A reasonable bin here would be all applications with a delinquency less than 6 months ago. In the end, we want a total model that does a good and repeatable job of prediction. Modelers are reluctant to inject prejudices or norms (6 months—half a year—that is a norm of how people tend to think and organize time) when the total prediction suffers significantly. But in this case, with millions of loans, and only a few hundred recently delinquent, how we bin would hardly cause the overall predictions for the population as a whole to move in any direction. The value of binning is to keep models simpler, able to be understood and explained, and also to avoid *data mining*, a phrase that historically has had a pejorative sense about it. It means chasing after and enshrining accidental bumps and valleys that happen in the data. Besides the incoherence of data mining, it often performs less well when applied to similar but not identical data that often does not have the same accidents. Anyway, binning is another word for clumping things.

The attribute creation cannot really be done by machine, that is, by computers pretending to be a person. But it turns out that these days the binning can be done automatically in any number of ways. One can buy or rent software that just keeps making bin cut after bin cut and looks for an effective division of the variable, one that predicts well without having such small cells that the answer is unreliable. However, even then, modelers will usually make some adjustments to the software suggestions. For instance, if the software suggests a bin of 1–5 months and 6–12 months, but 1–6 and 7–12 work, it is only a miniscule bit less predictive, so we might make the latter a bin conforming with human ways of breaking time up into quarters of a year.

A big company with a big modeling staff has the work force to make hundreds or thousands of variables to send off to the binning software. Smaller companies with scorecard interest may start by purchasing predefined attributes from the repositories. To quote an internet ad from Experian: "Premier Attributes (SM) provides lenders with the most comprehensive attribute set containing over 1700 credit attributes across 48 different industries. Our attributes summarize the essential data on a credit report to help you better understand a consumer's full credit behavior for improved lending decisions."[1]

The top variable in the two segments that I find, and expect that you would find, whether for Ever Delinquent loans on any other segmentation of loans, is something very close to Average Amount of Available Revolving Credit Over the Past 12 Months at the Card Level. This is computed as follows: Identify all revolving accounts. Subtract balance from limit for each. Take the average of that number. This is the credit liquidity of the borrower, what they could borrow if they need to. Basically, it's how much money is lying around, in so far as that can be told from creditors only. It's analogous to knowing the wealth of a person, though it has flavors of what their credit companies have thought about them over time (to raise their limits) and their current needs for debt and their usage of credit. This is a data-mining exercise. I have thoughts about what it all means, but I do not know, nor does anyone. Some variables work well, some less well, altogether they data mine a probability out of big data that is fairly predictive for the purpose. That is the lure and the danger of all big data.

The median person has between 2000 and 3000 on average that they can still borrow on their credit cards. This is a number that goes through quite a range of values, and it is not at all outlandish to thinking of it as simply a continuous number, the more the better; but making it continuous does not make it substantially more predictive than chunking it up into bins, and the bins are easy to understand. In my experience, it is typical to begin by looking at attributes by themselves, making an information chart to show how correlated it is with the Y variable we want to predict. Here is the information value chart for this top variable. (It was started by means of some machine learning software that picked the bins, and then slightly tweaked to use round numbers.)

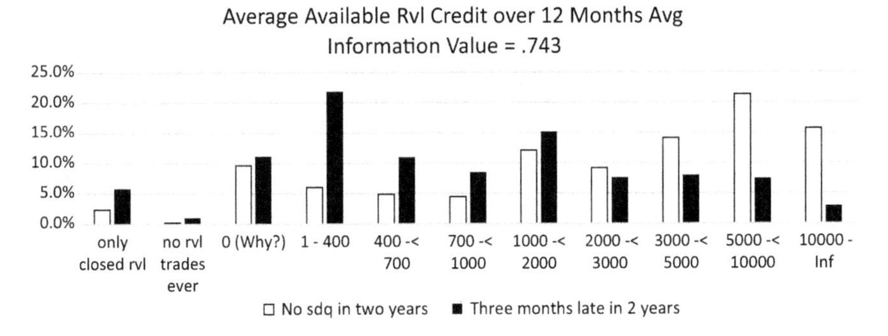

There is a blue bar (white bar in print version) and a red bar (black bar in print version) for every *bin*. For every bin, we calculate the share of all goods and the share of all the bads that happen. The blue bars total 100% because 100% of all the good loans are in one of those bins or another. The same for the loans that became delinquent. If a bin holds 10% of the population and represents 10% of goods and 10% of bads, then it is not special and not predictive. But when the blue share of all goods is appreciably higher than the red share of all bads, then that bin is overproducing goods relative to bads. We want more of that. If the red bar is a lot taller than the blue bar, then that means being in that bin sends a risky signal. Imbalance between red and blue bars is what gets a credit score started. Those bins *mean* something.

The first bin on the left represents consumers that have had revolving cards and now do not. This is a group that becomes delinquent at more than double the average rate of our applicants. Then there is a very tiny group, which has never had a revolving card, but in this tiny group, the red bar is much taller than the blue bar; so, this is a risky group too. The third bin represents people who do not have anything left to borrow—exactly. That seems impossible, so it is probably a quirk about missing data. This group is very average, probably because there is something both screwy and meaningless about most of the data here (but I do not know). It may well be that these borrowers may be distinguishable from each other in risk based on some other variable, such as age of trade lines or past delinquencies. In that case, we would interact the attribute, or perhaps just that bin, with that other variable.

Continuing to move right, there is then a steady and dramatic march as more and more revolving funds are available to consumers. Small amounts of available funds are much riskier than large amounts of funds. The reader can generally tell what shares of loans are in a bin just by looking at the blue bar, the share of good loans. This is not always true, but it is true for high quality loans because most borrowers in *every* bin go 2 years without a delinquency—99.4% on average. This data set is all from a period after 2008 when times were good in this data set. Still there are 7223 loans that went 3 months late in 2 years, enough to train a model on, to be ready for worse times.

So, not many of these borrowers stumble in any bin (in the post-crash years), but a tip-off to a much greater chance of stumbling is being in a bin where the red bar towers over the blue bar. In the category of having only 1−400 dollars remaining before hitting the limit (as an average over 12 months for all revolving trades), about 6% of all borrowers, are 22% of all future delinquencies. On the other hand, for the 15.6% of borrowers with at least 10000 dollars on average, the right most bin, we have 15.7% of all good borrowers but only 2.9% of all the borrowers that run into trouble and become 3 months late. So being in this bin is pretty good insurance that the borrowers will *not* have a problem.

We can make a decent Lorenz chart with just this one variable. The Lorenz curve is known for depicting how well (but usually poorly) distributed wealth or income is, in a society. But in the credit profession, we borrow it to show how variably loan failures are distributed along a scale of credit scores.[2] We are hoping for separation, although in the income and wealth spheres these are thought of as inequalities among people, and thus bad things to have in a population because it means people at the bottom are hurting and angry. It is really a chart that shows how anything at all can be distributed very differently for various gradations of something or other. In this Lorenz chart, all the loans are sorted by the weight of evidence for each bin of Avg Avail Credit. The X-axis shows how the loan sorts, riskiest loans on the left, and most likely to succeed on the right. The Y-axis shows what percent of bads (loans that go 3 months delinquent in 2 years) are represented by that percent of loans. With just this variable and with just the bins shown, the loans in the riskiest 7% of bins have about 23% of bads these are on the left), while those in the least risky 21% or so (the right part of chart) have only about 3 percent of the bads. A strong Lorenz chart is very rounded: the slope is high at the left and nearly flat on the right.

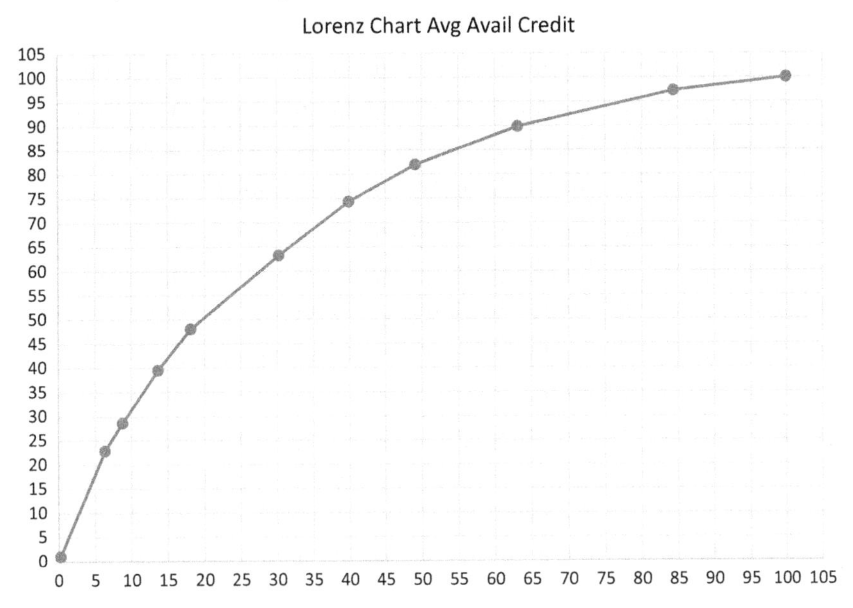

Now one might ask what does this variable *mean*? Available credit could be high because the borrower asked for and was granted high limits, closing out cards with lower limits. Limits could be high because the borrower has had his or her limit raised as he or she paid back his or her loans for many years. There are, frankly, a lot of stories that all lead to high available credit. The value is strongly correlated with income (0.22), and, to a lesser extent, with the age of the borrower (0.13). Although it is perfectly legal to use this variable in a model despite these correlations, it does not seem much of a *Character* issue—it seems much more to me to lie in the economic stress camp. A good deal of what gives a good credit score is the economic wherewithal to avoid serious economic issues and is only partly a scorecard on past payment behavior. It is possible that a lender could reject it or modify it for *mission* reasons, since it gives some advantage to well-off applicants in underwriting and pricing. The confounding problems are that something like it is certainly in every scorecard of financial risk: the one most likely to pay a loan back is one who barely needed it in the first place.

Endnotes

[1] From the ad for *Premier Attributes from Experian,* at https://www.experian.com/decision-analytics/premier-attributes.html. I reviewed it on August 4, 2019.

[2] A *Wikipedia* URL for Lorenz charts is www.en.Wikipedia.org/wiki/Lorenz_curve, last edited on July 9, 2019 and reviewed by me on July 15, 2019."In economics, the Lorenz curve is a graphical representation of the distribution of income or of wealth. It was developed by Max O. Lorenz in 1905 for representing inequality of the wealth distribution." Following is a longer quote from that URL:The curve is a graph showing the proportion of overall income or wealth assumed by the bottom x% of the people, although this is not rigorously true for a finite population (see below). It is often used to represent income distribution, where it shows for the bottom x% of households, what percentage (y%) of the total income they have. The percentage of households is plotted on the x-axis, the percentage of income on the y-axis. It can also be used to show distribution of assets. In such use, many economists consider it to be a measure of social inequality.The concept is useful in describing inequality among the size of individuals in ecology and in studies of biodiversity, where the cumulative proportion of species is plotted against the cumulative proportion of individuals. It is also useful in business modeling: e.g., in consumer finance, to measure the actual percentage y% of delinquencies attributable to the x% of people with worst risk scores.

CHAPTER TWELVE

Calculating weight of evidence and information value

Abstract

This chapter illustrates some variables that are highly correlated with delinquencies in mortgages. Such variables include the percent of credit card limits used right now, the number of trade lines a borrower has that never reached 2 months delinquencies, the total of all limits, the total of installment limits, the number of recent inquiries, and the number collection accounts. I show how we calculate the weight of evidence of each bin of each variable and the calculation and illustration of the information value of the whole variable. It is a practical foray into key parts of making a credit score.

I continue as a practitioner, accepting the system for the moment, to describe what real modelers do with the data. As mentioned, the information value of a variable is a good way to pick candidates for models. When there is a high information value, that means that variable used to make the bins is important to prediction. Information value starts by assigning *weight of evidence* (WOE) for each bin. The information value is a sort of weighted sum of the WOEs of each bin that tells how worthwhile that variable is in predicting delinquency (or whatever). This particular model is one that predicts future delinquency for a particular segment of all borrowers, the segment of borrowers that have been delinquent at least once. It seems like a complicated calculation, and the reader may wish to skip my explanation, with my blessings. But it is not hard if you have to do it a few times. Look it over and see if you can follow. If not, then skim ahead.

The WOE calculation takes a few steps, but simple arithmetic ones. There is nothing sacred about this arithmetic, but it sets up the variable for working well in the logistic regression, which is commonly used. Slightly different treatments would work as well but then we would have to do a bunch of things differently, with perhaps a very slight improvement in predictiveness but a large additional burden understanding why. As AI matures, however, the "why" will be increasingly lost.

To get the WOE for a bin—and let us take as our example the bin "available credit more than zero but less than $400"—we calculate what

Credit Data and Scoring: The First Triumph of Big Data and Big Algorithms
ISBN: 978-0-12-818815-6
https://doi.org/10.1016/B978-0-12-818815-6.00012-1

share of all bads come from that bin and what share of goods come from that bin. 15.4% of all the people that go 2 years without becoming 3 months behind are in this group, but 31.8% of all the people that become delinquent are in this group. In this bin, bads double, going from about 0.4% overall to 0.8%. Even though 0.8% may still seem small, in the excellent economy of the population period that still ends up being 31.8% of all the bads. To get the WOE, the percentage of all goods is divided by the percentage of all bads, $15.4/31.8 = 0.41$, and the natural log of that number is the $\text{WOE} = \ln(0.41) = -0.72$. Why take a log? It just goes with the logistic regression we are doing. Basically, it is just a measure to show the bins change the probability of a borrower stumbling. Basically, when that log differs significantly from zero by a good bit (say by more than 0.1), it is a predictive bin.

The information value adds up the WOEs, but weights the WOE when adding them up, giving bins the highest weights when goods and bads differ by a lot, not in a multiple sort of way, but in an absolute way: that particular bin has a lot to say about a *lot* of loans. Mathematically, a weight equals the bin percent of goods minus the bin percent of bads. Do not worry that the weighted WOE will be sometimes negative and sometimes positive, thus canceling. This cannot happen. When WOE is negative (bads happen a lot), then this thing I call weight (for want of a better word) is negative—and the two multiplied is positive.

We can do the information value calculation using other variables, for instance, Revolving Utilization for the Current Month.

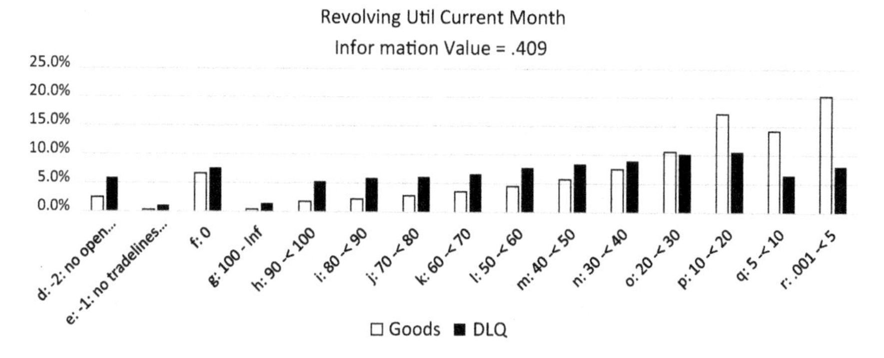

The WOE is greatest when there are blue (white in print version) bars towering over orange (black in print version) bars (which is matched somewhere else by orange bars towering over blue bars). We are looking for imbalance. The greatest WOE is in the second bin, "No Trade Lines of

This Type." The orange bar is four times the blue bar. However, this is a tiny little bin, so it does not really help the information value much. The biggest contributor to information value comes from the bin on the right: small revolving credit users (but not zero): 0.001−5% utilization of limit. These are people that do not use their revolving credit much, or at least only a small share of how much they could. The good share is larger than the bad share by a healthy ratio, and there are a lot of loans in this bucket, about a fifth of all loans. Thus, the information value of that bin is higher than the information value of any other bin, 0.112.

This variable has a strong correlation with our top variable "average available credit" (0.27), the most of any two variables in the scorecard. The connection is intuitive: if a borrower does not utilize much available credit, then there is more available. It is, however, much less correlated to income (−0.04) than average available credit, which rises with incomes (correlation of 0.23); in fact, it goes the other way a bit. It looks like wealthier people can use up all their limits even better than less wealthy people can. However, what is left and available, which surely is magnified when credit card companies or HELOC providers grant a high limit, is much greater for wealthy people, as expressed by average available credit.

A moderately important variable is the percent of trade lines a borrower has had that were 2 months late. Given that this is a model for people that have been at least 30 days delinquent at some point, much less than half our applicants, it is not that predictive. It is less predictive than how intensively a person uses the credit available of them today.

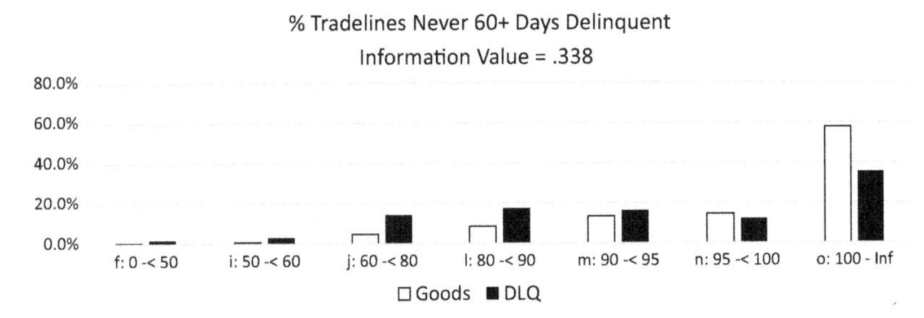

The below variable is decently predictive all by itself. In addition, it does not disappear in significance when joined to other credit report variables, so it is incrementally a helpful variable in predicting future mortgage delinquency and will appear in our next scorecard. Lower limits have more bads and higher limits have more goods.

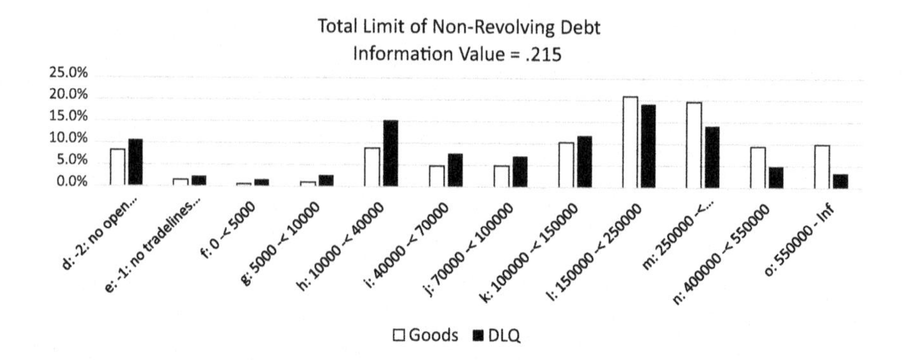

More than most variables, this is one interconnected to the nature of the data set (mortgages applications). Observe the following chart.

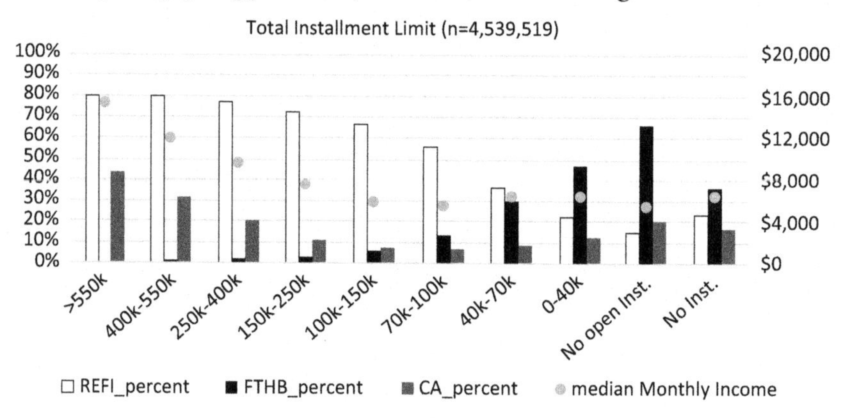

The small buckets (70 K and below) and buckets without installment debt are filled with first time homebuyers (the orange [black in print version] FTHB bars)—and in a period where these were scarce. In general, larger limits are associated with refinancing (blue [white in print version] bars). Also, as non-revolving limits rise, there is a decided tilt toward Californians (gray bars) and higher incomes (yellow [light gray in print version] dots—monthly income shown on right), because homes in California cost so much. Because California has had remarkable home price growth in the sample period, home price growth may be entangled with the excellent relative performance of those buckets. By the approach I have described, this variable possibly deserves to be in a credit model. But is some of the affect accidental (California doing well) and are some of the consequences really desirable (making it easier for refinances to come in the door and raising the bar on first time homebuyers)? Perhaps the positive effect of being in those buckets could reverse if California home prices crash again—which they seem to do every 10 or 20 years. Those are the tough questions one always need to wrestle with, and which can be operationally answered in many ways, such as answered by removing variables from models, neutralizing the effect on FTHB and lower income, and changing limits. The plethora of alternatives is one of the head spinning parts of modeling because it requires not just math and computer skills but judgment calls.

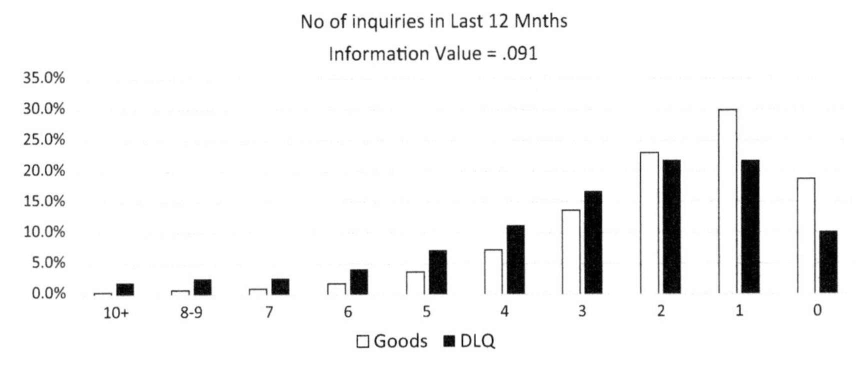

Inquiries on credit imply that a borrower is trying to borrow money. Probably this too is connected to credit liquidity: people who have lots of inquiries, that is, needing some money, are more likely to have a future delinquency.

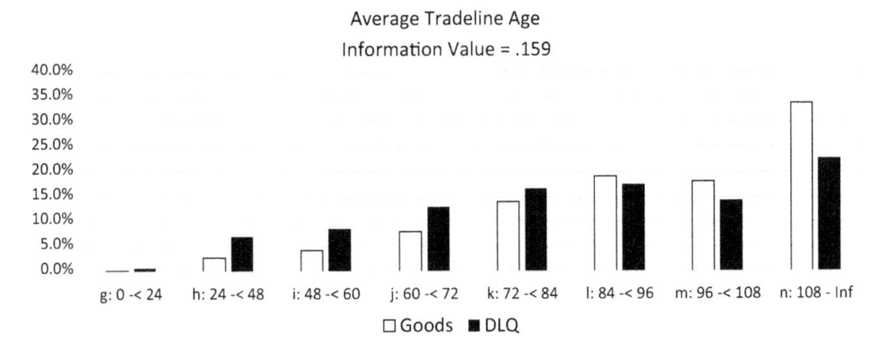

A higher average trade line age is a positive factor for credit safety. This particular variable has a huge correlation with the age of the borrower. However, the variable used is not age of the borrower but age of the oldest trade line, a time-honored variable in scorecards.

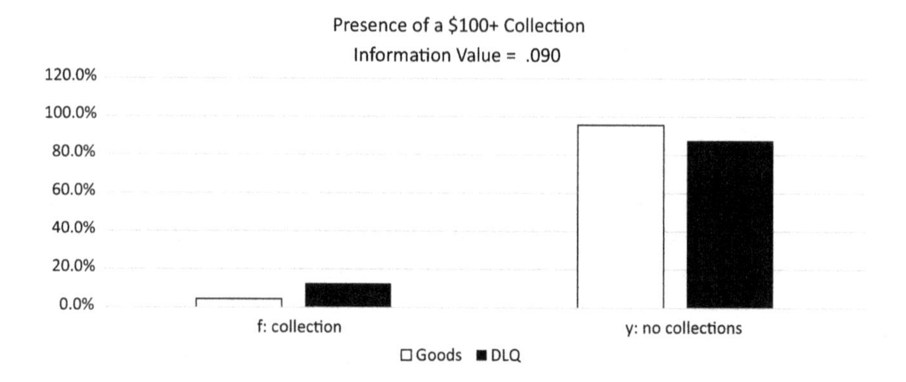

Collections on people's records are clearly very predictive, though the information value is not huge because only a tiny percent of people have a collection. There are no public records or liens in this scorecard because these are being wiped out by the CRAs, but we can use collections.

As I have pointed out many times now, credit scores have components of fairness, accident, and correlation with accidental issues—not to mention correlations with income, age, loan type, and location that take some thinking through.

CHAPTER THIRTEEN

Regressions

Abstract

This is a practical chapter of how modelers pick variables and combine them to make a credit score. Usually, variables with high information value end up in a model, but often one variable might be so similar to a second variable that while each is predictive, neither adds any extra oomph when one is already in the model. In the end, the combination that best predicts delinquency or default or whatever bad thing there is becomes the method of credit scoring. Therefore, if for whatever reason the borrower would look bad on the variable retained but good on the variable that is dropped, they will appear to have a bad credit score. This is one way that arbitrary things result from regressions, though on the whole regressions are the best way to get fairly simple credit scores that are more accurate for a population, if not the individual.

I showed a few strong variables in the previous chapter, but how do modelers pick winners and how do they put variables together? It starts of course by creating variables that have worked in common practice and prior experience, and then by following hunches and creating ones. Commonly now, we can rent software to estimate the *information value* of the variables. Usually, ones with high information value are going to end up in a model, but not all of them, because many variables with high information value are highly related to one another. Some particular variable all by itself could make a big difference, but it might be so similar to a second variable that all by itself seems predictive, that does not add any extra oomph when one is already in the model. For instance, months since 60 days delinquent would be a predictive variable but so would months since 90 days delinquent and so would number of trade lines ever delinquent. They probably do not all end up in a model because they are so connected and touch many of the same people. Therefore, we are always thinking what sorts of variables are really families of variables, wanting to make a more predictive model that is not too terribly complicated.

At the same time, we would be thinking of segments we wish to model. Segments are partitions of the population. For instance, the group of borrowers that have had a trade line problem or late in the past vs. a segment that has never had this. Segments are conveniences. There is nothing that can be done with segments that cannot be done by creating a gazillion

Credit Data and Scoring: The First Triumph of Big Data and Big Algorithms
ISBN: 978-0-12-818815-6
https://doi.org/10.1016/B978-0-12-818815-6.00013-3

interaction terms. Nevertheless, if you think that some bunch of consumers act differently than some other, or we just have completely different data opportunities for one bunch as opposed to another, it is easier to call it a segment and create a different model for that bunch of borrowers.

Every segment would have a different model, some only a little different, but some segments might be enormously different. The segments are hit or miss as the variables defined. The first notion has to be that there is only one segment because segments complicate things enormously. Experience and intuition are the only way to get hitting and missing done faster. Once segments are assumed, the goal is to do the best job possible predicting the probability of delinquency, or whatever we are predicting, for the borrowers in that segment. I should be clear that *machine learning* could replace both modelers and intuition. Machine learning is just a bunch of ways of setting regression tryouts on autopilot and turning out great festivals in interaction, cut-points, and segmentation that can predict a little better than a person for the sample being used, and also a little better for a similar sample that was not used to train the model. I probably have the same regard for machine learning as John Henry had for steam power, but I think I correctly see that as computers replace us, we understand less and less about what we are concluding. The way we can use machine learning now without that problem to too great an extent is to let the machine suggest all sorts of complex things and then to imitate its best ideas with bins, segments, and variable interactions that we can make sense of in conversation.

To illustrate modeling (and ignoring machine learning): let us say we guess that three segments make sense. One segment is ever delinquent—and we will call that Segment Dlq. This is convenient because all information on being late: how late, when late, what the borrower was late on, did it go to collection, were their liens and public recorded all those variables go in the ever-delinquent scorecard and cannot go in a never-delinquent scorecard. Then let us say that we split up the never delinquent group into a segment that is getting a refinance loan and a segment that is not: Segments Refi and Purchase. The never delinquent groups, well over two thirds in this data set, involves people that have never failed to make any payment ever, on this record. We are thus left with variables whose only goal is to determine if these people are on the way to trouble, through stress, poor prospects, bad choices we will never know. Most will never have a problem but the signals that predict higher rates of future problems will have undeniable repercussions statistically (that is, for group averages) and go into scorecards.

Moreover, let us say that there are 26 variables that have a high information value for at least one of the segments, which conveniently allows us to pretend we have variables A–Z. In addition, let us make up the order of information value for these invented variables:

Segment Dlq: A B C D F G H I J K L M N O P

Segment Purchase: A C E G I J K M N O Q S U X Z

Segment Refi: D E F G P Q R S T U V W X Y Z

Putting variables together typically implies regressions, though this is not the only way to do this. Much of the public is familiar with basic linear regression. Linear regression does precisely fit the situation with a dichotomous outcome: a borrower is either bad or good. Linear regression predicts continuous things, such as income or blood pressure or GDP or bushels of wheat. What is predicted is the Y aka dependent variable of the regression. The regressors aka independent variables aka X variables predict the Y, aka dependent variable. For instance, one might predict how much wheat will be produced in Nebraska. Knowing nothing about it, some reasonable predictors might be:

- Some constant (this could be zero), usually called.
- How many bushels were produced last year? (the first variable is called X1.)
- How many acres are claimed to be in devoted to wheat? (X2)
- How many inches of rain there are in the growing season? (X3)
- How many sunny data there are in the growing season? (X4)
- What is the price of wheat at planting time? (X5)
- What is the price of alternate things that might be planted? (X6)

I will stop there with pretending to know what goes into this sort of prediction. However, each of these independent variables has a level. The levels are multiplied by the parameters of the model—it is the parameters that the modeling process figures out—and an income is predicted. The constant is just a starting point, and can be zero, though usually it is not. (Someone is going to plant wheat even if nobody will buy it. Maybe he will make his own bread with it.)

Giving, bushels = $\beta_0 + \beta_1{*}X_1 + \beta_2{*}X_2 + \beta_3{*}X_3 + \beta_4{*}X_4 + \beta_5{*}X_5 + \beta_6{*} + €$.

You read that as Beta zero + Beta One times Variable One + Beta Two times Variable two etc., and you do that for all your variables, then there is still an error €, the Greek letter epsilon which is the error term, because you almost never predict anything perfectly. The model will also predict a standard deviation for that error, which indicates how close that prediction is likely to be. The computer is going to figure this out, presuming there are a lot of years worth of X variables and a lot of years of Ys too (bushels of wheat grown in different years). Computer or not, it takes data to get a model.

Let us say that the model predicts that Nebraska will produce 44.6 million bushels (yeah, I looked up what a reasonable answer would be). In addition, let us say the standard deviation of € is two million bushels. For problems that fit into the linear regression world, 95% of the time, the final answer will be within two standard deviations of the prediction. Therefore, 95% of the time Nebraska would have 40.6 million to 48.6 million bushels of wheat. The way these models work is that they are made to minimize the sum of all errors added together, actually the sum of squared errors—but you can get a text book if you care that much—so the key to these models is that errors are as like to be above the prediction as below it, and the real answer is likely to be closer to the prediction than to any other point.

However, when we predict whether someone will be delinquent or not in 2 years, that is not a level. Either they are delinquent or they are not. The answer is discrete aka categorical aka not continuous. There is a quite a difference between the possible answers, and nothing allowable in-between. We, hotshot economists, call that a dichotomous dependent variable. We can predict a probability for someone to be delinquent, say 1%; but there is no equivalent to a standard deviation in this case. If the person is delinquent, then they are 100% delinquent, the probability they are delinquent is 100%, and we missed by 99%. If they are not delinquent, then we missed by 1%. Better, but pretty dumb. Even dumber is if our model predicts the probability of someone being delinquent to be 200%. Linear regression models do things like that.

Therefore, we do not use linear regression. To be honest, linear regression models often work pretty well, particularly if you just chop off answers at zero and one to avoid being laughed at for predicting probabilities with less than 0% chance of happening or more than a certain chance. However, the most proper sorts of regressions, or the ones I have seen, are logistic models, probit models, and discriminant analysis, and the most common of these (in my experience) is the logistic model.

In the logistic model, the probability of delinquency $= e\wedge(\beta_0+\beta_1{}^*X_1+\beta_2{}^*X_2 \ldots)/[1 + e\wedge(\beta_0+\beta_1{}^*X_1+ \beta_2X_2 \ldots)]$ where "e" is not an error term but this magic number, the *natural log*, which happens to be a little bigger than 2.7. This number pops up all over the place in math, like another great number π (the ratio of a circle to its diameter). The two numbers seem to come right from God, and I cannot explain them. Look them up, but it will not help: their ubiquity is a mystery, whether you are spiritual or not. The symbol " ^ " is my symbol for exponent, so read it as "to the": the expression says to exponentiate e to the number calculated in the parenthesis. (I could perhaps avoid this " ^ " if I knew how to use a good equation editor, but as of this writing I do not, so the reader is stuck with " ^ ".) If the thing in parentheses looks a lot like a linear regression, that is because it is. In addition, the whole numerator is divided by 1 + e to that very same exponent that looks just like a linear regression (because it is).

One of the many beauties of this expression is that it is a number (the numerator) over that same number plus one (which is the denominator)—which happens to keep economists from being laughed at. If the numerator is really big, then the final answer, and the probability, is some big number divided by the big number plus one: like 999,999/1,000,000. That is: darn close to one but not quite one. This expression, which is the probability of delinquency or whatever, is never going to get as high as one, aka 100%, aka a sure thing. On the other hand, if the number is tiny, then you end up with the tiny number over one plus the tiny number. Therefore, you might have 0.000,001/1.000,001, a really small probability but ever so slightly bigger than zero. Meaning you can predict that something is unlikely to happen but will never predict zero, aka 0%, aka never-going to-happen. After all, *anything* can happen once (anything that hard science does not forbid).

The number we are going to find (that the computer is going to find) is still the old linear sum: $\beta_0+\beta_1*X_1+\beta_2*X_2$ ...—which also means we are finding all the Betas. If that whole mess, for instance, comes out to be equal to zero, the probability expression turns into $e^0/(1 + e^0) = 1/(1 + 1) = ½$. Therefore, that would predict that something would happen half the time. In our world, predicting that half of the borrowers will be delinquent is a lot, but sometimes you have a lot of bad stuff going on and that happens. Generally, the prediction is 1% or less, meaning $\beta_0+\beta_1*X_1+\beta_2*X_2$ ... is usually a negative number: $e^{-4.6}$ leading to $[e^{-4.6}/(1+ e^{-4.6})]$ is about 0.01 (1%). In the way we do credit scores, the β_1, β_2, β_3, etc. are rarely negative, and the X is rarely negative, so the constant β_0 is usually even less than −4.6, to make it all work. Nevertheless, this all depends on how we pick our X values.

Once we do that, then the model software *fits* the βs, meaning the computer picks the Betas, the influence of each bin of each variable, given the fact that every bin of every variable can be part of the equation, to make the whole much of attributes predict the probability of delinquency as well as possible—not for each individual person because that really cannot be known, but based on the history of a million, or millions of loans, that we feed the computer program. It does this by starting with a guess based on the basic correlations, then adds and subtracts a little bit to each Beta in thousands of runs to get good βs, in what is called a maximum likelihood prediction. That means it will find the βs that make this whole system the most likely to correctly predict all the specific delinquents and non-delinquents in the population, which may be millions of loans. It is trying to get as many guesses right as possible overall.

CHAPTER FOURTEEN

Getting a sensible model

Abstract

Judgment is involved in every step of scoring, starting with the big questions of what we even think we should be predicting. A huge issue is that predictions are not stable over time because the economy can be good or bad, people can lose jobs and not be at all like how they presented initially. A model that is best in one business frame is only mediocre in another. Modelers need to decide if they are scoring the probability of events that really threaten the enterprise or simply reduce profits. Models are usually measured by how well they order the consumers who fail vs. who succeed, illustrated with Gini, K–S, and similar statistics. I show some tricks for understanding the parameters if the modeler uses the common logistic form of regression.

Here is a mortgage modeler's tip that works with predicted probabilities that are small—and, except for particular years, places, categories of loans, most predictions, and actualities of mortgages having problems *are* small. Say the chance of default is about 1%, and that is a pretty common percent for these. That is true when the linear sum of β's (this is the second letter of the Greek alphabet, pronounced Beta) times the Xs is up to about −4.6 (negative 4.6), which is around what it does sum up to most of the time for these loans. That makes the numerator about 0.01 and the denominator, $1 + e$^$(\beta_0+\beta_1{*}X_1+\ \beta_2X_2$ ... generally, around 1.01. Well, 0.01 divided by 1.01 is just about 0.01, because the denominator, not much different than 1, does not change anything much. Dividing by something close to 1 has little effect. This may sound like nonsense at first, but it is taking advantage of the small probability of mortgage delinquency to rejigger that difficult looking probit division to only think about the numerator for most mortgages.

Well, the numerator is just a row of numbers times ones and zeros because of something else that happens to be true: we broke all the variables into bins that are either one or zero (on or off). That is just how we did it and over the years, I realized that I could use it to reimagine this probit

Credit Data and Scoring: The First Triumph of Big Data and Big Algorithms
ISBN: 978-0-12-818815-6
https://doi.org/10.1016/B978-0-12-818815-6.00014-5

expression into something a lot simpler. I presume I would have come up with different tricks if we had done something else, but this is what we did, and this is the probability of delinquency for most of these loans. Now what can we do with this trick?

Let us say that β on the variable 6inquiries is two and β on 0inquiries is one, with a difference between βs of 1. That means that the expression $\beta_0+\beta_1*X_1+\beta_2*X_2$ ... is 1 bigger when the variable 6inquires is *on* than when the variable 0inquiries is on, which means that the expression is e (= about 2.7) times bigger (more probable) when 6inquires is on than when the variable 0inquiries is on. If the difference in βs is 0.5, then multiply 2.7 by 0.5 (= 1.35), and when the Xs change, then the probability of delinquency would go up about 1.35 times.

Therefore, I use this trick to try to understand what a bin change means to most of our loans. What I am after is: does the result make *sense*? Judgment is involved in every step, starting with the big questions of what we even think we should be predicting. I have spoken to people from FICO. They tend to make a ton of sense. They are easy to speak to and can talk about every detail of the stuff they are predicting. I am not endorsing their product over anyone else. I am just saying that I am not the only one in the world trying to get this right. A huge issue that I worry about, particularly in the mortgage world, is that predictions are not stable over time. The population that is used is generally what you have, but as we have seen, some years (like 2007) were delinquency (and default and loss)-heavy while some years (like 2014) were delinquency-light. If you had a population that, say, spanned the period 2007—2014, and you did not control for year, then the computer program finding the best βs to predict what actually happened would think that βs that tended to happen more in 2007 were bad βs to have, even if they were not so bad. That seems a pretty dumb conclusion to come to, so we would put year in the model. The way to put year in the model is to make year (or even month, or combinations of year and state) into a bunch of variables that are either one or zero all the time, like number of inquiries. If the loan originated in 2007, then the variable Var2007 is one and Var2008, Var2009, ..., and Var2014 are all zero. If the loan originated in 2008, then Var2008 is one, and the rest of the year variables are zero.

The super-smart modeling program will get the annual βs right too, the right βs for the population. But there were about 15 times as many delinquencies in 2007 as in 2014 and that means that the program finding βs to predict delinquency, even if it were not fooled into thinking that all things 2007ish were bad, would still give a lot more weight to what predicted well in 2007 than in 2014, because there are so many more delinquencies to predict in 2007. Not that it is such a bad thing. It would mean a model that gives more importance to a year with big losses, that threaten insolvency, than to a year where a bit of a miss would hardly be felt.

There really is no simple answer here, whether to leave it 2007ish or to give more weight to 2014 (which can be accomplished in numerous ways, one being just to put in extra copies of 2014). This sort of thing is what economists have to think over, and talk over, and argue about, and report to their bosses, and bosses eventually have to make a call. There are lots and lots of places for math but perhaps just as many places for judgment—the art: picking variables, picking segments, picking populations, and picking outcomes. A lot goes into it. That is why I think it is really worth making this as human as possible. Not that I do not understand how fallible humans are.

Now how does the modeler tell outside of the regression statistics (which are pretty hard to understand) if the model is a good one? That is one of the hardest things to do of all. In fact, the most acute and experienced modeler could be flat-out wrong if the years do not go as expected. A model might be finished in 2019 and go into effect in 2020. Will 2020 be like 2007 or 2014 or something quite different from both? Even if βs on all the variables are about right, β_0 is going to be set by the computer to predict the whole mess about right. If the population we are modeling contains the meltdown, that is loans originated in 2005 through the middle of 2008, then the predictions will be a lot higher than if the population is for loans that originated after the middle of 2008. Those borrowers did not face the same home price drops or unemployment rise. Those economic impacts, even if we could measure them and model them precisely expost (things like home price change and interest rates, which only work so-so retroactively), are not known exante. Therefore, any absolute prediction is bound to miss, maybe by a country mile.

Therefore, we judge a model, not by absolutes, but by relatives. This is the old *grade on a curve* notion. Do the loans that have lower scores go delinquent more often than loans with higher scores? We typically sort all loans we want to look at from lowest score to highest score. Let us say that the scores were really perfect. The low scores all went delinquent until the score got above some level, and then nobody had a delinquency. The loans would make a picture like the blue (gray in print version) line below:

In this picture the X-axis is the sort order, meaning that below the 5% mark are the 5% with the lowest credit scores. The Y-axis is the percent of all bads (blue [gray in print version]) and the percent of all goods (red [black in print version])—as in the information value pictures.

In this picture, 10% of all the loans go bad. In addition, because this is a perfect score model, the 10% with the lowest scores all go bad, and the rest are good. That means the blue line at 10% with rise up to 100% on the Y-axis, because all the bads happen for the first 10% of loans, sorted worst to best, by our perfect score. At the 10% point, no loans have succeeded, so the red line is still stuck on the zero height of the Y-axis. All the rest of the loans succeed though, so from the 10% X-axis point on, the red line rises 10% for each 9% increase in loans—and both blue and red have to hit 100% (meaning that all goods and bads have happened because we have passed through all the loans).

A more likely result is the next picture. Twenty percent of the bads are caught in the lowest 5% of scores, and 34.4% of all bads come from the lowest 10% of scores. It is not a great scorecard, but it basically gets things right. The picture changes a little from bad year to good year—usually a little flatter in a bad year because all sorts of stuff happens to anybody in bad years—but the picture does not change much.

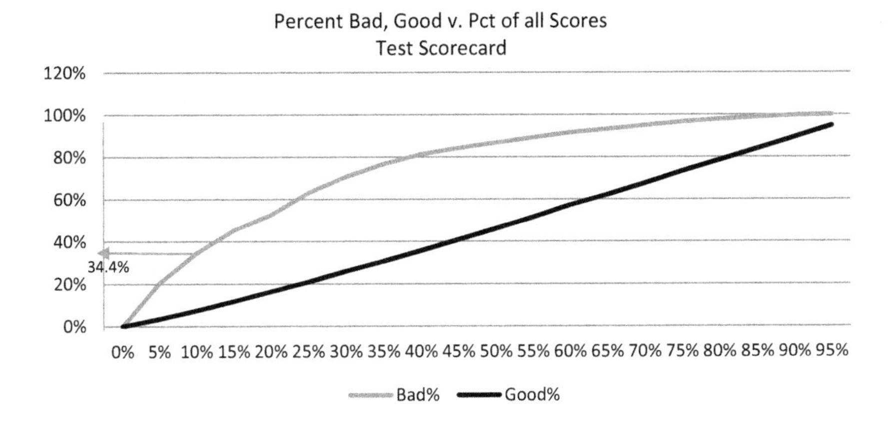

A common calculation made on the picture is the Gini coefficient, which really is just one way of describing how steeply the blue line rises compared to the red. In the picture, one is supposed to think of the whole rectangle described by the four corners X = 0%, Y = 0%; X = 100%, Y = 0%; X = 100%, Y = 100%; and X = 0%, Y = 100%. The Gini coefficient = A/(A + B), where A + B is half of all the area. Because A + B = ½, this is the same as multiplying A by 2. The Gini can never be quite equal to 100 because even with the perfect score, the blue line is not vertical; but it could, theoretically, get close. This way of doing things allows us to compare the sorting order of scores on the same population. Change the population and all bets are off. Some populations have a few risky people in a sea of safety and produce higher Gini coefficients than more mixed bags. If everyone is delinquent, the Gini coefficient is zero all the time!

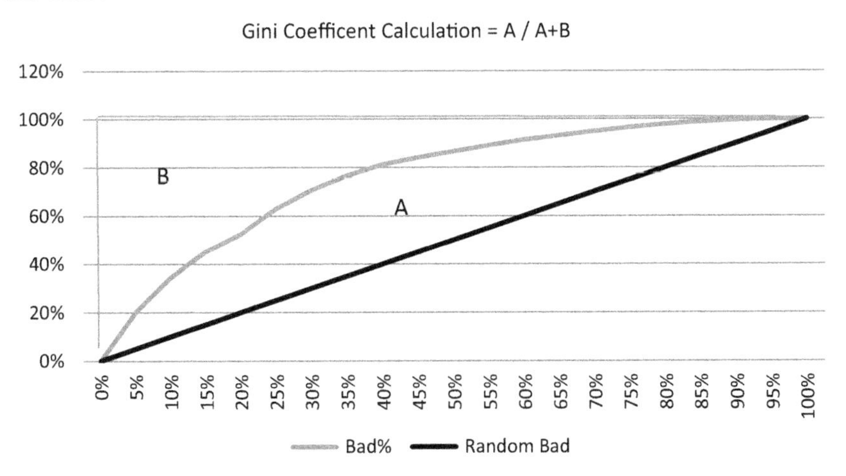

There is usually some point, as scores rise, where the good loan share starts climbing faster than the bad loan share. That is the point of greatest difference. In addition, the difference in heights of the two curves at that point is called the Kolmogorov—Smirnov statistic (often shortened to K—S), another common way of comparing scorecards. The K—S is just another descriptive statistic, however, everyone mentions it, so I did. Personally, I prefer the Gini.

Maximizing the Gini coefficient or K—S statistic both work pretty well, but they both ignore the shape of the *bads* curve somewhat. This does not matter that often, but another way to pick a scorecard is through cut-off analysis. Maybe the company wants to say yes to 90% of applicants and wants to do that and eliminate the worst loans possible while doing that. Then the comparison would be as in the chart of cut-off analysis. We would look at our favorite sample of loans, make our scorecard, draw this picture, and cut off 10%. If at the 10% cut on the line, we draw a horizontal line similar to the Y-axis (and all this can just be done without drawing the pictures of course), that will show what share of the bad loans we would be cutting out. If some other scorecard, possibly with a slightly lower Gini or K—S, happened to cut out a slightly higher percent of bads at that cut-off, then that might be the scorecard to use. It is possible to get very high and mighty about it all, mixing business and statistics. It does not tend to make much difference in my long experience: generally, all the statistics go to together. However, if there is a big staff, it is probably wise to look at all such variations, these and, of course, the many variable combinations, cuts, and interactions possible, in the making of scorecard options. But what the shape statistics show is, hopefully, how much commons sense is behind it all.

By the way, these methods of comparison only work when comparing scorecards that are developed on the same population of loans. Different populations have different Gini's and K—S, even with the same scorecard. Usually, populations with a few tough loans in a sea of safe ones have the highest Gini's. When the population is not very different in score, then the Ginis are lower—for all scorecards.

In addition, this short and rushed description of modeling is all that I will provide in this book. Credit modeling is just a category of all modeling, the problems very much like medical problems. Will a patient last 2 years without a relapse of cancer is mathematically the same as estimating if this or that loan will last 2 years without a delinquency. To really do it takes classes and mentoring and experience. The problems and the data in the fields are entirely different; however, and I have tried to convey some sense of the credit world kind of problems and how credit data figures in to this.

CHAPTER FIFTEEN

Credit scores on the same borrower differ between CRAs

Abstract

This chapter extends the idea of comparing borrowers at the different credit reporting agencies (CRAs), at the same moment, to FICO scores. It turns out that a common version of the FICO score differs quite a bit between scores, in part because of data differences but also because of the arbitrariness inherent in models that become credit scores. The gap between the highest and the lowest scores is greater than 50 points nearly a quarter of the time, and several percent of the time, it is greater than 100 points. The gap is larger when the average or median score between CRAs is low.

As a modeler for a creditor, I felt confident that my models were right for any group of a thousand. I never thought that I could forecast individuals, however. As a consumer, I realize that I have to live with these models, but I know they are only true statistically and could be miscasting any one individual. That brings me to the issue of the chapter: what happens when different models come to different results about any single person? As I pointed out in a previous chapter, one year, 2007 in particular, had terrifically more dire results for everybody than loans made in, say, 2011. That means that models made for 2007 and 2011 are different depending on factors that have nothing to do with historical credit. A model is a model. It is an average prediction based on the time, place, and data set on which it is built. It is not a replica.

There are lots of credit scores, and in particular, there are lots of FICO credit scores. All FICO scores have traditionally been built with one repository and period at a time, and then different FICO scores are predicting different things, even though all these FICO scores are called generic. I think they do this to sell the latest, greatest thing, though I presume they would tell you they have figured something out, or the environment has changed. However, there is typically an additional charge for the new thing. Now each new model will come up with a different answer for the very same data inputs. If this were not true, then what does it even mean to say that the model is new? What might be surprising is that even FICO scores

Credit Data and Scoring: The First Triumph of Big Data and Big Algorithms
ISBN: 978-0-12-818815-6
https://doi.org/10.1016/B978-0-12-818815-6.00015-7

with similar names, serving similar customers with similar purposes, can nevertheless come up with strikingly different answers for the same person at different CRAs. VantageScore does not do this to the same degree. Since they are owned by the three CRAs, they assure that the same models, variables, and Betas are in place, regardless of the CRA. If scores differ, it is because the data differ. FICO scores have also grown more alike in recent versions from one CRA to the next, though they are not identical. I think both represent a false congruence, however, despite the fact that it is less alarming to get the same score from the same data. This answer does not so plainly point to the randomness in all scores but there is a randomness in all scores. In some ways, the differences in scores by repository are more honest.

I noticed that, when my son applied to college, he was allowed to take the SAT repeatedly and many schools would just use his highest score. Now of course he got different scores for the same test on different dates. I presume that it was good for the College Board to sell numerous test sessions. In addition, I presume it looks good for the college to show higher SAT scores for new students. Moreover, it certainly behooves wealthy parents who can pay for test after test and want their children to go to the best schools. However, it is a fake number. Each SAT is probably fair enough, but if a student gets a 600 one day, a 650 another day, then a 700 the third, it is artificially constricting to say he or she got a 700 on the test. What he or she got was between 600 and 700 each time, and that is most true, because the test result is very, very random! The same for credit scores. They are very, very random. They simply cannot understand why someone has the track record they have and only have a limited power to predict what will happen to those people in the future. It is a worthwhile classification *for the creditor*. However, it is only a classification that borrowers have to live with—it does not define them, and it does not determine their future.

Now both the PERC and FTC papers a few chapters back find a fair number of errors on credit reports but claim that those errors do not tend to create significant difference in credit scores. However, what these studies never examined was how much scores could just plainly vary, regardless of data errors! Somewhat amazing really, that they it did not occur to them, but, unless artificially smoothed, they do, and they do a lot. In addition, I am not even talking about all the missing material that is never sent to CRAs, or missing because the CRAs made a deal with state attorneys general or played nice with furnishers. Scores are highly erratic, for data reason, but also for model reasons.

The most widely used scores are by FICO, and one set of these, developed at a specific point in time, some years ago, but common for the most important debts even today, is what is used in the statistics above. However, those are pretty important scores. They are used for numerous mortgages in the United States. Approval depends on them. Costs are set from them. The FICO generic score that the charts in this chapter are based on is a predictor of probability of a borrower going 3 months late on any of the debts that show up in a credit report. FICO does not show a probability; it shows a number on a scale of 300–850; but this is now true of every major score. This is the number that people are looking for, hoping it is high, with practical and emotional repercussions if it is not. Most scores are on the upper end of that scale; that is just how they make the scale. It is not a linear scale, but a logarithmic scale. An easier expression of this is that the chance of delinquency doubles with every drop of some constant amount of points (about 40 in my experience). The United States average credit score is now about 700.

Having said all that, let me show you our first chart about how different scores can be at the three national CRAs, covering many millions of loans and a number of years—but all scores are on the same people at the same time. Once again, I am keeping individual CRAs anonymous, calling them CRA1, CRA2, and CRA3. The distributions of FICO scores are different at the three CRAs, though not by much.

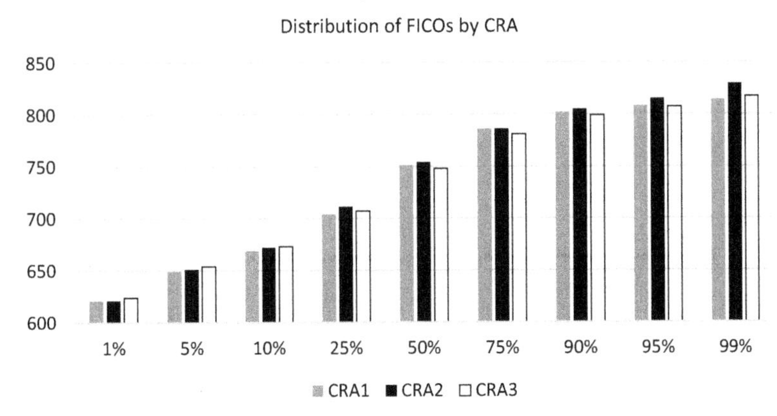

The problem is not in the broad distributions. Overall, they are at least fairly close. Matched individual to individuals, however, the differences are large. Here is a table that shows how different they are, categorized by the middle repository. The "gap" in these tables is the highest CRA score minus the lowest CRA score, both scores run on the same individual at just about the same moment. The data do not change with timing.

Middle score	Average gap	Median gap	% Gap >50	%Gap >100
<500	51	47	46%	6%
500–619	47	42	39%	5%
620–639	41	35	29%	3%
640–659	38	33	25%	3%
660–679	36	31	23%	3%
680–699	36	30	22%	3%
700–719	35	29	21%	2%
720–739	34	29	19%	2%
740–799	28	23	11%	1%
>800	22	18	4%	1%

There are a few big take-aways in this chart. One is that the *median* difference of top from bottom is usually larger than the measure of a big difference in the PERC paper. Only for people with credit scores over 740 is the median variation not over 25 points, but the reader may recall that a 25-point change in score was what PERC needed to see to think an error in data was worth fixing. This occurred between 0% and 2% of the time, depending on which of the two error papers one reads. What we are seeing is just moving from CRA to CRA causes that much change *usually*. For individuals with a middle FICO score below 660, fully a quarter will find at least a 50-point difference between their lowest and highest FICO scores, despite the fact that we are talking about the same person at the same time.

Following is a charted view of similar information, the difference between the highest and lowest Classic FICO scores at the 75th highest percentiles depending on the median credit score bucket. So, for example, the three scores at different CRAS for an individual might be 695, 710, and 720. The median bucket is 710-719, and the difference between high and low is 25 points. That is about the 75th percentile of such differences; and a quarter of all people in this median bucket have at least this much difference. I think it is obvious at the 75th percentile, for a quarter of applicants, that there is so much volatility that it behooves them to try to have the highest score used—at least in many contexts.

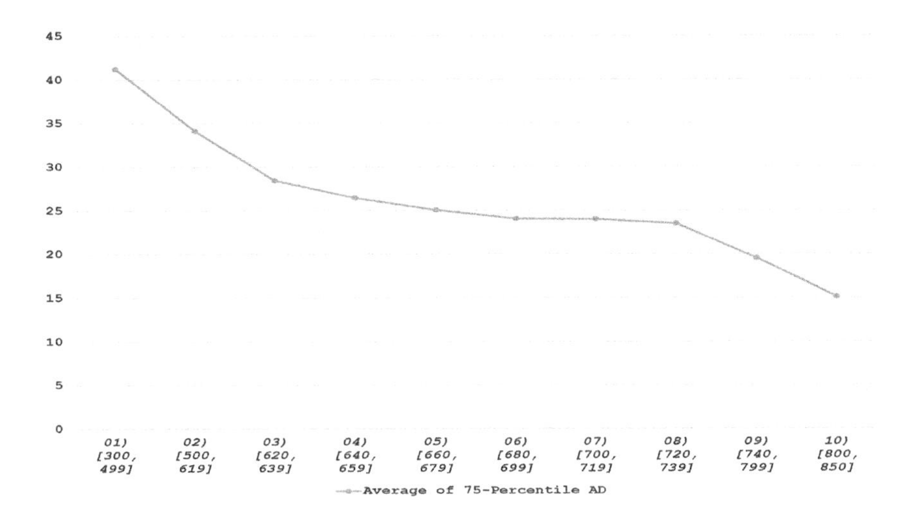

There are many kinds of loans that require a credit score above some level. Then there are the effects on rates, which can be dramatic. Here are some common costs in 2018.

Table: APR Rate Sheets by a Credit Union.

	Credit card		Auto loan	
FICO	**Rewards**	**Secured**	**<36 months**	**<60 months**
740+	9.24%	11.24%	3.39%	3.89%
739–700	11.74%	13.74%	3.89%	4.39%
699–660	12.24%	14.24%	5.14%	5.64%

As a practical matter, it may behoove a creditor to obtain all three scores and take an average, or take the middle score. What this does is take the volatility of model and data difference nominally out of the problem. It slightly improves the forecasting power to do this, but remember that the inaccuracy of models can never be erased. All forecasts contain the possibility of a great deal of error: that is life. The cost to get three scores is secret and varies with the market power of the creditor, but it should not cost any party of size to get all credit scores for one or two borrowers for 10 dollars. Even for very large buckets (60 points), the number where any one score is in a different bucket than the median is usually near a fifth.

It is also the case, in my experience, that the median score is a better predictor than a random score, and the average score is a little better predictor than the median. But just a little better.

Are the scores just done differently at each repository? That answer is yes, for FICO, but probably a lot of it is a slightly different period and so different loans are going into each model. However, I cannot stress enough that this does not does not make any particular model wrong, or another right. A whole suite of models that create a broad spectrum of scores for a particular individual could all be about equal in predictiveness. There is no precise score for any person, just like it cannot be foretold with accuracy how someone will do in college and beyond. I realize that readers expect that there must be a correct score for every person because everyone does get one; but that score is really not that person's signature, just a prediction assigned to a fact set associated with that person. The modeling assigns the weights to the age of oldest trade line, number of this or that late, liquidity of credit, number of inquiries—all the things that tend to go into scores. That we give it such social weight is our normative, judgmental mind at work. If you believe that changing credit cards and not holding on to old accounts is a bad thing or if you think raising limits on credit cards is good—well you will agree with the normative choices of credit scoring. However, many conclusions of the scoring approach only make sense statistically.

Needing to use credit, using credit, these are clearly not in themselves indicative of someone with financial strength. Yet having zero credit activity is a bad indicator in models. This does not mean that there is some problem with zero credit activity, only that in that group there are people with other problems that are not explained. Apparently, some significant share of people that never use credit do so because they have trouble, or have had trouble, with credit. A well-known case that is similar concerns alcohol use. Someone who drinks one glass of wine a day, and for years, is very unlikely to come to harm, or commit harm, if she drinks a glass of wine. Some significant share of former alcoholics, who do not now touch alcohol, would on the other hand be taking a terrible risk. Any danger-of-alcohol score would paradoxically show zero alcohol use as risky, a bizarre result. The same occurs for credit. Not using credit is a risk factor!

This confusion about what credit scores mean and are good for explains how scores can differ so much from one repository to another without meaning that one score is good or bad. These FICO scores are just about equivalent when kept to the group level. There is only a hair's difference between the success of a FICO score at Experian and one at TransUnion, and even the hair's difference flips about for this or that geographic or temporal cut. They are all *true*, meaning they all have a good Gini coefficient or area under the curve (AUC) or r-squared because they do not have to come to the same conclusion about any individuals.

A thousand low-scored borrowers will be genuinely and correctly predicted to have 10 times as many delinquencies as a thousand high-scored borrowers, by somewhat different scoring models and somewhat different data. Individuals do not matter to creditors' bottom line. They can be wrong about any individual they deal with, but only need to limit the number they are wrong about. Statistics are fine with large creditors, because we individuals *are* just a statistic to any large organization. That is all we can be, because scale is what organizations are all about.

However, scores, AI, algorithms, and websites are applied to us as individuals. Our feelings *of* group membership are profound. We are prepared to accept our slot and even crave to be slotted. Nevertheless, we feel and experience things individually. But people do not actually live and feel as a group. There is no consciousness that encompasses that thousand people with high scores or that thousand with low scores and no or costly credit. That second group will genuinely have something like 10 times as many delinquencies. However, there will be individuals in the high-scoring group that fail to pay back their debts and many individuals in the low-scoring group that do.

CHAPTER SIXTEEN

The credit industry outside the United States

Abstract

Unfortunately, I have little international economics background, and not even a lot of travel under my belt. However, I feel that I can work on the internet to get a reasonable idea of international practices in ecommerce, credit usage, credit reporting, and credit scoring. As it turns out, countries do not share credit data or reputations: everyone starts out at zero. I turn first to the major Credit Reporting Agencies (CRAs) to see what countries they claim to work with, but on their lists are both minor countries and countries that do little business with them. I decide to cover the 20 largest economies and countries with over five million in population but among the 10 highest in per capita income.

My career for the last quarter century or so included credit analytics in the United States. In that capacity, I became familiar with credit reports, laws, and practices in this country. It was only gradually that I came to question choices made, began to think about alternate paths, and observed technology outrunning the original intents of the industry, public, and government. In that time of course, I was also a consumer and a user of credit products myself, getting my own mortgages, relying more and more on ecommerce of all sorts, on computers to track my savings, and on credit cards instead of currency (and avoiding the collection of ever-more-trivial pennies), transferring funds and brokering stocks on my iPad. The day came when I felt I was so wise, and had so much time on my hands, that I would write a book about credit. In addition, when I began that project, I just assumed—I genuinely assumed, unthinking—that the United States was the only market on earth where our practices would be of interest to anyone who might read this book. It had barely occurred to me to wonder what happened outside our borders. I suppose this insularity makes me an Ugly American, but not an irredeemable one I hope. As I began to discuss the idea of writing a book on credit with Elsevier, my editor (at that time) thought it should be internationalized. His point was to broaden the audience, and, after an initial resistance, I agreed he was right. It quickly came home to me that I was

Credit Data and Scoring: The First Triumph of Big Data and Big Algorithms
ISBN: 978-0-12-818815-6
https://doi.org/10.1016/B978-0-12-818815-6.00016-9

living in a narrow mental framework, and this was an opportunity to learn something about the world.

Now of course there was the problem of finding out what happened in other countries, despite the fact that I had barely traveled, surely had lived in no other nation. Making virtue out of necessity, I turned to the internet, to learn what I could, surely starting this effort with the most United States centric point of view imaginable. I think that the topic and the country I became used to were not horrible for this bias. Credit scores surely got their start in the United States; we are the leader in consumption practice worldwide. As the reader will see, there are all sorts of flavors to how credit is collected, shared, treated, and foretold—throughout the world, and even the modern first world. I started by assuming that America was a paradigm, and then retreated to the opposite notion that the American experience was unique, but both were exaggerated.

I tried following the big three CRAs, which certainly are constant in the United States, and almost synonymous with the credit world here, guessing they might bring their practices with them. Each claim to be in large swathes of the world, presumably doing something in all these parts that is a continuation of what that they do here.

Experian lists its "Global Sites" as: Argentina, Australia, Austria, Belgium, Brazil, Bulgaria, Canada, Chile, China, Colombia, Czech Republic, Denmark, France, Germany, Greece, Hong Kong, India, Indonesia, Ireland, Italy, Japan, Malaysia, Mexico, Netherlands, New Zealand, Norway, Peru, Poland, Russia, Singapore, South Africa, South Korea, Spain, Switzerland, Taiwan, Thailand, Turkey, UAE, United Kingdom, United States, Venezuela, and Vietnam.[1]

Equifax says they serve Argentina, Australia, Brazil, Cambodia, Canada, Chile, Costa Rica, Ecuador, El Salvador, Honduras, India, Malaysia, Mexico, New Zealand, Paraguay, Peru, Portugal, Russia, Saudi Arabia, Singapore, Spain, United Kingdom, Uruguay, and the United States.[2]

TransUnion claims to be in South Africa, Kenya, Rwanda, Zambia, Namibia, Botswana, Swaziland, North America, Canada, United States, Mexico, Brazil, Dominican Republic, Chile, Puerto Rico, Costa Rica, Nicaragua, El Salvador, Guatemala, Honduras, Colombia, India, Hong Kong, Philippines, Europe, and the United Kingdom.[3]

However, after a bit of digging, I came to believe that the activities of the companies are often minor (relative to the role they have in the United States) in many of these countries, and often the countries on the list are not large on the world economic stage. These are three companies, large companies, trying to extend wherever they can, trying to appear genuinely international, because that is certainly their business goal. However, they have competitors throughout the world, and they just cannot repeat their United States experience elsewhere. Indeed, that is normally impossible because the conditions and laws are so different. Generally, all three are qualified in data management, technology, modeling, legal issues, and talking the talk of credit stuff; but they adapt to the conditions, laws, and industrial organizations of countries in which they try to establish themselves.

What struck me, in fact, after chasing down a few countries and internet articles, is that there is no consistent *world* at all in credit matters. Despite many common intents and overlapping markets, it is done nation by nation, with hard borders. Oddly, countries just do not share credit data, even ones that are strongly connected, such as countries of the European Union or countries served by the same CRA. For instance, Experian says they serve 14 countries, but no consumer can take advantage (or be disadvantaged) in one of those countries for debts paid or unpaid in another of the 14 countries. Besides non-overlapping data, many countries have something significantly different about their credit apparatus from every other country: laws, companies, who supplies scores (if there is any scoring), what is known, who contributes, etc. What this tells me about credit reporting, scoring, and security is that it is inextricably politicized at the national level, with some commonalities from historical ties and geography. In most countries, credit data is not owned by the consumers (e.g., the United States). In other countries, the data is aligned with things weirdly invasive (China with its cameras, India and its eye-scanners).

In recognition of the national distinctions, it struck me that the way to approach this was to do it nation by nation, making sure that I first of all cover the (economically) major countries separately while bringing out the commonalities where I can. I admit that I do this somewhat blunderingly, trying to hit all the main countries in the world from a consumer market point of view. I have no opinions about what are the noblest countries, or most interesting, but I can look up the monetary and tradable value of their business activity on the Investopedia website.[4] My plan is to say what I can about countries on one of two lists: First, I am looking for countries that have a significant consumer and credit economy. The 20 countries with the largest economies are the United States, China, Japan, Germany, United Kingdom (including England, Scotland, Wales, and Ireland), India, France, Brazil, Italy, Canada, South Korea, Russia, Australia, Spain, Mexico, Indonesia, Turkey, Netherlands, Saudi Arabia, and Switzerland. According to *Investopedia*, these 20 countries account for over 80 percent of the global economy. But a country that we think of as modern and developed might fail to be on this list simply because it has a small population, so I also add 10 countries (with population at least five million), ordered by the measure of per capita, which will allow some smaller countries into our group: Singapore, Norway, United Arab Emirates, Kuwait, Austria, Hong Kong, Denmark, Netherlands, Sweden, and Belgium.[5] Then I allow myself to rope in a few other countries, which strike me as noteworthy.

My approach then, the best I can see to do, is to scan the internet, which *is* largely transnational, to report what I think is key about the use of credit data and scores in any country that is in any of these groups, listing the countries alphabetically. Where websites' languages are not English, I use Google Translate to make it mostly understandable to me. Hopefully, I bring some expertise, to understanding how to translate what is on the website to some sense of reality of what is really going on in that locations. All websites throw in some spin. I think I can usually take some of that out. I am usually first trying to bring out the energy of the consumer market, the development of ecommerce, how people obtain things and pay for things. Are they spending their own money with checks and debit cards, or are they spending money, largely on credit cards, that they need to repay? Is credit a large part of every-day personal finance, with credit cards or, say, with mortgages?

As with many first instances of financial innovation, debit cards were first created in the United States. Though there is more than one story of how they started, the website *PocketSense* states that The First National Bank of Seattle issued the first debit card to business executives with large savings accounts in 1978.[6] These cards were ecommerce tools that behaved like a check. In the 1980s, the nationwide debiting system took hold, built on the credit card infrastructure and ATM networks already in place. Now, debit cards, labeled and administered by the major credit card companies, are available in almost all countries, and often the debit card can be used to withdraw cash from ATM machines. In many countries, particularly in Europe east of the United Kingdom, debit card dominates credit cards—which means that people are spending their own money that they have already accumulated. Lending is less feverish in this case, less widespread. This is in contrast to economies like the United States and United Kingdom, where most purchasing comes with a loan, or which could be a loan (credit card), and trust is more crucial.

Where trust is crucial, it may be that a homogeneous population in the home country gives rise to trust and mutual support, at least usually, by virtue of simple affinity. Where that is weaker, there are increasing degrees of recordation and evaluation of debt repayment, used to establish reputations that are not taken for granted. An important wrinkle in the recording of debt repayment is whether or not positive repayment is recorded, as well as failures. In many countries, only failures are available, and are gradually less of a blemish as time passes since the failure. This is very different from the United States and some other countries, where paying on time for a long time is a counteracting positive.

Next, what is the degree of scoring or modeling done with this held data? It is one thing for creditors or other contract-offering entities to come up with their own notions of what is acceptable. The extent that extenders of credit rely on models is a measure of robotic response to consumerism, and sets the society up for robotic responses on all sorts of matters. The internet was originally driven by pornography because that was a way to make money on the medium. Scores in financial matters are worth money too, and extend analytic acceptance and use. Then, at some point, the idea of scoring becomes a sort of norm in decision-making in all areas.

The last area to address is the legal framework for all the foregoing. In the United States, the Fair Credit Reporting Act (FCRA) and its regulators (including the state attorneys general) have defined the legal landscape of credit and credit scoring. It followed a certain path in the United States, largely because it mostly evolved prior to the internet and hacks galore. I will be trying to figure with the internet, not really very well I must admit, what is the legal setting in the various countries.

In total, I hope I try getting the flavor of each country, and where they are on the path to Algocracy in credit matters.

Endnotes

1 The list of Experian Global Sites is obtained from the Experian website at www.experian.com/corporate/about-experian.html reviewed by me on June 5, 2019.

2 The Equifax list is obtained from its website at www.equifax.com/about-equifax/company-profile/, reviewed by me on June 5, 2019.

3 The TransUnion list is obtained from its website at www.transunion.com/about-us/global-locations, reviewed by me on June 5, 2019.

4 The list of top economies, that I used, is available at www.investopedia.com/insights/worlds-top-economies/, reviewed by me on June 5, 2019.

5 The list of countries with high per capita income, that I used, is available at www.en.Wikipedia.org/wiki/List_of_countries_by_GDP_%28PPP%29_per_capita, reviewed by me on June 5, 2019.

6 *From A Detailed History of Debit Cards,* written by Eric Tilden, for *PocketSense* at https://pocketsense.com/detailed-history-debit-cards-5462528.html, updated November 8. 2018. It was reviewed by me on August 14, 2019.

CHAPTER SEVENTEEN

List of practices by country

Abstract

This is an alphabetic list of countries and their credit practices, in so far as I could discern that from the Internet. Countries do not share data, only some share laws, and everyone starts at zero in any new country. There is quite a spectrum. On the one hand are a group of relatively modern, consumerist, credit-loving countries, with clear-cut laws and credit algorithms their citizens have mostly accepted, including Australia, Canada, Germany, Malaysia, Singapore, South Africa, the United Kingdom, and the United States. On the other end are a number of countries with very rudimentary credit apparatus, such as Russia and all of Africa apart from South Africa. In the middle are many countries of the European Union that are well off but reluctant at this time to have their citizens take on credit, for instance, Belgium and the Netherlands. China and India stand apart for the intrusive directions that credit is taking.

Australia

Australia is relatively small, with only 25 million people, but it is in the top 20 economies in the world. It is also very westernized, high tech, formerly a dominion of the United Kingdom, and friendly to the United States and the West. Tourism is a very big business there, and Western credit cards are accepted almost everywhere. It is not surprising that they would handle credit similarly to the United Kingdom and United States (which are similar to each other). Australians seem to accept debt handily, as quoted from this article from Finder.Com.[1]

> *Australians' Household Debt Nears Highest Worldwide ...*
>
> *Australian household debt has steadily risen over the past three decades as more of us aim to own homes and continue to rely on products such as car loans and credit cards. In fact, the ratio of household debt to income has more than doubled between 1995 and 2015, going from 104% to 212%, according to the OECD Data released in 2015 ...*

Both negative and positive data about debt paying is kept. However, the United States collects positive data for 10 years while Australia does so for only 2 years.

Credit Data and Scoring: The First Triumph of Big Data and Big Algorithms
ISBN: 978-0-12-818815-6
https://doi.org/10.1016/B978-0-12-818815-6.00017-0

There are four national CRAs in Australia. Equifax is the largest credit agency in Australia, followed by Experian. These are two of the three national CRAs of the United States and these names will appear in many countries. The other two Australian credit bureaus are Dun and Bradstreet (an important financial data firm in the United States too though not a national CRA) and the Tasmania Collection Service. Each of the credit reporting agencies operating in Australia has to send any consumer who asks for it a free copy of her credit file every 12 months.

The Equifax site in Australia shows a timeline for the company now called Equifax and previously called Veda.[2] Most of the action comes in the last 10 years. The site claims the data they have are collected from banks credit unions store credit issues, payday lenders, telecommunications providers, utility providers, the Australian Securities and Investment Commission, and the judiciary system. Equifax Australia creates its own credit score. It ranges from 0 to 1200, but always comes also with the quintile that the consumer is in, relative to other people that are scoreable in Australia.

They model their own credit score. FICO, the leading credit scoring company in the U.S., has no presence in Australia. Equifax claims that the ingredients for their credit score are as follows: Credit Limit 3%, Repayment History 30%, Adverse Events 10%, Personal Information 3%, Credit Report Age 3%, and Credit Application 51%. This is far different from the usual American generic credit score in the reliance on Credit Applications, which are data that the consumer tells about himself/herself each time he/she wants to borrow, including facts such as age, number of children, employer, salary, and so on. Of course it is important, but it is not generic. Equifax in Australia must be exchanging data with creditors. In the United States, it would fall usually to the creditor to evaluate that separately from a credit score.

Like the American FCRA, Australia has a law that covers credit data, and it was passed decades ago. Again, from the Equifax cite:

The details inside your credit report, including how and when it can be accessed, are regulated by the Privacy Act 1988. This Act aims to balance the need to respect the privacy of individuals with the need to ensure credit providers have the information at their disposal to grant credit to consumers. You can access your credit report for free each year.

Your credit report cannot be changed unless information contained within it is found to be incorrect. If there is incorrect information on your report, the Privacy Act dictates it is your right to dispute this. You can do this by approaching your credit reporting body directly and asking them to investigate for you. Equifax has a Corrections Portal set up for this very purpose.

The Privacy Act 1988 (which had some revisions in 2014) covers much more than credit data, but it seems that Privacy has been identified in Australia as the key issue in the collection of credit information. In the United States, privacy is important, but its importance developed in time, long after the FCRA was first passed.

To sum up, Australia seems similar to the United States and perhaps a bit more Privacy-focused. It does use scoring but perhaps in a more context-driven manner. Still, it is organizing people by mathematical models.

Austria

Although among the top 10 countries in the world in per capita income, Austria does not seem to achieve this through routinized consumer lending or credit rating: there is little on the Internet to be found regarding Austrian credit services. The European Union generally has a thriving e-commerce; however, it is more focused on debit cards than the revolving credit cards of in the United States. Here is a quote from a website called VisaEurope[3]: "The European debit card market is twice as large as the credit card market and still growing - Europeans use Visa debit cards to spend more than €1.5 million every minute, while debit cards account for more than 70% of all Visa cards across Europe."

I cannot find a credit bureau (CRA) that seems to coordinate the credit information of Austrians. Threads on websites speak of each bank as making its own decisions. In general, credit practices seem low key relative to the United States and United Kingdom. There is borrowing. They are next to Italy in the ratio of household debt to income, substantial but nowhere near world-beating.[4] E-commerce seems mostly to be present for the purposes of currency replacement not for financing consumption.

With very little to go on for Austria, I rely on *Wikipedia*[5]: "In Austria, credit scoring is done as a blacklist. Consumers who did not pay bills end up on the blacklists that are held by different credit bureaus. Having an entry on the black list may result in the denial of contracts. Certain enterprises including telecom carriers use the list on a regular basis. Banks also use these lists, but rather inquire about security and income when considering loans. Beside these lists several agencies and credit bureaus provide credit scoring of consumers. According to the Austrian Data Protection Act, consumers must opt-in for the use of their private data for any purpose." To sum up, Austria seems less inclined to support debt consumerism and credit cards than the United States, and less interested in consumers proving they are reliable payers.

Belgium

Belgium does have numerous credit and debit cards, but credit cards are not used to run up the level of debt in the United States. All data on debts are held by the National Bank of Belgium. Access to the bank is via website. The website expresses the views of the Belgium political system, which is protective of Belgium consumers[6]:

> *The Central Individual Credit Register is an instrument used to curb excessive indebtedness. It records information on all the loans contracted by natural persons for private purposes as well as any overdue debts relating to these loans. It is compulsory for lenders to consult the Central Individual Credit Register before granting any loans.*
>
> *Mission: The recording and supply of this information to lenders aims to strengthen the means of preventing the excessive indebtedness of private individuals.*

A social networking site in "Belgium called The Bulletin: The platform for Belgium's International Community" put it this way[7]:

"Belgium has strict laws which are intended to prevent lenders offering loans to people that they are then unable to pay - if you were to be offered a loan "recklessly" then the lender would find itself unable to enforce the payments due and would probably have to write the loan off and clearly no lender wishes to place itself in that position."

"Consumers have little say in where their data is as well as extremely limited access to it. Regulations give consumers the right to glimpse your file once every 12 months for free on AnnualCreditReport.com. If you want further access to your own data, you are required to pay for it." This last is from Yahoo Finance.

If I correctly understand, Belgium does not allow credit scores at all.[8] Belgium has not only nationalized health care but also a private system that is more significant that in many European countries. The retirement pensions are generous. It is much more sedate and protective of citizens that the United States.

Brazil

Brazil is on the list because it is a huge country, with over 200 million people and, as a result, has a market economy in the world's top 10. Compared to the United States, it is a poor country, but it is middle of the road internationally. It is an OECD country, with much less debt than average among the OECD. Health care in Brazil is free. The pension system is generous but it probably outruns the national income of Brazil. It does not have a centralized credit reporting system. Per BusinessInsider.Com and the Center for Latin American Monetary Studies[9]:

> *Brazil formerly had no formal credit scoring system. Lenders generally relied on negative reporting alone, and debts were removed from the credit register as soon as they were paid off.*
>
> *But that's changing. Starting in 2012, Brazil's government set rules for the creation of positive credit bureaus, leading to a coalition of the country's five biggest banks to form a credit research agency, the International Financing Review reported.*
>
> *Other global companies, like Experian and Fair Isaac Corporation (FICO), have also stepped in and established their own systems in Brazil.*

FICO did purchase GoOn in Brazil December 12, 2018.[10] "Founded in 2002, GoOn provides risk consulting for the entire consumer credit lifecycle, and has hundreds of customers in banking, retail, credit cards, student lending, insurance and real estate." However, most Internet entries are very dated, and the data management and scoring seem today much less organized and pervasive than in the United States.

Canada

Canada is not only adjacent to the United States but also has markets highly integrated with ours. It is not surprising that their credit system is fairly similar to the United States. Still, it is not a perfect mirror for the US system. Canada borrows heavily and has one of the highest ratios of debt to after-tax income in the world. Canada does have higher taxes than the United States, a higher pension base, and nationalized health care—but these are not like Norway, Netherlands, and Denmark, which have even higher ratios of debt to after-tax income. Canadians are relatively overextended.

Two of the US CRAs have branched over to Canada, Equifax and TransUnion, who together control the market. Equifax on its site speaks of developing its databases in the last decade, meaning that the credit systems in Canada have had substantially less time to mature.

The CRAs are not as closely aligned in Canada as in the United States. Here are some relatively frank words (compared to the United States) from Equifax Canada[11]:

Credit bureaus have different sources for collecting information, and not all creditors and lenders report to the two major credit bureaus. This means that each of your credit reports may contain different information. Creditors keep the credit bureaus updated with your account status and payment history — two factors that contribute to your credit scores.

... As a result, your credit score may vary between the major credit bureaus — even if all of your creditors report to both credit bureaus.

... many creditors report to both major credit bureaus, some creditors may report to only one or none at all....

Credit bureaus collect the following types of information:

Personal information, such as your name and address

Credit account information, also known as "tradelines"

Inquiry information

Public record and collections information ...

How is your credit information used?

Most people are aware that banks and credit card companies leverage information provided by credit bureaus to make certain types of lending decisions about you. But, other companies with permissible purpose can also pull a copy of your credit report.

Equifax distributes FICO scores, per the FICO article FICO *Extends Distribution Agreement with Equifax for FICO Score in Canada.*[12] The pictures scores on the Equifax site show a similar range to FICO and Vantage in the United States, 300–850.

The TransUnion site in Canada seems to make its own credit scores and also stresses that subscribers do not all report to both bureaus.[13]

The laws covering the collection of credit data are governed by provincial law. "Generally, those provisions establish an obligation for customers of TransUnion to advise consumers if the information obtained from a consumer reporting agency is used to decline a benefit ... At the federal level, the Personal Information Protection and Electronic Documents Act outlines the requirements for organizations that use, collect or disclose personal information during the course of their business activities."

Federal Law of Canada requires that consumers agree to the passing along of their information to the Credit Bureaus. In the United States, the same is true, and every consumer who borrows money does indeed sign something which says that consumer data will be sent to a CRA. The consumer does not need to sign it in the United States but will not get credit in that case.

China

China is not an OECD country (though Russia is). It does not have either the robust health care or pension systems of Europe. It has focused on managing its citizens and creating a class of rulers with vast incomes. It has perhaps the most interesting approach to scoring, seemingly invasive by the US (and my) norms. Its national government is attempting to build a *social score*, or, at least, this is the allegation. Allow me to excerpt some of a breathless 2015 article from BBC.[14]

> *In most countries, the existence of a credit system isn't controversial. Past financial information is used to predict whether individuals will pay their mortgages or credit card bill in the future. But China is taking the whole concept a few steps further. The Chinese government is building an omnipotent 'social credit' system that is meant to rate each citizen's trustworthiness.*
>
> *By 2020, everyone in China will be enrolled in a vast national database that compiles fiscal and government information, including minor traffic violations, and distils it into a single number ranking each citizen. ... Users are encouraged to flaunt their good credit scores to friends, and even potential mates. 'A person's appearance is very important,' explains Baihe's vice-president, Zhuan Yirong. 'But it's more important to be able make a living. Your partner's fortune guarantees a comfortable life.' ...*
>
> *[A firm called] Sesame rates the online financial transactions of those using Alibaba's payment system, in addition to data it obtains from its partners including the taxi service Didi Kuaidi, rating whether users bothered to settle taxi payments.*
>
> *Controversially, the company does not hide that it judges the types of products shoppers buy online. Someone who plays video games for 10 hours a day, for example, would be considered an idle person, and someone who frequently buys diapers would be considered as probably a parent, who on balance is more likely to have a sense of responsibility,' Li Yingyun, Sesame's technology director told Caixin, a Chinese magazine, in February.*
>
> *The Chinese authorities are watching the pilot process very carefully. The government system won't be exactly the same as the private systems, but government officials are certainly taking cues from the algorithms developed under the private projects .... A lengthy planning document from China's elite State Council explains that social credit will 'forge a public opinion environment that trust-keeping is glorious', warning that the 'new system will reward those who report acts of breach of trust' ...*

Details on the inner workings of the system are vague, though it is clear that each citizen and Chinese organization will be rated .... A national database will merge a wide variety of information on every citizen, assessing whether taxes and traffic tickets have been paid, whether academic degrees have been rightly earned and even, it seems, whether females have been instructed to take birth control....

A more recent article in the Atlantic adds even more emotion,[15] but it brings out two contrasting themes. On the one hand, "The country is racing to become the first to implement a pervasive system of algorithmic surveillance. Harnessing advances in artificial intelligence and data mining and storage to construct detailed profiles on all citizens, China's communist party-state is developing a 'citizen score' to incentivize 'good' behavior." The positive side is "that because lack of trust is a serious problem in China, many Chinese welcome this potential system."

This is possible because the country has become so digital so quickly, and, of course, the state is involved in every corporate action. Brookings writes[16]:

"As US-based card payment companies like American Express, MasterCard, and Visa strive to set up shop in China, Chinese consumers are increasingly using their mobile phones to buy goods and services. In effect, the country has leapfrogged from cash to mobile payments, bypassing the payment cards system."

Summarizing, I will point out the obvious. China is not a free society. Its Internet firewalls are well known to the world. Commerce in China is emerging in what could be a digital fishbowl, every purchase available to the government, cameras everywhere, in combination with facial recognition software. China is not hiding the fact its way of using these data to create a social score for every citizen. Indeed, it seems to be going out of its way to advertise the fact. If China wants to have a correlation to membership in the Communist Party or law-breaking or sending emails that complain about government or having children that do well in school, they can and will do so. People with higher scores will be more highly correlated with the behaviors or successes that the Chinese government values.

But models need to have a Y, a value to predict, otherwise they are just rules stipulated by people. If there is a Y, then there must be some mathematical truth embodied. No doubt people that buy math books will have children that do better in school than people that buy cigarettes or play most video games. Some provinces and some nationalities are more likely to be members of the Party, or officials. A model will predict good and bad behaviors, as defined by whoever directs the model. The second effect is that a high score, because it is itself a reward, and quite possibly a very significant award (which conferring the right to travel to a foreign country) will *induce* the behaviors that raise it. Chinese parents are well known for spending a small fortune to help their children score highly on school entrance exams. Presumably, this same effort will go into raising credit scores. Of course, even in the United States, there is anxiety to have a higher credit score, and while the ways to achieve a high credit score are basically just making money, not getting into deep debt, and paying back debts in full and on time, there is a numerological passion to our score craving.

The Chinese are the bogeymen of this American generation, as Japan was a couple decades ago, and before that the Russians. I have come to know dozens of Chinese professionally, and at least a couple very well. Perhaps I am biased, because they have mostly become friends.

The Chinese credit score worries me. The problem with this is that it so convenient to believe that the Chinese are engaging in new forms of thought control, convenient from us because it shows how relatively free we are and convenient from them because they really seem to appreciate groupthink. But the many Chinese I have really met and worked with have improved my life. I somehow do not feel that the score will turn out to be as imposing as promised. Meanwhile, our US use of scores is almost by stealth turning out to be constrictive.

Bloomberg recently wrote an article titled: "China's Most Advanced Big Brother Experiment Is a Bureaucratic Mess."

"Suzhou's Osmanthus social-credit program has won national awards, but many residents have never heard of it." The article implies that the whole program is moving along slowly, has muddled goals, and is largely a propaganda exercise of the government. It is meant to be scary, though perhaps it is mostly scary to us, advanced by some poor translations. According to the *Bloomberg* article, the Chinese themselves have barely thought about it. Hence, the story is still out on the social score.

Denmark

Norway, the Netherlands, and Denmark are numbers 3, 2, and 1 on a list of the highest ratio of debt to disposable (after tax) income. From that statistics, one might think they are fast spenders, consumption-driven, and in trouble. This is not true for any of these countries. All are relatively wealthy companies, with high tax rates, high pensions, secure jobs, low national debt, nationalized health care, and most of their borrowing is for durables.

According to the Denmark National Bank, people in Denmark have a very advanced financial system, a lot of wealth, and a lot of debt.[17] They borrow to sustain a solid life style and do not feel they need to pay off the debts before retiring because of their high pensions. "In line with the trend in most of Denmark's neighbouring countries and other advanced economies, the value of the assets held by Danish households — their homes, equities, pension savings, bank deposits, etc. — has risen by more than their debt over the last 15—20 years.... In an international comparison, Danish households' net wealth relative to disposable income is at an average level. But Danish households differ from those in other countries in that they have very large balance sheets, i.e., large wealth as well as large debt. Particularly the high level of household debt has attracted considerable attention, nationally and internationally."

So, the citizens of Denmark are not buying small things with debt, but large, durable things. They buy small stuff with debit cards.

Per a website called Just Landed[18]:

> *Denmark, one can use a U.S. or other national card in Denmark, but the citizens of Denmark usually buy things with a Dankort card, which is a national debit card for Denmark ....*
>
> *There is debt in Denmark of course, and a firm considering granting debt can go to a credit bureau called Debitor Registret A/S, or the Debtor Registrar, run by a company called Bisnode ....*
>
> *It is simple - you enter the personal name ... and see if there are payment remarks on the person. You also get knowledge about which companies the person owes money and how large the amounts are.*

Experian also has a presence in Denmark and can be found under the website www.experian.dk/ [19]. While they do not appear to have a US style CRA, they have a *bad payer* list they call the RKI register. According to Experian:

> *Experian's RKI register ensures Danish companies and consumers against irresponsible credit. The registry can either be used preventively by avoiding purchase agreements with new bad payers or follow-up where companies are advised if an existing customer is registered as a bad payer.*

There seems to be no accepted credit score as in the United States. There is much less invasion of privacy, no law that allows creditors to send all data to a CRA. If a borrower has not failed to pay back a debt and can manage the debt, (s)he is assumed to be a good risk. Trust of strangers is not the issue that it is here in the US national debt is low. Taxes are high. Pensions are secure. Health care is nationalized.

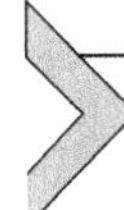

France

Per the website *BusinessInsider*[20]

> *France has no major credit reporting agency. Instead, to pursue a mortgage, for instance, you'll need three months of bank statements and paperwork to prove your income, as well as proof of marital status (if applicable) and the sale contract, according to the French Property real estate service.*
>
> *The files only relate to a person if they have written bad checks, have participated in fraudulent activities, have been declared bankrupt or have bounced checks in France.*
>
> *A bank will dig into your financial records and require a healthy 15% (at least) down payment and fees amounting to an additional 7% ....*

Repeating this theme, a website called Complete France writes[21]: "In France, the Bank of France maintains files which are only available to financial institutions holding a license delivered by the Bank of France."

This is supported by threads on social websites, for instance, someone in Quora writes[22]: "There is almost no credit card/debit card in France. French credit cards are more like American debit cards. Almost all mortgages are true fixed rate mortgage (unchanged for whole time of the mortgage, not revised each five years or less like here in Canada). French people hate debts/credits etc ..."

Per the OECD site (see Austria), France has significant household debt but not high in relation to peers. It has nationalized health care and moderate pensions. It is not a highly consumerist society but a largely assimilated and trusting one at present.

Germany

Germany, as does a lot of Europe, prefers cash to credit. From a website called *The German Way and More*[23]:

> *North Americans are often frustrated by the lack of credit card acceptance in Germany. Americans and Canadians, so used to paying with plastic, are dismayed to discover that once they stray from the tourist circuit, their AmEx, MasterCard, or Visa credit cards are often useless in German-speaking Europe ....*
>
> *The Bundesbank, Germany's central bank, recently estimated that 79% of financial transactions in Germany are settled in cash, while in Britain and the USA that figure is under 50%. A typical German walks around with the equivalent of about $123 in cash in their wallet, nearly twice as much as Australians, Americans, the French or the Dutch typically carry. There is little talk of a 'cashless society; in German-speaking Europe.*

However, there is credit in Germany, and a consumer society, albeit one less consumerist than the United States, German has a score somewhat analogous to FICO, called the Schufa, which is apparently relied on by a number of financial actors. It has inspired a good deal of resentment, as can be observed in the following article.[24] It is true this is just a blog and so amenable to be colored by the point of view of a blogger named Walter Palmetshofer, but it seems to be a large-scale issue.

> *Last week the Open Knowledge Foundation Germany (OKFDE) and Algorithm-Watch launched the project OpenSCHUFA. ... Already over 8.000 individual Schufa data request (30.000 personal data requests in total).*
>
> *Why we started OpenSCHUFA and why you should care about credit scoring. Germany's leading credit rating bureau, SCHUFA, has immense power over people's lives. A low SCHUFA score means landlords will refuse to rent you an apartment, banks will reject your credit card application and network providers will say 'computer says no' to a new Internet contract. But what if your SCHUFA score is low because there are mistakes in your credit history? Or if the score is calculated by a mathematical model that is biased?*
>
> *The big problem is, we simply don't know how accurate SCHUFA's or any other credit scoring data is and how it computes its scores. OpenSCHUFA wants to change this by analyzing thousands of credit records. ...*
>
> *SCHUFA collects data of your financial history — your unpaid bills, credit cards, loans, fines and court judgments — and uses this information to calculate your SCHUFA score. Companies pay to check your SCHUFA score when you apply for a credit card, a new phone or Internet contract. A rental agent even checks with SCHUFA when you apply to rent an apartment. A low score means you*

have a high risk of defaulting on payments, so it makes it more difficult, or even impossible, to get credit. A low score can also affect how much interest you pay on a loan.

An answer on the social website *Personal Finance & Money Stack Exchange* writes with apparent authority on the topic of *Credit Rating in Germany* that "they take your zip code and your neighborhood into account when calculating their score. Also moving often affects the score negatively."[25] This sensitivity to where you live is not allowed in the United States but does play a role in other countries where there is less public attention to the rights of subgroups in the population.

Hong Kong

Hong Kong was part of England from 1842 to 1997. In 1997, it was returned to China with a degree of independence that I think most assumed would just erode with time. However, Hong Kong surprised us all recently with its degree of resistance to control by China. Moving past politics, Hong Kong is certainly a well-established market-driven consumerist society.

Visitors have no problem using any of their usual e-commerce plastic says Finder.Com[26]: "When you travel in Hong Kong, you can use your credit cards freely. Mastercard and Visa are more popular than American Express and Discover cards, but there are ATMs and places where the latter two cards are also accepted. Most ATMs in Hong Kong won't charge you fees for cash withdrawals."

The Hong Kong dollar is pegged with a precise ratio to the American dollar. There is surely a pull to the West that is ever present. Hong Kongers are shoppers, consumers, and e-commerce users. If consumerism is modernity, they are as modern as the United States.

Like the United Kingdom, Hong Kong uses the term CRA, standing for Credit Reference Agencies (Credit Reporting Agencies in the United States). These data are presumably by the Personal Data (Privacy) Ordinance of Hong Kong, intended to safeguard the privacy of individuals in relation to personal data. This was passed in 1996. At the time it was futuristic and seemed protective. However, this law was deemed sufficient onto its own. Apparently, there is no regulatory body responsible for it, not that the regulatory bodies in the United States have been very helpful, in my view. I think it is a little bit useless and lacks the sensitivity to the Internet and hacking threat of the General Data Protection Regulation passed by European Union.

The only consumer credit reference agency in Hong Kong is TransUnion. The following comes from their website.[27]

> *The company has been operating in Hong Kong since 1982 and began managing the city's consumer credit reporting system in 2003. As the only credit reference agency in Hong Kong, TransUnion currently maintains records on 4.95 million consumers in Hong Kong.*
>
> *The company serves over 100 members in Hong Kong who are mainly banks and financial institutions. TransUnion compiles credit reports based on data received from its members as well as public sources of information. Consumers can order a copy of their personal credit report either online, by mail or directly from TransUnion's office.*

However, TransUnion has been accused of having lax security for its data by newspapers (including the South Morning China Post) in Honk Kong, which apparently found it easy to obtain data on anyone it wanted.[28] Reporters say they were able to bypass checks using identity card numbers and publicly available information.

> *The Firm, which has records of 5.4 million people in city, denies cyber breach, saying data was fraudulently accessed.*
>
> *The privacy commission said the incident might be related to security loopholes involving the procedure for obtaining credit reports.*
>
> *Hong Kong's Monetary Authority and privacy watchdog have called on major international credit bureau TransUnion to improve its online authentication procedures after a local newspaper claimed it could easily access the personal credit files of public figures in the city ...*

However, when I (Eric) checked the Hong Kong website today (July 7, 2019), trying to understand their approach to credit scores, it contained this blurb:

"TransUnion takes security very seriously. In response to a recent incident with our consumer credit report service, we have temporarily suspended all online consumer credit report services in Hong Kong with immediate effect. We will update the market once we resume operations. If you would like to purchase our Credit Report, please click here to make an appointment and visit our office in person. Sorry for the inconvenience caused."

So, this is not quite like the Equifax hack in the United States but the CRA seems porous and either artless or understaffed. In regard to credit scores, they also seem somewhat clumsy, describing them as follows:

> *Credit Score ranges from A to J, where A is the highest score. It is one of the references credit providers may use as part of the credit approval process. In addition to Credit Score, credit providers may also consider the applicant's risk tolerance, internal credit ratings, as well as the applicant's financial status and other personal information.*
>
> *In addition to credit history and enquires, other information in your credit report is also used to calculate the Credit Score. Any changes in the records might trigger a reassessment of the Credit Score.*

India

India is an immense country, virtually tied with China in population at well over a billion, but much poorer. It is fifth in the world in the size of the economy, behind the United Kingdom, with a population less than a 20th of India. It is a sprawling place, and using credit cards is not their first priority.

There are four credit information companies licensed by Reserve Bank of India. The largest of the four, formerly The Credit Information Bureau (India) Limited (CIBIL), was started in January 2001 but purchased by TransUnion in 2017. Also operating there, from 2010, are Experian, Equifax, and a firm called Highmark; they also have licenses from the Reserve Bank of India.

To my American ear the TransUnion-CIBAL website describes the data behind their CIBIL score in somewhat vague terms.[29] "Based on millions of updates received by TransUnion CIBIL from a strong member base comprising banks, financial institutions, state financial corporations, non-banking financial companies, housing finance companies and credit card companies, the credit file information is broad and in-depth. It delivers insights into a consumer's borrowings across lending institutions, helping you identify risk areas and disburse credit faster and with greater efficiency at all times." The mention of millions of updates, a broad range which simply means that this is not a small and local sort of thing, is most telling because it tells so little.

India happens to be home to something called Aadhaar, described by *Wikipedia*[30]: "The world's largest biometric ID system … Aadhaar (English: Foundation) is a 12-digit unique identity number that can be obtained by residents of India, based on their biometric and demographic data. The data is collected by the Unique Identification Authority of India (UIDAI), a statutory authority established in January 2009 by the government of India, under the jurisdiction of the Ministry of Electronics and Information Technology, following the provisions of the Aadhaar (Targeted Delivery of Financial and other Subsidies, benefits and services) Act, 2016."

Aadhaar includes an iris scan and one bank, Axis, now allows customers to access their funds without any paperwork; they simply have to allow a scan of their eye. Obviously, each one of us can be identified uniquely, now in any number of ways. Fingerprints, DNA, the teeth of skeletons seem to come up in the news. But the physical connection to credit seems far more invasive than what is allowed in the United States. Admittedly, it may only be a marginally greater threat to our privacy. The United States has had social security numbers since 1936. These uniquely and permanently attach to persons, just without a biometric tag.

FICO is also in India, doing its capitalist best to enter every market, joining with a firm called Lenddo which, per the *Lenddo* website,[31] "was founded in 2011 and its main focus initially was to improve lives of the emerging middle class in developing countries by providing micro loans for specific purposes." The following FICO article comes from an announcement by FICO, reported at a website DataQuest.[32]

New FICO credit scores lets lenders expand access to credit in India

Analytics software firm FICO announced the launch of the FICO Score in India and the roll-out of an alternative data score, FICO Score X Data India, in partnership with Lenddo. …

FICO Score for India is based on traditional credit data available from any of the major credit bureaus in India. FICO Score X Data India, in partnership with Lenddo, evaluates alternative data such as that from a consumer's digital footprint (web or mobile device) to produce a score for consumers who don't have enough traditional data on file with one of the Indian credit bureaus to produce a FICO Score for India. …

The introduction of these scores is timely given the government's recent efforts," said Dattu Kompella, managing director in Asia for FICO. "India's Ministry of Finance recognizes that lack of financial inclusion forces the unbanked into informal banking sectors where interest rates are higher and the amount of available funds much smaller.

Indonesia

Indonesia has over 260 million people, fourth in the world after China and India (both with well over one billion), and the United States with well over 300 million. Pakistan and Brazil are fifth and sixth. Like Brazil, Indonesia is on this list because, despite being rather poor per capita, its size in population vaults it into one of the top 20 market economies in the world. It does have a firm, called Perfindo, which shows intent but not yet the achievement of establishing a centralized credit bureau.[33]

Typically, widespread credit card and ATM use precedes CRAs. However, Indonesia makes using plastic somewhat harder than Western countries. From an article called *ATMs in Indonesia: Credit cards and fees* on the website TransferWise comes the following post[34]:

When traveling in Indonesia, you're likely to run into parts of the country where plastic isn't widely accepted. That means you're going to need to have cash on hand during your trip. But how do you get your hands on Indonesian rupiah?

Luckily, ATMs can be found pretty easily in Indonesia, so getting the cash you need shouldn't be too much of a chore. However, ATMs are less common in Indonesia than in many parts of the Western world ....

ATMs in Indonesia are common in bigger cities and in tourist hotspots, like Bali. In more rural areas, though, you may have a hard time finding one ....

Visa and Mastercard are most widely accepted in Indonesia, but credit and debit cards are mainly only used in bigger cities and tourist hotspots like Jakarta and Bali. Many places will only accept cash, so it's a good idea to always have some on hand. In generally, credit utilization lags the West by quite a bit but it is starting to get used.

Italy

Italy is not one of the leaders in the world in its ratio of debt to after-tax income, though it has a substantial ratio. So, they do borrow money in

Italy, just not like the United States. But Italy has one of the highest pensions in the world, as a percent of earned income before retirement according to the World Economic Forum.[35] It also has a fairly high tax rate and national health care. Unfortunately, Italy as a country is highly leveraged and may not be able to continue it all.

In the 10 years even before 2011, Italy has become much more allowing of credit cards.[36] However, there is nothing like FICO or the credit repositories in the United States that are inclusive of most debts. In general, cash is used more in Italy than in the United States but many cars and expensive electronics are bought on credit.

There is something like a CRA in Italy, though less sophisticated, that can be accessed at the *Banca D'Italia* website which advertises *Access to Central Credit Data*[37]:

> *The service allows to know the data transmitted to the Central Credit Register by banks and financial companies regarding their debtors. The service is free.*
>
> *The Centrale dei Rischi is an information system, managed by the Bank of Italy, which collects information provided by banks and financial companies on the credits that they grant to their customers and on the related guarantees.*
>
> *Who can use it?*
>
> *The natural persons in whose name the information is registered, or their guardian, ... bankruptcy trustee or other bankruptcy procedure body which is responsible for representing the companies, person with power of attorney, ...*
>
> *auditors and auditors of companies, institutions, etc....*

The organization of the Central Credit Register seems pretty haphazard, but it exists. Italy is growing more consumerist, borrowing more nationally and at the household level. However, it lacks much of the credit infrastructure of the United States.

Japan

Health care is nationalized. The population is aging, while the pension systems if falling behind. Japan's use of credit is substantial but nowhere near the top of OECD countries (See Austria for site). It is a rich country in many ways, but probably sliding. A number of sites point out that most individuals use cash, but, when they do borrow, the money is repaid promptly. Per an article from an International travel and ticket-selling firm called Matcha, the use of credit is lower in Japan than in the United States but growing.[38]

It does not seem as if Japan has credit scores as the United States or some other countries with similar economic clout.[39] "Japan ... does not have a centralized bureau or set of bureaus through which they learn about an individual's credit score. Instead, most lending institutions such as large banks, credit companies, etc. conduct their own credit reconnaissance to determine whether they feel comfortable extending credit or a loan to an individual." Japan is one of the most homogeneous nations in the world, as well as one of the oldest. It is not surprising that mechanisms to achieve trust, such as credit scores, are not central.

Malaysia

Malaysia is not on my list of big markets or high per capita countries, but it does seem to have a credit infrastructure that is quite a bit like that of the United States, which is why I include it. Indeed, it took me a minute to discover that a colorful website about credit scoring concerned Malaysia is not from the United States. The website is called *CompareHero, your trusted financial comparison platform*, and includes the following text[40]:

> *Your credit score is a three-digit number, typically between 300 and 850, that represents your creditworthiness and relates to how likely you are to repay debt. This helps banks and lenders evaluate your application for credit or loans. Credit reporting agencies calculate these scores based on their own proprietary models. Your score will never factor in personal information like your race, gender, religion, marital status, savings or deposits information, salary details or criminal records.*
>
> *Why is a Credit Score important?*
>
> *A credit score plays an important role when you want to apply for a financial product from a bank, including a personal loan, mortgage, car loan, or credit card. Banks, financial institutions, and even businesses use your credit score to evaluate the credibility of your financial health. It helps them understand the risks they might face if they decide to lend money to you. The higher your score, the better it is and the higher the chance of getting your applications approved. Essentially, it is an indicator of your financial health ....*

However, this seems to be a very classy advertisement and does not seem to be from the credit bureau of Malaysia, which is Bank Negra Malaysia's Credit Bureau.[41] Bank Negra is the regulator of banking for Malaysia. Their description of the credit bureau is

"Bank Negara Malaysia's Credit Bureau is established under the repealed Central Bank of Malaysia Act 1958 and continues to operate under the

Central Bank of Malaysia Act 2009 (CBA). It has been in operation since 1982. Like other credit bureaus in the world, the Credit Bureau essentially collects credit-related information on borrowers from lending institutions and furnishes the credit information collected back to the institutions in the form of a credit report via an online system known as the Central Credit Reference Information System or CCRIS."

They have a credit report, about which they write:

The Credit Report contains the following credit-related information of a borrower:

(1) Outstanding Credit(s)

All credit facilities obtained by the borrower, which are still outstanding, either under - the borrower's own name; a joint name with another borrower(s); a name of a sole proprietorship or partnership where the borrower is the owner of the partnership or the business; the name of a professional body where the borrower is the member of the body; or the name of a corporation.

Credit facilities that have been fully settled are excluded from the credit report.

(2) Special Attention Account(s)

All outstanding credit facilities under close supervision of the participating financial institutions.

(3) Application(s) for Credit

All applications approved in the previous 12 months and pending applications for the borrower.

Who Can request the Credit Report

Financial institutions upon any credit application and during the review of creditworthiness of existing customers; Any individual for own credit report; Registered credit reporting agencies which are approved by Bank Negara Malaysia, with prior consent from the borrower; Any individual for credit report of own business(es) i.e. sole proprietorship, partnership or professional body; and Any company for its own credit report.

Its e-commerce seems reasonably complete in larger cities but not in rural areas, where cash is required. The laws for banking seem well-developed, except that while Malaysia is multicultural, its official religion is Islam, and Muslims represent around three-fifths of the country. Islam is uncomfortable with debt, and a separate banking system supports the Islamic community.

Mexico

Mexico is a fairly large country, with over 130 million, but still just one-tenth of the size of India. It is far poorer than the United States but middling in the income spectrum of the world at large. It has a healthcare system which seems fairly nationalized but better care is available for those who can pay. Pensions are now widespread but often insufficient. In short, many are struggling, and it is not a highly consumerist economy. There seems to be an intermediate degree of credit bureau/credit score maturity in Mexico, based on the following article posted on the Circulo de Credito website in 2017[42]:

> *Círculo de Crédito, the fastest-growing credit bureau in Mexico, can provide credit scores on nearly twice as many people, thanks to its adoption of an innovative score from analytic software firm FICO. Since it has been using the FICO® Extended Score to score people with little or no credit history, Círculo de Crédito has increased the percentage of people who can be scored from 45% to around 85%.*
>
> *Some 10 million Mexicans lack enough credit history to calculate a risk score, which makes it harder to get approval for a loan or credit card. FICO worked with Círculo de Crédito to develop a customized score based on the high correlation of an individual's risk with the risk level of people who live at the same house.*
>
> ...

Círculo de Crédito has 45% market share in Mexico, with more than 2600 clients in different sectors, including financial institutions, retail, microfinance, telecommunications, and government institutions. The credit bureau offers customer data, value-added products such as scores, and customized solutions.

The Netherlands

Norway, the Netherlands, and Denmark are numbers 3, 2, and 1 on a list of the highest ratio of debt to disposable (after tax) income. From that statistics, one might think they are fast spenders, consumption-driven, and in trouble. This is not true for any of these countries. All are relatively wealthy companies, with high tax rates, high pensions, secure jobs, low national debt, nationalized health care, and most of their borrowing is for durables.

The Netherlands is one of the 10 countries described in piece called *Many countries don't use credit scores like the US — here's how they determine your worth*, which appears in an Internet publication called Business Insider, written in 2018[43]:

> *[In]The Netherlands, a person with a steady income who isn't defaulting on any existing debts (like missed bill payments) is generally likely to be judged creditworthy.*
>
> *Unpaid debts are registered to the Bureau Krediet Registratie (BKR), the governing credit registry bureau, finance consultant Peter Gibney told Just Landed.*
>
> *If you do end up with a negative mark, you could have it for the long haul. Negative marks on the BKR disappear five years after the initial debt is discharged, according to the BKR.*

This is seconded by the following characteristic answer to a Reddit Internet post regarding the topic[44]:

> *In the Netherlands you don't get a positive score, but instead you get a negative one: you are less likely to get a certain loan if you already have some registered at BKR (or when you are registered as someone who missed a few instalments). Banks and such will also ask for proof of income and proof of (long term) employment for many loans.*
>
> *You can also see what information is registered about you at BKR, but there's no immediate reason to do so. Companies that care about it are able to request it themselves.*

I naturally wondered how you get a credit card in the Netherlands and how you use it. I ran into this language from the website Amsterdam Tips[45]: "The use of credit cards in the Netherlands is not as well established as elsewhere with most payments being made by cash, debit cards or via internet banking. The thrifty Dutch have much less of a consumer debt culture than say US, UK or Australia and many shops in Holland still do not accept credit card payments."

However, there is quite a lot about mortgages; and it is possible to borrow 100% of the value of the home, and at fairly low rates. However, there are no credit scores involved, just bank decisions. Nevertheless, the Netherlands is just behind Denmark in an international ratio of household debt to household income after taxes. But, like Denmark, the Netherlands has high taxes, nationalized health care, and high pensions. That is, there is not the pressure to pay off the home prior to retirement that is experience in the US.

Norway

Norway, the Netherlands, and Denmark are numbers 3, 2, and 1 on a list of the highest ratio of debt to disposable (after tax) income. From that statistics, one might think they are fast spenders, consumption-driven, and in trouble. This is not true for any of these countries. All are relatively wealthy companies, with high tax rates, high pensions, secure jobs, low national debt, nationalized health care, and most of their borrowing is for durables.

Norway is per capita one of the leaders of the world, but it contains only 5 million people, the size of a large city in the United States. It is blessed with oil, gas, hydropower, fish, forests, and minerals.

Credit and debit cards are both used extensively in Norway. Experian has a Norwegian website, but it does not seem to have obvious products for consumers. It is advertising its long history and worldwide footprint in analytics. There seems to be nothing about credit scores on it.

On the other hand, there are allusions to a credit record in Norway on the Experian cite.[46] There is apparently a common place where disappointed debtors record the problems as they see it, that borrowers can see, and potential creditors can see, translated into English by Google as "Payment Notes." It appears that the creditors will decide for themselves how to interpret the data here.

Russia

Russia is an OECD country but has a low ratio of household debt to after-tax income. Russia is certainly a less consumerist country than many in the West. Cash is the most common way to pay for things, though foreigners can use credit cards in many places. But borrowing is not the rule for population, not even e-commerce.

> *Russians have low levels of financial understanding. Just 59% trust banks and more than 60% are not willing to take responsibility for their financial security," according to the Financial Education and Financial Literacy Project run by the website Right About Money.[47] According to that website, only one in five Russians believes they will be dealt with fairly in the financial markets ....*
>
> *Russians also have no obvious incentive to save. This has traditionally been a managed economy where individuals pay no income tax. The burden is entirely on employers. Individuals have little idea how much the government collects and how much they contribute through lower wages. In such an environment, encouraging retirement saving is difficult.*

They have a beginning credit bureau, called Experian Interfax. Here is language on that site[48]:

> *Experian Interfax Credit Bureau in association with Sberbank and Experian.*
>
> *Experian Interfax credit bureau aims to improve transparency in the Russian retail lending market, reduce credit risk and provide consumers with better access to credit. Experian Interfax is owned by Interfax Information Services Group,*

Sberbank, Russia's biggest bank, and Experian, a global leader in providing value-added information solutions to organizations and consumers.

Experian Interfax started business activities in March 2006. The bureau's clients include over 200 banks as well as mobile phone operators, collection agencies and insurers. The bureau is energetically expanding operations, introducing borrower evaluation scoring and anti-fraud systems and developing new software solutions for banks .... Consumers and small businesses benefit from the bureau because it helps lenders make better credit decisions which, over time, will reduce costs and enable greater access to credit on more favorable terms.

Equifax and TransUnion also have a presence in Russia, but it seems backward even relative to Experian Interfax.[49] It is of course hard to tell who is ahead or behind by looking at these websites, but it is clear there is not much to be ahead or behind about. Russia is a largely totalitarian, still-managed society, where freedom is doled out. The Internet is not yet under the control of the Kremlin, but this seems to be more a matter of relative backwardness. In April 2019, a bill to do just that passed. It is not ready yet for the tyranny of scoring and machines, as it still has to work out the tyranny of Man.

Saudi Arabia

From the website *Just Landed, Saudi Arabia,*[50] I can glean that there is e-commerce here in that people have bank accounts and can get debit cards easily. But there also appear to be restrictive limits on what consumer are allowed to do with credit cards. So far as I can tell, it is less consumerist and less credit-loving than the United States.

There appears to be just one credit bureau, called Simah.[51] Their site is much more conservative and less sales-aggressive than corresponding CRAs in the US Simah started in 2004. I think that its own answers to "frequently asked questions" are pretty clear (shown below). There does not seem to be any score, similar to the FICO score. I think this is more of a consortium rather than a law-driven grip on the citizenry with the awesome mystery of the FICO score. However, it is a start in that direction, and nothing seems to prevent it from getting to that dispassionate AI level in 10 or 20 more years. Here is what they write:

What is the Saudi Credit Bureau (SIMAH)?

SIMAH is a credit information agency that collects, analyzes and provides detailed and up-to-date credit information on both individuals and institutions in the Kingdom of Saudi Arabia .... SIMAH began its operations in April 2004.

... SIMAH's ownership is shared by ten Saudi Arabian banks operating in the Kingdom of Saudi Arabia .... The Saudi Arabian Monetary Agency (SAMA) is responsible for licensing, supervising and monitoring all of SIMAH's activities. ...

SIMAH maintains a central database of credit information related to its clients (consisting of individuals and institutions), which is periodically collected and updated by bureau members .... bureau members' clients can benefit from SIMAH credit reports by remaining aware of their previous and current credit transactions and their creditworthiness, helping them to make the best financial decisions possible ....

SIMAH takes strict technical measures to ensure the security of all credit information it collects. It is impossible to illegally access the credit database due to a number of complex, technical measures taken by SIMAH to safeguard its credit information.

Singapore

The *Huffington Post* blog *Life* implies that three countries Singapore, Malaysia, and Hong Kong "have leapfrogged the US and UK in terms of technology and they have much more comprehensive databases."[52] The countries are not all that comparable. Malaysia has over 30 million people, Singapore but five and a half million, and Hong Kong with seven and a half. The gross domestic product is similar, however, so Malaysia is individually much poorer. However, so far as I can tell through Internet sites, its credit management is much more sophisticated than Honk Kong with Singapore seeming more in line with Malaysia.

According to *Money Smart* website, in an article called *How to Apply for Credit Cards in Singapore – The Complete Guide,* Singapore travelers can use their plastic everywhere there.[53] The availability of debit cards and credit cards seems to me to be similar to the United States, per Money Smart. And as described by the website *SingSaver*, credit scoring in Singapore, available from the Credit Bureau of Singapore, is similar to FICO or any of the other scores in the United States.[54]

The Monetary Authority of Singapore seems to fill role much like the CFPB or FTC in the United States.[55] They provide an excellent website which has the appearance of a highly developed credit bureau and scoring system:

A credit bureau is an agency that collects and stores information on your credit history, such as loans, credit card applications and repayment records ...

For banks and finance companies, only 2 credit bureaus are allowed to obtain such information in Singapore. They are Credit Bureau (Singapore) and DP Credit Bureau.

What is a credit report? A credit report is a compilation of your credit payment history collected across all your banks. It is issued by a credit bureau to banks, finance companies and credit card companies when they make enquiries about you. You may also request a copy of your report from the bureaus.

The credit report includes information such as:

Basic personal profile data (excluding contact addresses and telephone numbers).

Records of all credit checks made on you.

Credit repayment trend for the past 12 months, including late payments on credit card bills.

Default records, if any — displayed from the date it was uploaded to the credit bureau.

Bankruptcy records, if any — displayed for 5 years from the date of discharge. If you are able to repay your debts in full, the Bankruptcy Order will be annulled and your bankruptcy record will be removed immediately.

Closed or terminated credit accounts — displayed for 3 years from the date the account was reported closed or terminated.

Aggregated outstanding balances.

Aggregated credit limits.

It sounds like the United States.

They have two credit bureaus (the same as CRAs), Credit Bureau (Singapore) and DP Credit Bureau. The latter is now run by Experian, as well as the Money-Lenders Credit Bureau (MLCB). I could not enter the Credit Bureau (Singapore) site, though the entry paths shown on Google look US-like.

South Africa

South Africa has a population of 58 million, but a total economy just on a par with Malaysia, Singapore, and Hong Kong (one-tenth of the number of people.) However, the United Kingdom and South Africa have historic ties, similar laws and finance, and South Africa has a very modern credit system similar to the United Kingdom. South Africa has a very easy-to-use and widespread banking and ATM network, and all the e-commerce travelers could want, per *Capetown Magazine*.[56] Applications and credit card use seems widespread, according to *Business Tech*, January 8, 2019.[57]

The 230-page National Credit Act was passed in 2005. It seems similar to the US FCRA (reviewed briefly). The following from the Banking Association of South Africa describes it neatly.[58]

> *INTRODUCTION TO THE NATIONAL CREDIT ACT*
>
> *Credit enables people to spend money they don't have, spend more money than they earn, use credit for ordinary purchases, use credit even when they have cash and use debt to pay off debt. The use of credit and poor money management skills often leads people into a situation of over-indebtedness where they are unable to service credit agreements.*
>
> *The National Credit Act (35 of 2005) is part of a comprehensive legislation overhaul designed to protect the Consumer in the credit market and make credit and banking services more accessible. The National Credit Act (NCA) was introduced "to promote and advance the social and economic welfare of South Africans, promote a fair, transparent, competitive, sustainable, responsible, efficient, effective and accessible credit market and industry, and to protect Consumers."*

CRAs are usually called credit bureaus in South Africa and there are four: Experian, TransUnion, Compuscan, and Expert Decision Systems. "South Africa has a robust credit reporting system .... But the rest of Africa generally has very poor or non-existent coverage, and changing that is a daunting challenge."[59] Credit scores are used, as in the United States, and described similarly, for instance, on the South African TransUnion site.[60]

> *Your Credit Bureau score is designed to show you, by way of a number ... how your credit standing compares with other consumers ....*
>
> *This, along with your employment history; your income and affordability assessments as well as the type of credit for which you are applying, may affect the outcome of your credit application.*

Your Credit Bureau score is calculated using a formula that evaluates how well or badly you pay your bills, how much debt you carry and how all of that stacks up against other borrowers. In effect, it tells you in a single number what your credit report says about your management of existing credit.

Generally, the higher your score, the better. A TransUnion Consumer Credit Score, for example, can range from 0 to 999 or from poor to excellent.

That is not the scale of a FICO score; however, FICO is trying to take root in the country.[61]

South Korea

South Korea has over 51 million individuals and is 12th in the world in the size of its economy. South Koreans are avid credit card users. Both locals and visitors can use credit cards in most stores and restaurants. Visa and MasterCard are the most widely accepted types, with some high-end hotels and restaurants accepting American Express.[62] Per *Frommers*, "For smaller restaurants, outdoor markets, and bus fare, cash is necessary. However, don't carry excessive amounts of cash. If you do, use a money belt (since pickpockets are prevalent in the cities' crowded public transportation systems)." In general, South Koreans have a debt problem.[63] Consumers owe too much, well over a trillion dollars collectively. They do so under some fairly clear and organized law from the FSS, the Financial Supervisory Service.[64] "The purpose of the Financial Supervisory Service is to contribute to the growth of the national economy by (1) promoting the advancement of the financial industry and the stability of financial markets; (2) establishing sound credit order and fair financial transaction practices; and (3) protecting financial consumers, such as depositors."

Credit Bureaus seem to have come late to South Korea, but there is one now, called KCB in English. Here is part of their website: *KCB at a Glance.*

"To prevent recurrence of a financial crisis, and further strengthen the domestic financial industry, major financial companies in Korea formed consensus on sharing credit data with each other. 18 major financial companies in Korea built KCB together by participating as shareholders, and since its foundation, KCB has been operated through transparent and fair governance to make sure that it will benefit the financial industry as a whole."

I could not tell when the website had been updated, but it appeared only moderately slick. It has a history page which indicates the firm was founded

February of 2005. It has a section on the history page called 2017 to 2019, which has not entries after 2017. It offers something called a "k-score," which seems to be a sort of credit score, but I could not find colorful pages about any credit score, what it contained or meant.

The delinquency rate for loans in Korea is, however, several times lower than in the United States and reflects a much greater social discomfort in welshing on debts. It is rising now, per an article in the Pulse of April 26, 2019.

"The delinquency and non-performing loans (NPL) ratio of South Korea's credit card companies have been on the rise, underscoring the looming risks in the colossal consumer debt amid protracted economic slowdown."

Summary: South Korea is a consumerist credit-loving country, with cultural tendencies to pay back debts and somewhat behind the United States in the collection and mathematization of credit data.

Spain

According to Megan Horner, writing *Using a Credit Card in Spain* for the *Finder* website[65]: "Spain, where you'll find cultures as diverse as its geography, continues to depend on tourism as a major source of revenue. This is good news for travelers because local businesses have adopted new technologies to keep with changing times. What this basically means is you'll have no significant problems in using your credit card when you're in Spain." However, the locals prefer cash, according to an article *For Payments in Spain, Cash Still Reigns* at PYMNTS.Com.[66] Generally, there does not seem to be the reliance on credit cards that exists in the United States. "In Spain, however, some old habits die hard, and that includes the country's preference for physical currency. No matter what new payments tech comes along — or how convenient or secure it claims to be — Spain still likes to pay with cash. Other nations may have been won over by technology, and the Spanish government has made efforts to limit cash usage by consumers, but Spain's population has made its preferences known."

In Spain, the main credit rating agency is called ASNEF (Asociación Nacional de Establecimientos Financieros/National Association of Established Financiers) and they hold files of bad payers in Spain. According to ASNEF[67]:

Spain is no different than other countries whereby your activity in regards to finance is monitored by credit rating agencies and decisions related to your credit profile are checked against such records. If you need any kind of loan ranging from a car, boat, home or consumer product, then your personal profile will be checked against a credit rating agency.

The files stored by ASNEF are managed by Equifax Servicios Sobre Solvencia y Crédito S.L. which is the Spanish subsidiary of the UK and US equivalents. There are two types of checks that you can make and its easiest to do it through a third-party site called "Einforma" who are connected directly to Equifax which means that you can easily execute your credit report query online in the comfort of your own home.

Check 1: Check if you are on a list of bad debtors

Check 2: Request Full credit report

The website does not appear to have anywhere near the sophistication or hyperselling energy of the US sites. There does not seem to be a regular credit score in Spain, though one, the Finscore, is marketed as such, but not by ASNEF. According to *BusinessInsider*, quoting the Bank of Spain, Spain tracks "virtually all the loans, credits, bank endorsements and risks in general that financial institutions have with their customers." However, good credit is more about staying off a bad credit blacklist, according to Spanish law firm Velasco Lawyers.[68] Once on a blacklist, consumers remain there until the debt is paid off or 6 years passes.

To summarize, Spain is more rule- and observation-based, without the same feverish interest in credit, or numerological evaluation, in the United States.

Switzerland

With less than 9 million people, Switzerland is small, but with a per capita income just ahead of the United States, the people are so well off that the nation has the 20th largest economy in the world. It is also the nation in the world with the highest wealth per individual. The Swiss have extremely high pensions, but these may not be funded adequately, according to the article *Are Switzerland's pensions too high?* according to an article on the website SWI swissinfo.ch[69] The Swiss also have high taxes and nationalized health care. Thus, it does not seem too alarming that, like some other European countries, the Swiss have one of the highest debt to after-tax income ratios in the world, as they do not need to pay down debt before retirement.

Switzerland is multilingual, largely German and French.[70] In 2017, the population of Switzerland was 62.6% native speakers of German; 22.9% French. The French-speakers, according to the academic article *Culture, Money Attitudes and Economic Outcomes* in the *Swiss Journal of Economics and Statistics*, are apparently more likely to borrow than the German-speakers, who tend to frugality.[71]

Switzerland has two gigantic banks, each managing almost a trillion dollars: UBS and Credit Suisse. E-commerce systems, including debit card and credit card availability, are available everywhere. However, credit is used more for durables than small items, as in consumerist nations such as Hong Kong, the United States, or United Kingdom. It has established laws that tilt slightly against more aggressive credit habits:

Quoting the remarkably complete website *Moneyland.Ch*[72]:

The Swiss consumer credit act … regulates consumer loans of between 500 and 80,000 francs which are issued in Switzerland. These rules came into effect on January 1, 2003. The regulations apply to credit cards, customer loyalty cards, private loans, leasing contracts and bank account overdrafts.

The consumer credit act defines which information must be included in consumer credit contacts. The regulations also limit the maximum effective interest rate which lenders can charge. …

Before a loan can be issued, lenders must consider a number of aspects of the applicant's credit history, including any irregularities in the way in which their rent or other obligations are met, as recorded by a credit bureau …

As of 2016, loan providers are no longer allowed to aggressively market consumer credit products.

Moneyland.ch also writes about the one principal credit bureau in Switzerland (similar to the U.S. and U.K. CRA):

The ZEK (Zentralstelle für Kreditinformation) is the go-to credit checkpoint for all lenders that issue consumer loans, credit cards and car leases, in accordance with Swiss consumer credit law …

The bureau operates a central database which only credit-issuing companies like banks and loan-providers have access to. …

The database contains positive, negative and neutral information. A borrower's creditworthiness is shown to lenders in code form. Information that builds the credit histories of borrowers in Switzerland and Liechtenstein includes the following:

Personal information: surname, name, birthday, address, civil status

Credit history: details about installment-based, account overdraft, cash, fixed, or payday loans. History of all open or denied credit applications, plus both ongoing and expired loan agreements.

Credit card use: Records of blocked credit cards, poor credit repayment and credit card debt.

Rental contracts: records of leases, rentals and purchases.

Official data: Records of bankruptcies and court orders.

Important: Every time you apply for a credit card, a record of that application is added to your credit history at ZEK. If the application is denied (if a bank only accepts applicants with excellent credit, for example), your credit record will be negatively impacted.

Right to your credit history: As a borrower, you have the right to request a copy of your credit history from the ZEK.

There is a credit rating process but it's less definitive that in the United States and reviewed more judgmentally by lenders, who do not regard credit as the same sort of commodity that say, the U.K., Canada, the U.S. and Malaysia do. The controls are similar, the sharing of data as assertive, but the algorithmic mystery and certitude somewhat less.

Turkey

Turkey has 83 million people, the 17th largest country in the world. It is relatively poor per capita, though wealthier than the much larger China, and is the 17th largest economy in the world (depending on how it is measured). While Islamic countries are typically uncomfortable with debt, Turkey has a 20th century secular focus, which includes more Westernized economic tendencies, including use of debt and credit cards. Secularism may have lost ground, however, with the rise of Islamist and strongarm President Recep Tayyip Erdogan, whose career spans decades, but came into his present office in 2014. In 2016, there was a coup attempt on the Turkish government, famously blamed by Erdogan on Fethullah Gulen, long in the United States but a former religious leader in Turkey. Since 2018, in part after a spectacular spat between their Erdogan and Trump, in part because strongman President Erdogan has seized evermore perilous control over the Central Bank, the economy has been floundering, and for a flux of reasons, beyond me to untangle, I think that Western style credit practices will be on hold for a few years.

Before more recent troubles, e-commerce was well established in Turkey.[73] "Turkey, a popular tourist destination, is a credit card—friendly country." The locals also use credit extensively. Turkey had set a goal to be cashless by 2023 and seemed to have an innovative financial sector.[74] A firm called KKB served as their CRA. Its *History* is on its website.[75]

There appears to be no credit scoring in place. However, quantitative sorting of credit seemed on its way, as a new bulletin was issued by FICO announcing its entry into the country in 2014, though with a lack of updates since.[76]

In short, Turkish society and credit practices await developments.

United Arab Emirates

The United Arab Emirates consists of seven emirates, something like states in the United States. The most well-known one, at least in the United States, is Dubai. Dubai is commercial and westernized, with exotic malls and the world's tallest building. The United Arab Emirates overall has over 9 million people, with per capita income almost the highest in the world. Not a lot of the people are rich, but the very rich leaders of this oil-based economy create a middle class with a generous welfare program. So far as I can tell, these welfare recipients can also get credit cards as needed. However, a generally more conservative society helps restrain consumerism.

There seems to be, as in Saudi Arabia, a single credit bureau, called the Al Etihad Credit Bureau.[77] They describe themselves as owned by the government. Here is what they say:

"Al Etihad Credit Bureau is a Public Joint Stock Company wholly owned by the UAE Federal Government. As per UAE Federal Law No. (6) of 2010 concerning Credit Information, the company is mandated to regularly collect credit information from financial and non-financial institutions in the UAE. Al Etihad Credit Bureau aggregates and analyzes this data to calculate Credit Scores and produce Credit Reports that are made available to individuals and companies in the UAE."

The credit bureau seems to be a money-making organization, selling scores and data. Here is the part that describes how to buy scores and what the buyer gets. In many ways, it is like the FICO score and sets the user up to be classified by a fundamentally unexplained algorithm.

WHAT IS THE CREDIT SCORE?

It is a three-digit number that predicts how likely you are to make your loan and credit card payments on time. The number ranges from 300 to 900. A low score indicates a higher risk, whereas a higher score indicates a lower risk ... The Credit Score will help financial institutions make better-informed decisions, process credit card and loan applications faster and provide preferential benefits for those with high scores ....

The Credit Score is calculated using information from various sources, like banks, finance companies and telecom companies. Your Credit Score is dynamic, and changes according to the most recent information in your Credit Report. Missing or delaying a payment beyond the due date, frequently utilizing all your credit card limits, or taking on additional loans or credit cards may lower your Score. Overall, reducing the number of credit cards, consistently reducing outstanding balances, and making payments on or before the due date will improve your credit score.

United Kingdom

The United Kingdom is comprised of four countries: England, Ireland, Scotland, and Northern Ireland. It is very much like the United States in that people use both debit and credit cards, with a bit of a tilt in the United Kingdom toward debit cards compared to the United States. While Brits buy a lot on credit, they seem to owe quite a bit less than citizens of the United States. The *Average UK household debt now stands at record £15,400* is the title of an article from *The Guardian* January 6, 2019.[78] At today's exchange rate (August 14, 2019), that is only $18,634, which is about one-seventh of the average household debt in the United States.

Like the FCRA, the United Kingdom has the Consumer Credit Act.[79] It was passed in 1974, nearly the same time as the FCRA. In fact, national attention to the problem of money lending probably precedes the interest in the United States. The United Kingdom has the two of our three major CRAs as the United States (Experian and Equifax) but the third CRA in the United Kingdom is Call Credit.[80] The letters CRA stand for Credit Reference Agency in the United Kingdom (and some British Empire countries as well) instead of Credit Reporting Agency in the United States.

FICO has tried to establish a presence in the United Kingdom but without success. Instead, each repository creates its own score, with slightly different scales. There seems to be no rush to bring them together, as in the United States. There are also some extra facts in the scores in the United Kingdom, such as the number of changes in address made by the applicant. However, there is much more alike between the American and English systems of handling credit. And scoring is an algorithm that rates people dispassionately, has been accepted, and is past the critical moment of being questioned.

United States

The United States is a large country, third in the world with 329 million according to the latest United Nations Population Division estimates, at the website Worldometers; but dwarfed by China at 1420 million and India at 1368 million.[81] But it has the largest economy of any nation, 19 and a half billion in 2017, from the same website.

Per *Consumer Debt Statistics & Demographics in America - Debt.org* the "median household income hit $61,372 in 2017, according to the U.S. Census Bureau. That's almost $20,000 more than it was in 2000. But the typical American household now carries an average debt of $137,063."[82]

People in the United States are awash with credit cards, consumerism, and debt of all kinds. Most adults have credit cards, and credit cards are used more than cash. Education debt alone is now about a trillion and half dollars. Three Credit Reporting Agencies, Experian, TransUnion, and Equifax, receive regular updating of negative and positive information on a voluntary basis from all major lenders but not, generally, service providers who charge after the service has been delivered.

Most judgments about credit, but also many about tenancy, employment, receipt of cell phones and cable, etc., are made via credit score. The most used credit scores are made by the FICO company, but CRAs separately, and Vantage, a jointly owned company of the CRAs, makes credit scores that are used.

Endnotes

1 Consumerism in Australia is described in an article titled Australians' Household Debt Nears Highest Worldwide/Discover how Australia's Personal Debt Compares to Other Countries and Pick Up Tips to Improve Your Finances. It was updated on Finder on May 22, 2019, at www.finder.com.au/

australias-personal-debt-reported-as-highest-in-the-world and was last reviewed by me on July 14, 2019.

[2] The Equifax website in Australia is at https://www.equifax.com.au/personal. I reviewed it on August 15, 2019.

[3] The information on Austrian credit habits comes from VisaEurope at www.visaeurope.com/making-payments/and was last reviewed by me December 2, 2018.

[4] The Organization for Economic Co-operation and Development (OECD) is a group of 34 member countries that discuss and develop economic and social policy. OECD members are democratic countries that support free market economies. A website containing statistics that they gather concerning household debt is at https://data.oecd.org/hha/household-debt.htm, I reviewed this last on August 15, 2019.

[5] My understanding of Austrian credit markets comes in part from Wikipedia at www.en.Wikipedia.org/wiki/Credit_score#Austria. The page was last edited July 2, 2019 and observed by me on July 8, 2019.

[6] The National Bank of Belgium wrote about The Central Individual Credit Register July 9, 2019 at www.nbb.be/en/central-credit-register/central-individual-credit-register and reviewed by me on July 14, 2019.

[7] Bulletin: The platform for Belgium's International Community is at www.thebulletin.be/credit-rating-belgium and was reviewed by me on July 14, 2019. The name of the article is Credit Rating in Belgium, posted Jul 19, 2016.

[8] For information about how Belgium copes without the CRAs, see the article How Belgium Deals With Credit Without Equifax, Experian, and TransUnion by Ethan Wolff-Mann, Senior Writer for Yahoo Finance, contributed September 22, 2017 at www.finance.yahoo.com/news/belgium-deals-credit-without-equifax-experian-transunion-114323975.html and reviewed by me on July 14, 2019.

[9] My understanding of the credit reporting in Brazil is largely from the BusinesInsider article Many Countries Don't Use Credit Scores Like the US — Here's How They Determine Your Worth by Christopher Curley Aug. 20, 2018, is at www.businessinsider.com/credit-score-around-the-world-2018-8#7-brazil-. It was last reviewed by me July 15, 2019.

[10] FICO's efforts in Brazil are in their announcement titled FICO Acquires GoOn to Advance Growth in Brazil made December 12, 2018 at www.prnewswire.com/news-releases/fico-acquires-goon-to-advance-growth-in-brazil-300764026.html. It was reviewed by me on July 14, 2019.

[11] The Canadian Equifax site, at www.consumer.equifax.ca, was reviewed by me on July 15, 2019. Credit Scores are discussed in detail at a subsection of that site, with the URL www.consumer.equifax.ca/personal/education/credit-score/how-are-credit-scores-calculated/.

[12] FICO Extends Distribution Agreement with Equifax for FICO Score in Canada at www.fico.com/en/newsroom/fico-extends-distribution-agreement-with-equifax-for-fico-score-in-canada a press release August 8, 2018 and reviewed by me on August 14, 2019.

[13] The Transunion site in Canada can be found at www.transunion.ca. I reviewed this on August 4, 2019.

[14] The BBC article titled on Chinese Credit Scores: Beijing Sets Up Huge System by Celia Hatton on October 26is at www.bbc.com/news/world-asia-china-34592186. It was reviewed by me July 15, 2019.

[15] The Atlantic International Article, titled China's Surveillance State Should Scare Everyone, by Anna Mitchell and Larry Diamond, on February 2, 2018, is at www.theatlantic.com/international/archive/2018/02/china-surveillance/552203/. The URL was reviewed by me on July 15, 2019.

[16] A Brookings Institute article titled ORDER FROM CHAOS: What's Happening With China's Fintech Industry? was written by Wei Wang and David Dollar on February 8, 2018. Its URL, www.brookings.edu/blog/order-from-chaos/2018/02/08/whats-happening-with-chinas-fintech-industry/, was reviewed by me on July 15, 2019.

[17] According to a piece called HOUSEHOLD WEALTH AND DEBT on the website of the Denmark's National Bank on December 14, 2018.at http://www.nationalbanken.dk/en/

publications/themes/Pages/Household-wealth-and-debt.aspx. I reviewed this site on August 14, 2019.

[18] The Just Landed, Denmark article, is at www.justlanded.com/english/Denmark/Denmark-Guide/Money/Accessing-your-money and was last reviewed by me on July 15, 2019.

[19] The Experian website is at www.experian.dk/and last reviewed by me July 15, 2019.

[20] My understanding of the credit reporting in France is largely from the BusinesInsider article Many Countries Don't Use Credit Scores Like the US — Here's How They Determine Your Worth by Christopher Curley Aug. 20, 2018, is at www.businessinsider.com/credit-score-around-the-world-2018-8#7-france- It was last reviewed by me July 15, 2019.

[21] Particulars about how the Bank of France maintains credit files is from an article Credit Checks in France, published September 13, 2012 are taken from a site called Complete France, with URL www.completefrance.com/french-property/mortgages/credit-checks-in-france-1-1515796, last reviewed by me on July 15.

[22] The social website that I rely on for intuition into the French system is Quora, and the thread at www.quora.com/Is-it-true-that-theres-no-credit-score-company-in-France was reviewed by me on July 15, 2019.

[23] The website Language and Culture in Austria, Germany and Switzerland at www.german-way.com/germanys-cash-culture-geld-stinkt-nicht/contains a post April 13, 2016 from an author called HF, entitled Germany's Cash Culture: "Geld stinkt nicht". I last reviewed this July 17, 2019.

[24] The blog about the Schufa is the Open Foundation Knowledge Blog at www.blog.okfn.org/2018/02/22/we-crack-the-schufa-the-german-credit-scoring/written by February 22, 2018, by Walter Palmetshofer and reviewed by me on July 15, 2019.

[25] The social website Personal Finance & Money Stack Exchange with the article of Credit Rating in Germany includes an answer by someone named Freddie, who writes with detail and an air of authority, March 11, 2016, at www.money.stackexchange.com/questions/48187/credit-rating-in-germany. I reviewed it July 17, 2019.

[26] The information about e-commerce in Hong Kong was taken from the Finder.Com website at www.finder.com/using-a-credit-card-in-hong-kong The article, titled Using a Credit Card in Hong Kong, was written by Kliment Dukovski and last updated June 14, 2019. It was reviewed by me on July 15, 2019.

[27] The TransUnion website in Hong Kong can be found at www.transunion.hk/home, last reviewed by me on July 15, 2019. My belief that TransUnion is the only website in Hong Kong comes from the www.hongkongbusiness.hk/financial-services/feature/only-consumer-credit-reference-agency-in-hong-kong, from a website called Hong Kong Business, last reviewed by me on July 15, 2019. It describes TransUnion's role at some length.

[28] The issue about an apparent hack at TransUnion in Hong Kong come from the South Morning China Post in Honk Kong, by Danny Mok and Sum Lok-Kei. published November 29, 2018. It is at www.scmp.com/news/hong-kong/society/article/2175505/hong-kong-authorities-urge-credit-bureau-transunion-tighten, and reviewed by me on July 15, 2019.

[29] The website URL www.transunioncibil.com/was reviewed by me on July 15, 2019.

[30] Wikipedia's article about the biometric ID system Aadhaar is at www.en.Wikipedia.org/wiki/Aadhaar. It was last edited July 9, 2019 and reviewed by me on July 15, 2019.

[31] FICO's partnership with a company Lenddo is based on the Lenddo website at www.lenddo.com/about.html, reviewed by me on July 15, 2019.

[32] The FICO information comes from an article about the FICO announcement, at DataQuest, at www.dqindia.com/new-fico-credit-scores-lets-lenders-expand-access-credit-india/, reviewed by me on July 15, 2019.

[33] Information on Indonesia and Perfindo comes from the Perfindo website at www.pefindobirokredit.com/about-us/?lang=en, reviewed by me on July 15, 2019.

[34] The article ATMs in Indonesia: Credit cards and fees was posted July 19, 2018 to the website TransferWise at www.transferwise.com/us/blog/atms-in-indonesia. I reviewed the site on July 17, 2019.

[35] These countries have the most generous pensions by Rob Smith 2/21/18 for the World Economic Forum at https://www.weforum.org/agenda/2018/02/retirees-in-these-countries-receive-100-of-a-working-salary/, reviewed by me on August 14, 2019.

[36] Per the article Using Credit Cards in Italy at the website LIFE IN ITALY, PRACTICAL INFORMATION Posted on January 26, 2011 by Natalie at https://anamericaninrome.com/wp/2011/01/using-credit-cards-in-italy/. I reviewed the website on August 14, 2019.

[37] Access to Central Data Credit Data at Banca D'Italia site is at www.bancaditalia.it/servizi-cittadino/servizi/accesso-cr/. It was reviewed by me on August 14, 2019.

[38] The article on Japan comes from an article titled Using Credit Cards In Japan - A Guide To Money During Your Trip on the Matcha website at www.matcha-jp.com/en/5919. It was published July 6, 2018 and reviewed by me on July 15, 2019.

[39] Reiteration of the lack of a CRA in Japan comes from an article titled International Credit Reporting: The United States versus United Kingdom by Lauren Jackson for Self Lender on June 28, 1019. It can be found at www.selflender.com/blog/international-credit-reporting-us-vs-uk and was reviewed by me on July 15, 2019.

[40] The website CompareHero carries the come-on Find Malaysia's best credit card, personal loans & insurance deals and has the URL www.comparehero.my/. It was reviewed last by me on July 15, 2019.

[41] The Bank Negra URL is www./creditbureau.bnm.gov.my/CIfinancial.html and was reviewed by me on July 15, 2019.

[42] The website of Circulo de Credito is described at a FICO site with a URL of www.fico.com/en/newsroom/fico-and-circulo-de-credito-make-it-easier-for-millions-of-mexicans-to-get-credit-01-24-2017. I reviewed it on July 15, 2019.

[43] The BusinessInsider article about the Netherlands is one of 10 countries described in piece called Many countries don't use credit scores like the US — here's how they determine your worth, by Christopher Curley Aug. 20, 2018 at www.businessinsider.com/credit-score-around-the-world-2018-8. I reviewed it on July 15, 2019.

[44] The Reddit post at www.reddit.com/r/thenetherlands/comments/4wvj4u/how_to_get_a_credit_score_and_a_credit_report_in/was from 2 years ago and reviewed by me July 16, 2019.

[45] The website AmsterdamTips, in the article Living in Amsterdam: Credit Cards in the Netherlands, posted to www.amsterdamtips.com/credit-cards-netherlands on February 19, 2019 discusses the "thrifty Dutch." I reviewed the website on July 16, 2019.

[46] The Experian site in Norway is at www.experian.no/and was last reviewed by me on July 15, 2019.

[47] I relied on a website called Right About Money which has the article Consumerism Reaches Russia and Leaders Respond with a Financial Literacy Push by Dan Kadlec, posted July 26, 2018. It is at www.rightaboutmoney.com/consumerism-reaches-russia-and-leaders-respond-with-a-financial-literacy-push/and was reviewed by me July 15, 2019.

[48] The partnership between Experian and Sberbank, at Interfax, can be observed at www.interfax.com/txt.asp?rbr=27, reviewed by me on July 15, 2019.

[49] The Russian TransUnion website is at www.transunion.com/russia, reviewed by me on July 15, 2019.

[50] I learned about e-commerce in Saudi Arabia from Just Landed, Saudi Arabia, at www.justlanded.com/english/Saudi-Arabia/Saudi-Arabia-Guide/Money/Debit-and-Credit-Cards. I last reviewed this URL on July 15, 2019.

[51] The website of their credit bureau Simah is found at www.simah.com/english/Pages/default.aspx which I reviewed July 15, 2019.

[52] Huffington Post has a blog called LIFE with an article entitled How Do Credit Scores Work in Other Countries? It was contributed by Credit.Com, at www.huffpost.com/entry/how-do-credit-scores-

work_b_1723362, reviewed by me July 15, 2019. This article carries the opinion that Singapore, Malaysia, and Hong Kong have jumped ahead of the U.S. in credit databases.

[53] Money Smart, in an article called How to Apply for Credit Cards in Singapore – The Complete Guide writes about credit card usage in Singapore. It describes e-commerce in Singapore, at www.blog.moneysmart.sg/credit-cards/apply-credit-card-singapore-complete-guide/available, reviewed by me on July 15, 2019.

[54] A website called SingSaver carries an article Financial News and Advice in Singapore posted by Ryan Ong on May 13, 2019, that explains his idea of how to get a high credit score. The URL, www.singsaver.com.sg/blog/5-ways-to-get-the-highest-credit-score-in-singapore, sounds similar to myFICO in the U.S.

[55] The Monetary Authority of Singapore submitted an article Credit Reports and Credit Worthiness that sounds much like what is written by the CFPB or FTC in the United States. The website www.moneysense.gov.sg/articles/2018/11/credit-reports-and-creditworthiness, was reviewed by me July 15, 2019.

[56] Capetown Magazine has an article called A Traveler's Guide to Money and Currency in South Africa Son at www.capetownmagazine.com/money-south-africa, reviewed by me July 15, 2019.

[57] A website called Business Tech has an article entitled A Traveler's Guide to Money and Currency in South Africa at. www.businesstech.co.za/news/banking/292584/south-african-credit-cards-compared-2/, reviewed by me July 15, 2019.

[58] There is a PDF on the Government Gazette of South Africa with the 230-page National Credit Act, passed in 2005, at www.justice.gov.za/mc/vnbp/act2005-034.pdf. I reviewed in July 15, 2019. The Huffington Post in its LIFE posting, taken from Credit.Com discusses credit coverage in Africa generally at www.huffpost.com/entry/how-do-credit-scores-work_n_1723362, reviewed by me June 9, 2019.

[59] From the Banking Association of South Africa at www.banking.org.za/consumer-information/legislation/national-credit-act, reviewed by me July 7, 2019.

[60] TransUnion has a South African site, discussing credit scores there at www.transunion.co.za/education/credit-score which I reviewed July 7, 2019.

[61] The FICO effort to play a role in South African is documented in their announcement 1/17/10 (a number of years ago) at www.fico.com/en/newsroom/transunion-and-fico-unveil-enhanced-credit-score-for-south-african-market-01-17-2010 which I reviewed last on July 7, 2019.

[62] Opinions about currency in South Korea are derived from Frommer's article Money in South Korea at www.frommers.com/destinations/south-korea/money, reviewed by me July 16, 2019.

[63] The PULSE is an on-line article by Maeil Business News on 4/26/19 at www.pulsenews.co.kr/view.php?year=2019&no=264886 that contains an article about the delinquency levels in South Korean, entitled Delinquency rate of Korean credit card firms rises in Q1. I reviewed it July 16, 2019.

[64] Wikipedia describes the Financial Supervisory Service (South Korea) which oversees the financial industry and credit in South Korea. The entry, at www.en.Wikipedia.org/wiki/Financial_Supervisory_Service_(South_Korea) was last updated March 31, 2019 and reviewed by me July 16, 2019.

[65] Finder describes the e-commerce in Spain in an article updated July 15, 2019 by Megan Horner entitled Using a Credit Card in Spain. It is at www.finder.com/using-a-credit-card-in-spain and reviewed by me on July 16, 2019.

[66] The tendency of locals to use cash is found in the article For Payments In Spain, Cash Still Reigns at a PYMNTS.Com post Jan 15, 2018 at www.pymnts.com/cash/2018/payments-spain-cash-government-cap-debit-cards/, reviewed by me July 16, 2019.

[67] I got information on credit reporting and ASNEF from The Marabella Guide, which has an article entitled How to Get a Personal Credit Report in Spain posted November 28, 2015. It can be found at www.marbella-guide.com/how-to-get-a-personal-credit-report-in-spain/, reviewed by me on July 16, 2019.

[68] My information that Spain keeps a credit blacklist is derived from the Business Insider article Many countries don't use credit scores like the US — here's how they determine your worth by Christopher

Curley on Aug. 20, 2018. This can be found at www.businessinsider.com/credit-score-around-the-world-2018-8#5-spain-5, reviewed by me on July 16, 2019.

[69] The article Are Switzerland's pensions too high? was published on April 8, 2019 by Sibilla Bondolfi on the website SWI swissinfo.ch at https://www.swissinfo.ch/eng/pension-funds_are-switzerland-s-pensions-too-high-/44877268. I reviewed in August 14, 2019.

[70] Geographical facts about Switzerland come from an article in Wikipedia entitled Languages of Switzerland, edited July 3, 2019, at www.en.Wikipedia.org/wiki/Languages_of_Switzerland, reviewed by me July 16, 2019.

[71] The interesting article on cultural differences by different language-speaking populations in Switzerland comes from the academic article Culture, Money Attitudes and Economic Outcomes by Caroline Henchoz, Tristan Coste and Boris Wernli, published January 29, 2019 in the Swiss Journal of Economics and Statistics. It can be found at www.sjes.springeropen.com/articles/10.1186/s41937-019-0028-4, which I reviewed on July 16, 2019.

[72] The legalities of Swiss credit practices are described in the article The Swiss Consumer Credit Act at a website called moneyland.ch, at www.moneyland.ch/en/swiss-consumer-credit-act-definition, reviewed by me on July 16, 2019.

[73] Information on e-commerce comes from the Finder website, which has an article Using a credit card in Turkey by Kliment Dukovski, updated July 15, 2019. It can be found at www.finder.com/using-a-credit-card-in-turkey, and was reviewed by me on July 16, 2019.

[74] The financial intentions of Turkey are derived from an article Turkey: The Journey to a Cashless Society written January 2, 2019 by Soner Canko for the website Medici. It can be found at www.gomedici.com/turkey-journey-to-cashless-societylocals, and was reviewed by me on July 16, 2019.

[75] Information about the Turkish CRA called KKB can be found on its website, www.kkb.com.tr/en/about-us, observed by me July 7, 2019.

[76] The FICO announcement is at www.biia.com/fico-in-partnership-with-turkish-credit-bureau, posted August 4, 2014 and reviewed by me July 8, 2019.

[77] Information about the UAE credit bureau, Al Etihad Credit Bureau, comes from their website at www.aecb.gov.ae, reviewed by me July 16, 2019.

[78] From an article Average UK household debt now stands at record £15,400 in The Guardian by Miles Brignall, last modified on Jan 7, 2019 at https://www.theguardian.com/business/2019/jan/07/average-uk-household-debt-now-stands-at-record-15400. I reviewed it on August 14, 2019.

[79] The Credit Consumer Act in the U.K. is described in Wikipedia at www.en.Wikipedia.org/wiki/Consumer_Credit_Act_1974, edited June 8, 2019 and reviewed by me July 16, 2019.

[80] A website called Clear Score posted an article A guide to the credit reference agencies May 17, 2018 at www.clearscore.com/credit-score/what-are-credit-reference-agencies, reviewed by me July 16, 2019. It contains information about the CRAs in the U.K.

[81] Appears at Worldometers with website https://www.worldometers.info/world-population/population-by-country/. I last reviewed it August 14, 2019.

[82] Consumer Debt Statistics & Demographics in America - Debt.org is at https://www.debt.org/faqs/americans-in-debt/demographics/. I reviewed this on August 14, 2019.

CHAPTER EIGHTEEN

Data security

Abstract

Equifax was hacked and many other organizations as well, and hacking is likely to be a continuing problem of the information age. The FTC and state attorneys general forged a publicized settlement with Equifax in which they provide a limited amount of money or tools to consumers as compensation. The tools allow consumers to monitor the companies which monitor them—assuming the consumers want to spend large parts of their free time and thought on the problem. There are four options for consumers to protect themselves from identity theft: alerts, freezes, locks, and monitoring, each of which requires a lot of energy for consumers to pursue. It is possible for consumers to spend about a thousand a year achieving this modestly useful and exhausting business, whipped up by articles on the topics news and encouraged by the CRAs themselves, to whom this is a new source of profit from data collection.

Equifax had a data breach, which they announced on September 7, 2017. It was big news at the time. However, what was actually taken, by whom, and for what reason remains shadowy. It would be easy to sensationalize this data loss, to blame the CRA system for it, which collects so much personal data in one place. One might even point out that the data that was stolen from us to begin with has now been stolen from the thieves. However, I think that would be a cheap shot. I think this could happen to anybody. There have been so many public hacks that I really do not know what is safe or what to worry about anymore. Is it all out there already? Should I avoid going to my bank accounts and credit lines on-line? Today, the newspaper reports that some new breach at Facebook harvested some important data for 30 million people. Sony was hacked in 2014. The U.S. Office of Personnel Management was hacked in 2015. The Democratic National Committee was hacked in 2016, the year Russian bots showed up in Facebook. Target, LinkedIn, Facebook, eBay, Yahoo, Uber, and Chase—they have all had hacks, gigantic in that they say information on millions of people were leeched—to where? To the "dark web" says my son, as if that should both terrify me and explain everything. So, Voldemort has my social security number?

One thing all those hacked companies have in common is that they are still doing pretty well. Equifax stock closed at 142 on September 6, 2017—the day before its breach was reported. It dropped to 93 within a

Credit Data and Scoring: The First Triumph of Big Data and Big Algorithms
ISBN: 978-0-12-818815-6
https://doi.org/10.1016/B978-0-12-818815-6.00018-2

week, but it happens to be 142 (rounded) today (as I write on July 30, 2019). However, stock gyrations are hard to predict or explain. Earnings per share did not fall at all. Equifax earned $5.79 for 2018, as per *Yahoo Finance*. That was more than they earned in 2017. The state attorneys general made a big display of charging Equifax, and just recently, there was what I found to be a remarkably confusing and probably impotent settlement of the matter on the FTC website, which the FTC seemed to have negotiated[1]:

Equifax to Pay $575 Million as Part of Settlement with FTC, CFPB, and States Related to 2017 Data Breach

Settlement includes fund to help consumers recover from data breach ...

Equifax Inc. has agreed to pay at least $575 million, and potentially up to $700 million, as part of a global settlement with the Federal Trade Commission, the Consumer Financial Protection Bureau (CFPB), and 50 U.S. states and territories, which alleged that the credit reporting company's failure to take reasonable steps to secure its network led to a data breach in 2017 that affected approximately 147 million people.

In its complaint, the FTC alleges that Equifax failed to secure the massive amount of personal information stored on its network, leading to a breach that exposed millions of names and dates of birth, Social Security numbers, physical addresses, and other personal information that could lead to identity theft and fraud ....

As part of the proposed settlement, Equifax will pay $300 million to a fund that will provide affected consumers with credit monitoring services. The fund will also compensate consumers who bought credit or identity monitoring services from Equifax and paid other out-of-pocket expenses as a result of the 2017 data breach. Equifax will add up to $125 million to the fund if the initial payment is not enough to compensate consumers for their losses. In addition, beginning in January 2020, Equifax will provide all U.S. consumers with six free credit reports each year for seven years—in addition to the one free annual credit report that Equifax and the two other nationwide credit reporting agencies currently provide.

The company also has agreed to pay $175 million to 48 states, the District of Columbia and Puerto Rico, as well as $100 million to the CFPB in civil penalties ....

Today's announcement is not the end of our efforts to make sure consumers' sensitive personal information is safe and secure. The incident at Equifax underscores the evolving cyber security threats confronting both private and government computer systems and actions they must take to shield the personal information of consumers. Too much is at stake for the financial security of the American people to make these protections anything less than a top priority. For consumers impacted by the Equifax breach, today's settlement will make *available up to $425 million for time and money they spent to protect themselves from potential threats of identity theft or addressing incidents of identity theft as a result of the breach.*

It is impossible to understand what to do from this article, apart from being impressed by what seems like big numbers and the tough regulators that throw them around along with frightening new priorities for all of us. There have been flocks of articles trying to explain it in the last week, for instance one called *A step-by-step guide on how to file an Equifax data breach claim* from *CNBC*.[2] However, I found that the FTC had their own site explaining what to do, which I found pretty readable.[3]

Equifax Data Breach Settlement Affected by the Equifax breach? File a claim now. July 2019.

In September of 2017, Equifax announced a data breach that exposed the personal information of 147 million people. The company has agreed to a global settlement with the Federal Trade Commission, the Consumer Financial Protection Bureau, and 50 U.S. states and territories. The settlement includes up to $425 million to help people affected by the data breach.

If your information was exposed in the data breach, you can file a claim at EquifaxBreachSettlement.com for the benefits described below.

Not sure if your information was exposed? Use this look-up tool to see.

You can file a claim for:

Free Credit Monitoring and Identity Theft Protection Services

Up to 10 years of free credit monitoring OR $125 if you decide not to enroll because you already have credit monitoring.

There is also a section of this article for people who have actually been harmed as a result of this hack. I have never met anyone who says they have actually been harmed, except in so far as they had anxiety. However, this is not the sort of harm meant by this settlement. This leaves actual consumers with the choice to get free monitoring or $125 if they already have monitoring. Based on the prices that I have seen, the $125 will not come close to compensating them. Besides, from what I have been reading in the press, people are going to get much less than $125 because the pot of money to pay for it is insufficient. Therefore, the authorities recommend we get the free monitoring.

Despite what seems to me to be a minor value in bothering with this, I must admit that I found the first screen that the FTC sent me easy to use. They give me a link to a screen at Equifax, which had only a couple simple questions that I answered easily, before I learned that I was indeed a victim. Great. The next screen offering was also relatively easy to complete, except that I do not want the tedium and obsession of free monitoring. Therefore, unless I am willing to lie or to rationalize that I already monitor my credit myself (clearly not, what they mean, but hey ...) there is nothing at all in this settlement for me. But the screens are easy to use.

Doubtless, Equifax wishes the hack had not happened but their actuality to various governing bodies, separate and distinct from the monitoring services, seems to be $275 million, much less than 10 percent of revenue in a year, about a third of their earnings before taxes in just 2017. The sums larger than that mentioned in the settlement are probably either computer services they would be providing anyway or compensated for by what they will earn selling monitoring services far beyond what is given for free. It is not that I am outraged that they are not punished further. I am just pointing out that they the settlement is really one that gets them off the hook at a relatively small cost. But then they are paying for being victims.

Meanwhile, I read in my regular perusal of the on-line version of the Washington *Post* the article *Capital One says data breach affected 100 million credit card applications*. The thief, already apprehended, is surely not part of a team of brilliant programmers but a loose cannon who seems to have essentially caught herself with internet boasting. Still, she broke in and stole information on a 100 million users. I have a Capital One credit card myself now. Oops!

Moreover, this very week, I got a notice in the mail from a place called Palisades Eye Surgery Center that "my personal information may have been subject to unauthorized access or acquisition as the result of a cyber-attack." A weird entry-point to my private information, but does it really matter? Palisades wrote, after some chest-beating about all they had done to fight for my data: "As an added precaution we have arranged for you to enroll, at no cost to you, in an online, credit monitoring service for 1 year provided by TransUnion Interactive, a subsidiary of TransUnion, one of the three nationwide credit reporting companies. To receive Credit Monitoring, enrollment is required. You can sign up for this free service between now and October 14, 2019 using the Verification Code .... To enroll, simply go to www.firstwatchid.com, click on the Verification Code button, and follow the instructions."

I am further advised to "Add a fraud alert statement to your credit file at all three national credit-reporting agencies .... Place a 'Security freeze' on your credit account .... Remove your name from mailing lists of pre-approved offers of credit for approximately 6 months. Receive a free copy of your credit report by going to www.annualcreditreport.com." I presume the letter was written by a robot, and that robot assumes I not only have a lot of free time to worry about my cataract prescription being stolen but can do this with the speed and thoughtlessness of robots.

I am quite sure that from now as long as the mind can imagine, there will be computers and databases hacked in cases famous and obscure. There will be an endless struggle between cyber-criminals and cyber-cops. The CRAs are juicy targets but they know this, especially after the Equifax hack. While they seem to have escaped with their scalp this time, losing data is a business threat for them and the other CRAs, if only because they depend on Federal laws and regulations, which can be moved by public opinion. Speaking to their executives, I can confirm that all the CRAs are highly sensitized to security risks. They were before the big hack, but now are even more so.

Oddly, the hack could work to improve business at the CRAs. The repositories have jumped on the chance to sell products to fearful consumers. The alarmed public has three options in the Credit world—alert, freeze, and lock—for controlling access to their credit, none of which will really anybody from hackings but might, rarely, avert some credit-related mishap. A last exercise available is monitoring. Great, we can all spend our hours monitoring the firms monitoring us, except that they are paid to do it, and we pay to do it. The lock and the monitoring cost money, but people will pay it. People have been frightened into it, and they represent earning opportunities for the CRAs.

The fraud alert, mentioned in the letter to me from Palisades and long available per the FCRA, is a notice on a credit file that can be placed for free by a consumer. Following are excerpts from the article *What is a fraud alert?* From the website *Credit Karma*[4]:

What is a fraud alert?

If you've been the victim of identity theft or fraud, you can contact one of the three major credit bureaus to place a fraud alert on your credit reports, giving potential lenders and creditors a heads-up that someone may try to fraudulently use your identity to apply for a line of credit.

A fraud alert is a statement in your credit reports that alerts anyone reviewing the reports that you may be a victim of fraud or identity theft. This alerts creditors and lenders that they should perform more-thorough vetting — such as calling to check whether you're actually at a particular store trying to take out new credit — when verifying your identity before extending credit in your name ....

There are two main types of fraud alerts you can place in your credit reports: initial fraud alerts and extended alerts. The initial fraud alert expires after 90 days. Once it expires, the credit bureaus will automatically remove it from your reports. After the initial fraud alert is removed, you can then request another 90-day fraud alert if you think you're still at risk for identity theft ...

Even though a fraud alert is placed on your credit reports, there's no guarantee the alert will stop identity theft.

The fraud alert becomes part of what we have seen is a long and boring credit report and one hopes that the creditor who orders it smells a fish. Because nobody knows if they do, nobody with the anxiety level to get this will probably feel satisfied they have achieved much. Also, it just lasts 90 days. It probably does the job, but only for a short time, and is a lot of trouble. Though indisputably free, when I typed in "fraud alert" under Google, the first three responses are ads for paying services, designed to make consumers nervous and sign them to expensive monitoring services.

Next among options, maybe ward off some fraudsters, is the credit freeze, specifically offered as a free service nationally under the Economic Growth, Regulatory Relief, and Consumer Protection Act (passed in May of 2018). Here are excerpts from *How to Freeze Your Credit* from *NerdWallet*, followed as usual by my insightful summary[5]:

How to Freeze Your Credit

If you're dealing with identity theft, a credit freeze, also known as a security freeze, can offer peace of mind. No one will be able to open credit accounts in your name, which can save you the hassle and cost that come with having your identity stolen.

How do I freeze my credit?

You must contact each of the three major credit bureaus individually to freeze your credit; each has a slightly different process. Generally, you need to provide your Social Security number, birthdate and other information confirming your identity. Here's contact information for the credit bureaus, plus links with step-by-step guides:

Equifax: Call 800-685-1111 or go online. Check out a step-by-step Equifax credit freeze guide.

Experian: Call 888-397-3742 or go online. Here's a detailed walk-through on getting an Experian credit freeze.

TransUnion: Call 888-909-8872 or go online. Read our TransUnion credit freeze guide.

Once a credit freeze is in place, it secures your credit file until you lift the freeze. You'll need to lift the freeze temporarily if you want to apply for new credit ....

How do I unfreeze my credit?

You go to the credit bureau website and use the same credentials you used to freeze your credit to unfreeze your credit. You can also unfreeze your credit by phone or postal mail if you can provide the personal identification number established when the freeze was set up. Unless you use postal mail, unfreezing takes effect within minutes of requesting it.

When you are applying for credit, you can ask the creditor which credit bureau it will use to check your credit and unfreeze only that one. Or, if you're shopping for a loan and may make several applications in a short period, you may choose to lift the freeze at all three major credit bureaus ....

Who can access my frozen credit reports?

A credit freeze makes your credit reports inaccessible to most people, with [quite] a few exceptions: ...

Your current creditors still have access, as do debt collectors.

Marketers can see your credit reports for the purpose of sending you offers ....

What's the difference between a credit freeze and a credit lock?

Both a credit freeze and credit lock block access to your credit reports. However, a credit lock is a product offered voluntarily by a credit bureau, which may charge a fee ...

Is there a downside to freezing credit?

A freeze can give you a false sense of security — you may still be susceptible to credit fraud or other fraud involving your Social Security number.

It can be inconvenient because you need to remember to lift the freeze when you want to apply for credit .... [And remember or figure out how.]

if a thief steals information about an existing account, your credit may be used without your permission. It's still important to check monthly statements carefully for signs of fraudulent activity and to alert creditors immediately if you see something suspicious.

Note the last line: the consumer still has to be on the look-out for fraudulent activity, according to this article, so where is the peace of mind? Plus, a lot of people can still see the credit report, plus only a few will remember how to lift the freeze when they need to, plus it requires contacting each CRA, plus, and this is a big plus, the consumer has to remember to look for a freeze, not a lock. A lock is a minor variant on a freeze that sounds nicer and does not take any time to lift or remembering three PINS. It costs "just 24.99" per month at Experian but is free at the other two CRAs as of today, August 3, 2019. I supposed that is good, but where is the peace of mind locking up two repositories for free when the fraudster can just go to Experian for what they want. In addition, locks seem connected to costly monitoring services, not by requirement but by advertisement and suggestions. When I looked for the cost of a lock at TransUnion[6], it was shown as free under the name of but advertised with monitoring for $19.95 per month. Equifax may be slightly more subdued in advertising locks at this time—after all they are still reeling from the hack—but they offer it at the same price; $19.95 per month.

Why are there locks when a freeze will do? I do not know really. I do not think anybody quite knows. If the lock is just a freeze with a little twist to make it easier to unlatch, it seems like it ought to be free, or required by the regulator to be free. Who has time for all this? However, the really bizarre part of this is how partial a protection is offered by freezes and locks, and even less by alerts. These tools help protect only against identity theft as a means to get new credit, a matter with a perhaps frightening psychological evocation but one that is probably relatively innocuous that a consumer can easily prove is not her doing. However, this is a very minor misuse of personal information. Using the data to obtain passwords, get into bank accounts, blackmail, whatever evildoers can dream up: unaffected. In addition, even the credit freezing and locking requires the consumer to work with three different CRAs though they are all roughly the same for this purpose. That's a lot of trouble, a lot of contacts, and even if free, several new PINs are there to hang on to and remember when the need to unfreeze arises.

Conclusion

Having all our credit data collected in three places turns out to create extra burdens, psychological and real.

Endnotes

[1] The press release from the FTC is at www.ftc.gov/news-events/press-releases/2019/07/equifax-pay-575-million-part-settlement-ftc-cfpb-states-related and was reviewed by me on July 30, 2019.

[2] The *CNBC* site, with author Megan Leonhardt, published today *A step-by-step guide on how to file an Equifax data breach claim* Published at www.cnbc.com/2019/07/30/equifax-data-breach-step-by-step-guide-on-how-to-file-a-claim.html. I reviewed it on July 30, 2019.

[3] The article *Equifax Data Breach Settlement Affected by the Equifax breach? File a claim now.* carries only the date July 2019. It is at www.ftc.gov/enforcement/cases-proceedings/refunds/equifax-data-breach-settlement and was reviewed by me on July 30, 2019.

[4] The article *What is a fraud alert?* was published on March 12, 2018 on *Credit Karma* written by Deb Hipp at www.creditkarma.com/id-theft/i/what-fraud-alert/. I reviewed it on August 3, 2019.

[5] *How to Freeze Your Credit* by BEV O'SHEA on July 24, 2019 for the website *NerdWallet* at www.nerdwallet.com/blog/finance/pros-and-cons-freezing-credit/. I reviewed the piece on August 3, 2019.

[6] This can be found at www.transunion.com/blog/identity-protection/difference-between-a-credit-lock-and-credit-freeze. I looked on August 3, 2019.

Algorithms and individuals

Abstract

Artificial Intelligence or really digital algorithms that run our lives are common digital recipes. It is in our nature to recapitulate any successful sequence, but AI often replaces humans in a manner that lacks transparency, design, and accountability, and without empathy. A particular program called Compas, defended with a lot of statistical bravado, is used to make decisions about whether prisoners will be paroled. I find that the predictive power of Compas is slight, less than credit scores.

So much for hacking and identify theft. The Information Age is a lot of trouble. Computers bring all sorts of rashes and viruses, the aggravations of using new software, of remembering passwords, of speaking to robots, of hacking, and lying, of disassociation. However, complaining about all that (and cell phones—God!) is not why I happen to be writing this book or this chapter.

As I have come to notice how we have all been boiled by algorithms, I think I have come to understand why we have not noticed. They do not raise alarm bells. Just as we see a bird or animal in the forest only when it moves, we are attuned to experience certain things and not others. Algorithms are terribly common things, being just recipes, steps always followed. It is in our nature to recapitulate any successful sequence, and then to follow those sequences or build sequences into mechanical things. In a way, it is singularly human to reproduce successful acts and even incorporate them into things. We are the tool making animal.

But let me make this less abstract, with an example: the ordinary car. Cars are a common expression of a set of algorithms baked into a thing. There are a number of things about cars that make them feel good to us, to feel part of a human-centered world. One is that there is nothing really important about the car that is incomprehensible. The goals of each part, mixing the gas, breaking the speed, cooling the engine—those seem clear and defensible. Not that long ago, most people knew quite a lot about how their cars worked. They often fixed their car themselves, or tuned it, or painted it. They felt that it was understandable and that they understood it. I will

Credit Data and Scoring: The First Triumph of Big Data and Big Algorithms
ISBN: 978-0-12-818815-6
https://doi.org/10.1016/B978-0-12-818815-6.00019-4

call that transparency. It has always been important but it has also been disappearing as cars have more and more incorporated computers. Still, the goal of every car of a certain type is to do exactly, without any variation, what every other car of the type does. Familiarity can feel like transparency in many ways. What the car is and does can be seen and relied on and if not perfectly understood, at least largely understood. Cars are somehow human, and my response to them is human.

Cars also have something I will term design. They look a certain way, they have color and shine and feel, and sound a certain way, and convey a certain something about the status and needs of the owners. Design is inherently human. Animals cannot even see the design. Cars are not simply functional. They are not defined for us only by their goals. Car companies have design too. There are the reliable Japanese makers, highly engineered German makers, and refined British makers. There is human and social feeling there. I call this stuff design, the detectability of esthetic points that give us feelings about the thing beyond its obvious goals. I am not on a semantic mission though, and the reader can substitute whatever word she wishes. Hopefully, I have conveyed the general idea.

Another feature about cars is that they give drivers at least a feeling of self-control. We go where we want. We go when we want. The car does not just come along and whisk me somewhere. We wait patiently in our lane or perhaps we cut off the other drivers, we put seatbelts on and listen to whatever we want, call whomever we want, we buy the car we want, etc. I think it is pretty clear that there is empowerment here, control, pick your word.

Last, there is accountability, not perfect accountability, but cars are bought on reputation and with specs, cars come with warranties, most repair shops will do it again for free if they screw up the first time. They cost a good deal of money, so we do not buy them thoughtlessly, and we buy them with strong, usually kept, expectations. We need insurance. We pay our tickets. Police officers can pull us over, but the police officer must tell his name. Despite all the headaches, gotchas, disappointments, and restrictions, it is usually clear in some way or another what or who is doing what and to whom.

Transparency. Design. Empowerment. Accountability. The reader might have other words for them, but when these are missing people feel lost, passive, confused, and empty. That all comes from the world of stuff. The world before there was activity that could strongly imitate us as subjects.

However, computers and algorithms, more and more a part of our life, do imitate us, but generally lack all these features, all the time. They just spit out decisions. What characterizes our times, and almost surely even more so in the future, is the prevalence of what John Danaher calls "governance algorithms ... the increasing reliance of public decision-making process (bureaucratic, legislative and legal) on algorithms," supervised by computers. In an article in the Journal of Philosophy and Technology entitled *The Threat of Algocracy: Reality, Resistance and Accommodation, Philosophy and Technology*, he claims these "constrain the opportunities for human participation in, and comprehension of, public decision making."[1] He has lots of fancy words for it, but I think everybody knows that when they are on computers, or just dealing with people that are on computers (lenders, the IRS, Social Security, and police), that we and they are being nudged, forced, or led by some decision-making process that is not really in the room with us. There is a pretense, sometimes laughable, that we are talking to human beings like ourselves that have feelings or at least plans that care about wasting our time. But we know that we are subject to sheer calculation or rules applied over and over again that are shifted by this word or that, not by our goals or needs, but by the routes of algorithmic lines. This robotic, impersonal logic is operating on so many of our activities, making the most personal of decisions, in dating sites, making financial trades, deciding who gets probation from prison, and, *Who will click, buy, lie or die*, according to the book title by E. Siegel.[2]

Sometimes, it may be considered positive that there is no accountability, since nobody has to either wrestle with the right thing to do (if they happen to be one of those people that care about that) or accept blame. Typically, one has had to make an effort to avoid accountability by claiming "It is not my decision" or "I am just following the rules". It has now reached what seems to me to be an Orwellian point, with an algorithm called Compas, by a company that used to be called Northpointe, now calling themselves Equivant. My guess is that the name change is so they sound like nice and fair-minded people, rather than a penitentiary. Compas is an algorithm that is used to set prison sentences—through algorithms. Let me quote some critical and melodramatic reporting from something called Washington Monthly, by Rebecca Wexler[3]:

> *Rodríguez was just sixteen at the time of his arrest, and was convicted of second-degree murder for his role in an armed robbery of a car dealership that left an*

employee dead. Now, twenty-six years later, he was a model of rehabilitation. He had requested a transfer to Eastern, a maximum-security prison, in order to take college classes. He had spent four and a half years training service dogs for wounded veterans and eleven volunteering for a youth program. A job and a place to stay were waiting for him outside. And he had not had a single disciplinary infraction for the past decade.

Yet, last July, the parole board hit him with a denial. It might have turned out differently but, the board explained, a computer system called COMPAS had ranked him "high risk." Neither he nor the board had any idea how this risk score was calculated; Northpointe, the for-profit company that sells COMPAS, considers that information to be a trade secret. But Rodríguez may have been stuck in prison because of it.

This seemed beyond dating suggestions, investment formulas, suggestions for friends from Facebook, people I should network with from LinkedIn, articles I might like, and bots who pretend to be friends and tell me who to vote for. This is a person's life, and nobody to answer why. I thought I would look up Compas and Northpointe on-line and there was indeed some literature. This is the beginning of what I read:

COMPAS Risk and Need Assessment System Selected Questions Posed by Inquiring Agencies

Ease of Use:

Does your tool require an interview with the inmate? If so, what advantage does this offer? Northpointe designed COMPAS to allow for test administration flexibility. There are several options data gathering options, any of which are valid. The offender may fill out the self-report section on his or her own. There may be a scripted interview, in which questions are asked verbatim. The interviewer may use a "guided discussion" format to simultaneously gather the assessment data and enhance rapport and buy-in for the intervention process, using a motivational interviewing style. The choice is the agency's to make, depending on the skill level of their staff, the time available to collect the data, and the resources available for COMPAS administration. Does COMPAS rely on static factors (criminal history only)? How does this approach compare to the static plus dynamic measurement approach employees by other companies? COMPAS relies on both static and dynamic data to generate its risk and needs results. The use of dynamic measures allows for measures to change over time as behavior changes. These changes are included in the measures of risk and need. The dynamic factors also allows for the "overlay" of previous assessments on the latest assessment to visual see any change in risk and need scores. Is there a short-screen/pre-screen? COMPAS is scalable to fit the needs of many different decision points, including pre-screening. In applying the risk principle, many agencies select the Violence and Recidivism risk scales for pre-screening or triaging the case. Individuals that score higher on risk may then have a more in-depth assessment using additional COMPAS scales. Information previously entered into a COMPAS assessment is automatically imported into the second-tier assessment. This also allows for the distribution of the assessment workload over several offender processing points—e.g. pre-trial might turn just the scales needed to support a release decision then at post sentence, for example, additional scales would be added to their assessment in support of supervision and treatment decisions (case plan). How long does it take to administer the tool? This depends on the assessment information needs at a particular offender processing point and the scales that you have determined are necessary to inform a decision. COMPAS assessment can take anywhere from 10 minutes to an hour depending on the scale content and administration data collection style. When possible, we also encourage developing an interface between COMPAS and other MIS systems. These system interfaces are built quickly and are designed to eliminate redundant data entry.

The tell here is the constant braggadocio and salesmanship of this product that slices and dices human beings. It could be a middle of the night advertisement or a segment on Home Shopping Network. *It is a product that can be used quickly, slowly, include an interview, be completed by the inmate or an interviewer. However, it is always wise and right. Why? Because they use a Risk and Recidivism scale—a score by a different word. Moreover, scores mean that no individual really has the awful choice of whether to free another individual. Here is the defense of the score.*

Accuracy and Utility What is the theoretical framework for this tool? COMPAS incorporates a comprehensive theory-based assessment approach. It is designed to incorporate key scales from several of the most informative theoretical explanations of crime and delinquency including General Theory of Crime, Criminal Opportunity/Lifestyle Theories, Social Learning Theory, Subculture Theory, Social Control Theory, Criminal Opportunities/Routine Activities Theory and Strain Theory. On what population was the risk tool 'normed'? COMPAS offers several norm groups options at system configuration including community corrections, jail populations, prison inmates, and a composite norming group representing all of the above. Each agency, with guidance from Northpointe, decides which norm group(s) they wish to score the assessment against. In addition, COMPAS is normed to male and female populations as well. As sufficient data become available, the Northpointe R&D team can work with the site to design samples that will generate locally relevant norms. Has your tool been evaluated by an independent source? COMPAS psychometric data has been peer-reviewed and published in a number of professional journals including Criminal Justice and Behavior January 2009 and Journal of Quantitative Criminology June 2008. COMPAS psychometric reports are available from Northpointe upon request. Is COMPAS valid? The General Recidivism Risk scale was developed in a sample of presentence investigation (PSI) and probation intake cases. The outcome was any arrest (misdemeanor or felony) within two years of the intake assessment. We recently validated the General Recidivism Risk scale in a sample of 2,328 PSI and probation intake cases. We fit survival models in which the Recidivism Risk scale predicted any offense, person offenses, and felony offenses. The AUCs ranged from .68 to .71 in the full sample.

How dare you question this brilliant tool that has an AUC of 0.68 to 0.71? The AUC, the Area Under the Curve, it turns out, is just the area under the blue (gray in print version) line, which is section A plus the 50% under the know-nothing orange (black in print version) line. In fact, you can just get the AUC from the Gini and vice versa.

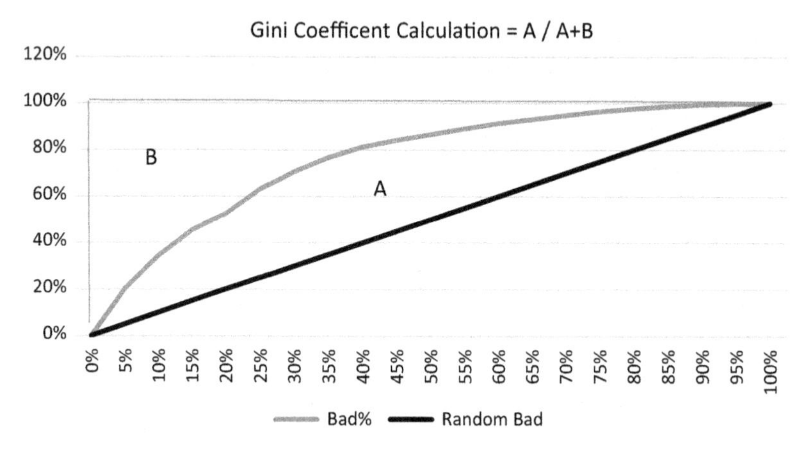

The Gini coefficient is 2 * AUC − 1. They are really the same thing. Therefore, an AUC of 0.71 means a Gini of 2 * 0.71 − 1 = 0.42. Reviewing the picture above, section A looks like around 42% of the sum of A and B. Yes, the Compas-picking line is better than the know-nothing orange line. But it is far from perfect. It is much less predictive than we typically find credit scores to be in predicting mortgage delinquency, and much, much less powerful than models which predict delinquency or default based on collateral value, loan amount, reserves, and all the other facts that emerge when a mortgage is made. Nevertheless, we also saw there was data error with credit scores. Here, with much fewer objective questions and all sorts of people answering all sorts of questions, on all sorts of scales, it is hard to see how the data could have fewer errors, but I do not really know. There are no details about the methodology behind the model, though I doubt it is really different in kind than what I have done to get a credit score. Let me neither presume too much nor flagellate the reader with breathless arguments. I think we can conclude that, more or less, the Northpointe is a re-arrest score, strikingly like the credit score I last worked on, which had outcomes of delinquency on a mortgage within 2 years.

Is COMPAS valid? The General Recidivism Risk scale was developed in a sample of presentence investigation (PSI) and probation intake cases. The outcome was any arrest (misdemeanor or felony) within 2 years of the intake assessment.

It is easy to argue that the score is racially biased, as does Pro Publica,[4] for very similar reasons that mortgage models have been accused of being racially biased. In addition, it is doubly easy to argue that the methodology is opaque, or driven by errors. It is opaque because it is proprietary. Opacity is one of the barriers to entry (to copy and sell as a competitor). However, opacity disguises data and modeling accidents and allows users to wonder about the true importance of inputs, which may work best on a large sample but not make sense in any one individual case. For instance, in credit scores, it might be the case that a 60 day late is more predictive overall than a 90 day late, given all the other inputs in the score; but there may be a perfectly good reason in a particular case for a 60 day late but not a ninety—say the person moved and the mail got screwed up for a while. It is important that the score by itself be taken as sacred, or it loses its power. This might be largely acceptable in the case of credit, but here it is a particularly crucial decision, whether to free someone or not.

On the other hand, because it is an important decision, because it must be made and has to be made, and because it is not at all clear that to me that any parole officer (surely not free from bias him or herself) would do better without this score—maybe the mystery and power of scoring, or AI as it is called these days, can be justified. Yes, I am turned off by the defensive crouch of the writer who tries to impress the reader with terminology and statistics; but maybe this is the way to make the score click, or at least to make the most money for this product, the real goal of the written material.

The problem is that the algorithms are taking the place of human decision, done (literally) robotically. There is nobody to blame, and no accountability, a hidden design, without form, not comprehended as a being or even an entity. Facebook wrote me this morning: did I see my sister-in-law's comment on something my niece said. It was tuned into me in some way, but not in a living way, not knowing me or caring about me, or capable of either. Of course, this is not really new fundamentally. Technology was joined to steam engines and cotton-growing, to mass communication and travel, to constant improvements in warfare, and to space exploration. It just did not pretend to be a person before recent times. I do not pretend to understanding humanity or the arc of our technologies and cultures, but it does seem as if something weirder than usual is happening: computers have allowed our self-interest to separate from us as agents and imitate us in the use of technology.

Endnotes

[1] *The Threat of Algocracy: Reality, Resistance and Accommodation, Philosophy and Technology*, by John Danaher, J. Philos. Technol. (2016) 29: 245. www.doi.org/10.1007/s13347-015-0211-1. See also a blog by the same author on the topic, part of a series called *Philosophic Disquisitions*, posted on January 6, 2014, at www.philosophicaldisquisitions.blogspot.com/2014/01/rule-by-algorithm-big-data-and-threat.html. I last reviewed this website on July 9, 2019.

[2] Eric Siegel published the book *Predictive Analytics: Who will click, buy, lie or die.* February 19, 2013. Available from Amazon at https://www.amazon.com/Predictive-Analytics-Power-Predict-, reviewed by me on August 12, 2019.

[3] Rebecca Wexler wrote an article for the June issues of the Magazine Section in *Washington Monthly* entitled *Code of Silence: How private companies hide flaws in the software that governments use to decide who goes to prison and who gets out.* It can be found at washingtonmonthly.com/magazine/junejulyaugust-2017/code-of-silence/ and was reviewed by me on July 16, 2019.

[4] This is from *Machine Bias - There's software used across the country to predict future criminals. And it's biased against blacks* in *Pro Publica May 23, 2016* by Julia Angwin, Jeff Larson, Surya Mattu, and Lauren Kirchner. It can be found at www.propublica.org/article/machine-bias-risk-assessments-in-criminal-sentencing and was reviewed by me on August 2, 2019.

CHAPTER TWENTY

Something like a conclusion

Abstract

I recap the book and my career. In writing the book my perspective shifted away from a career of making models to one where I perceived how much of our humanity is lost in an increasingly digital world where artificial intelligence makes so many of our decisions. Credit data piracy and scoring were the first intervention with AI that we faced, and I showed that it is only truish statistically. Yet it kicked our ass and seems here to stay. There is little we can do to stop this new world; but, somehow, we have to remind ourselves that we are individuals, with identity and autonomy, and that there is nobody home in AI. It is neither our master nor our friend. We and our experience are all that matter.

This is a book that could be said to begin with a frustration, which grew into a crusade, then faded into a book. Books are what people resign themselves to after they have given up trying to fix a problem.

I have had what many would consider a successful career, achieving moderately impressive models, software, and intellectual productions, all while making a living. One of those achievements, not completed alone by any means, but driven by me, was a credit score, which took advantage of something called "trend data" that the CRAs began offering. The notion of "trend data" is just that certain data that were in the databases of CRAs for the previous 3 years would be sold along with the credit report. This was not the break-through in format the CRAs claimed as justification for a large price increase. For instance, they had always shown the trend of consumer delinquency, they had always shown what the consumer owed on the bill, and they just had never before shown a history of the borrowers' payments on the bill.

It occurred to me at the time, however (unaware they would raise the price), that this could be the greatest thing since sliced bread in the credit scoring business because it would allow us to distinguish *transactors*—convenience users of credit cards who paid for stuff with a credit card but then paid off the entire bill every month—from *revolvers*—individuals who ran a constant balance on their credit cards, a terribly expensive way to borrower money. The latter might also suggest that the borrower is in such

Credit Data and Scoring: The First Triumph of Big Data and Big Algorithms
ISBN: 978-0-12-818815-6
https://doi.org/10.1016/B978-0-12-818815-6.00020-0

straightened circumstances that they simply cannot pay back the entire bill. Revolvers might not have delinquencies because they managed to pay the shamefully low minimums (usually 2% of balance) each month. By comparing the payment each month with the amount due the prior month, we would be able to distinguish the non-late but hard-pressed borrowers from the transactors and create a large, new, and mostly fair class of second-rate citizens, distinguishing them from the almost riskless first-class citizens who never had problems paying their credit card bill.

Well, it did, at first, turn out to be the greatest thing since sliced bread, it did improve the credit score to give points for paying back the bill each month. Among other wonders of this score, a person could improve their ranking rapidly, by simply adopting the habit of paying back their indebtedness right way. The current practice of credit scoring has a much longer period or rehabilitation, as age of oldest tradeline, and delinquencies age and become distant memories only over a long period. I was elated to be part of the cutting edge of this development.

Then the large banks simply stopped reporting current payment amounts. Nor did the CRAs even inform me of this change. It was only after the new score that depended on this data had gone into production that I learned that the data was dropping away, more each month.

They just stopped reporting it and I could do nothing about it. Cue the frustration.

The lost payment data made my credit score model less predictive and took away a variable I hoped would allow more people to be judged differently and thus to obtain mortgages sooner. It was striking to me that furnishers could get away with something, that seemed blatantly illegal under the FCRA, which calls for "accurate and *complete*" data. I tried to generate actionable outrage at the CRAs about the problem but that went nowhere.

I understand that at that point I was certainly not worrying about privacy rights or the true owners of that information. If I am honest, I have to admit that in my career I helped this societal shift to scoring, calibrating, and manipulating people by their data alone. It *is* ironic that what moneylenders provide, and what CRAs hold, is voluntary, while the data about our lives is taken involuntarily—but that was not my beef when I started this book. It had not yet occurred to me, as I peeled away the layers of obscuring fat to make a statistically reliable model, that nobody had signed up to be vivisected in this way. To be fair (to me), when I made these scores, I was always trying to explain how they worked. I had a vision that my models would be transparent, understood, and also give people a chance at redemption, ways to fix their ranking.

Predictive Analytics it was called in the first years of doing it. It was the latest thing, and I saw nothing wrong with what I was doing at the time. Then it was called data science, an entirely new trade and a new chance to get ahead. There was a brief flurry of national resistance to credit scoring and its opacity and biases, at the end of the last century. Then, surprisingly, the resistance to all things scoring or data-mined died down. The internet came along, and perhaps everybody was distracted or thought big data was worth it. My epiphany came years later, as did my chagrin over the payment data that was erased.

Therefore, I started the book wanting to model a bit better, cursing the constant barrage of technology and artificial intelligence that I saw in my personal life, but not seeing my own part in it. As I worked on the book in 2017 and 2018, I came to see that I had contributed to making the problem worse. I am not begging forgiveness—what did I know?—but from the work to put this book together, I came to a new view about it and my part in it. And, like new believers everywhere, I want to pass on my new viewpoint.

First, a recap of the book: In 1970, 50 years ago, the Federal government legalized the collection of all our credit data by three companies that have essentially all been in place over that period, but reached cruising altitude with FICO scores in the eighties. I had no sense for their stability before, but it boggles the mind. I think they know they have a good thing and so act mutually to protect it. They have a common trade organization, which speaks for them, manages data collection for them, and manages a system that pretends to fix errors but does not do that. In addition, we consumers have somehow accepted it all as the status quo, with what seems a kind of willful ignorance. All of us are told whenever we want to start using some new pipeline of credit that our failure to pay can be sent to these companies, but I did not even know I had agreed to it. Probably you did not know that either. When the data that is vacuumed up was hacked from the Equifax cupboard, hacked, and led many to worry and complain about Equifax, there was no thought to just dismantling the whole thing. The only cure offered was to monitor all that data they collect, and that seemed sufficient, so long as it came with a few ounces of flesh. A new big business for these companies is profiting on our fears about that data that was hacked. In addition, we are largely accepting of that, too.

Those companies collect, hold, and sell whatever data creditors want to give them. When the creditors think it is too much trouble to send some data to the three companies, the CRAs simply allow the deficiency. That the payers do not object, that the creditors do not object, that the *regulators* do not object—it all surprised me. It still surprises me. I think we have become numb to data about us being all over the place, and that it might have all sorts of gaps but that is not our look-out, and we also have accepted the narrative that our lives are now a corporate asset. That the CRAs act together about it, this is the result of a stalemate in which they each figure there is no killing blow to be landed, so they accept a triopoly. When there are complaints from state attorneys general, the three companies bow as one, throwing away data but maintaining their equality and business model.

All the data they have is modeled and it gets a number and we get that number. FICO got that going, a trend setter in human formulas—boiling data down a bunch of disconnect stuff to something that means more than all the isolated factoids. That score, and many things AI, is far from precise and differs depending on which CRA provides it, though you would not know from the internalizations of the score. I walked through some features of how this credit score is made. It is far more arbitrary than it looks and only works statistically on large groups. It was never meant to speak for a single soul. Nevertheless, we live with it as if it is a grade in high school that stops us from going to the college we want to. Bitch, moan, accept. Most not only accept that they must live with that number but now take it as insight into their deepest character, particular if a good grade. In addition, what part of this has not spread to other countries soon will, albeit with twists and turns in each nation.

This all went down in the United States more than a generation ago. This data was the first major consumer data used. The FCRA the first law about private and personal data. Credit scores were the first great AI. But it was only first. Since that happened, it touches us everywhere. AI has multiplied many times. Most of what we do has a digital component and our data trails are tracked and held by numerous entities that care even less than CRAs about whether it is right. These entities then use that data to manipulate us in any way they can, usually to make money. Big data has been lauded for years. Now we are starting to fear it but far too late. The old data intrusions seem almost quaint. Imagine what Google has on most of you now, or Facebook, or Snapchat, or Amazon, or your firm, or your computer, or television, or cell phone. China can pretend to, and perhaps even achieve, a social score that forms opinions about consumers regarding their political life, spiritual inclinations, personal habits, and affiliations, and reward or punish them for each. This is the data mining and AI that we asked for. Some people stay in jail now because of AI. A few get married.

End of recap.

Now I am not a big fan of human intelligence. I am not sure that the decisions made today are any worse from a logical point of view. However, today these decisions are increasingly digital and unfeeling. They lack humanity, empathy, transparency, design, accountability, nor confer empowerment. Those warm and fuzzy features have disappeared from much of the market. They might make a bit of a comeback here and there with all the surveys we answer after phone calls, or through compassionate candidates, or nurturing mothers. I do not pretend to predict every current in culture. But the data collection, hacks, scores, AI, digital opportunism, robots, voice mail, and all that stuff: I think it'has come to stay and will grow and metastasize in unforeseen directions: social scores, chips under the skin, those are for sure—but there are all sorts of unexpected developments ahead. Each one of us will deal more and more with non-human pretenders to humanness, or humans buffered in some way by digital fabrics that keep us further apart.

There is, admittedly, little, maybe nothing, that an individual can do to alter the direction of civilization, technology, billions of people whipping up ever-greater dust. Maybe we will destroy ourselves but probably not. However, we will probably always be individuals, probably always *be* humans, even if the world around us is decreasingly human. Anyway, this conclusion only applies while we are human individuals. I wanted to tell you, the world, or maybe just get it off my chest, that credit scores and AI are a combination of luck, error, power, and statically truish things that are often wrong or wildly wrong. And that they very truly threaten our sense of ourselves and of what it is to be autonomous and accountable, to make up and own our minds, to judge and be empowered, and to care about one another. I think if I can make that point, and you can accept that point, if only in part, that this will lessen the ill effects. The worst ill-effect is not that you tolerate the robots. It is that you start to think they are people.

If you cannot change the course of this world of technology, just do not buy into it too deeply. What you make of it is up to you. We are individuals, first, last, and always—so long as we remember it. We can know it even if the scores do not. Do not become that score. We can bitch if we want, try to fight it if we want, or just give in or look for the good things. There will always be an infinity of problems, and while for part of a lifetime some of us might postpone them, they will rise up and smite us. But we do not really have to be the stooges of technology. It will screw with us at times, and we will forget passwords, and we will get hacked. We will be separated from people. We will lose sleep. We will also use technology, save some time, make reservations, move money, and buy things in the middle of the night. AI might send us on some very good dates or get us movies that we like. Nevertheless, AI is blundering, thoughtless, clumsy, and often wrong. And there is nobody home. Literally nobody. It is nobody. You are somebody. All I ask is that you get it.

Keeping that in your mind, knowing something of this world is all I can offer. In addition, you only have it if you want to have it. Your sense of identity depends on your appreciating how assaulted it is and that you need to keep insisting on it. It was too easy for credit scores to replace us. You barely knew it. But now you know. If nothing else, I hope you can see how arbitrary your score is on a personal level, how information about you is vacuumed up with all kinds of holes put there by people and groups looking out for themselves and not you. You can see the regulators simply making it up as they go along, CRAs making it up as they go along, so they can go along longer. I doubt you can stop any of it. However, you can stop believing it.

APPENDIX 1

U.S. (and a little bit of European) law

Abstract

There are numerous laws in the United States regarding credit, repeated with many differences in every country with markets. This chapter attempts to say something about every important law in the United States that bears on the four categories of Making Loans, Collecting and Recording Debts, Managing Credit Report (including the most important law, the FCRA), and the complicated and probably lost cause of Data Privacy and Security. California in the United States and the European Union in its General Data Protection Regulation have outstripped Federal U.S. law in its attempt to protect consumer privacy, though I suspect they will make little difference.

There is quite a bit of law that has some impact on how we use credit to approve loans. This is a review of the law. Throughout the text, I tried to point out that it is only sometimes binding and understandable or current; but there are laws and the ultra-students of credit data would need to know it.

I divide categories of relevant law into four.

(1) Making Loans: modestly pertinent to our undertaking this project.
(2) Collecting and Recording Debts: minor relevance.
(3) Managing Credit Reporting: critical.
(4) Data Privacy and Security: a lost cause, but an important lost cause.

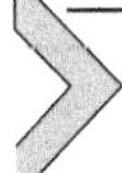

Making loans:

Truth in Lending Act (TILA, 1968)
Equal Credit Opportunity Act (ECOA, 1974)

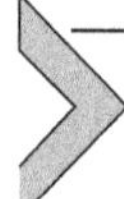

Collecting and recording debts:

Fair Credit Billing Act (FCBA, 1974)
Fair Debt Collection Practices Act (FDCPA, 1977)
Credit Card Accountability Responsibility Disclosure Act (CARD, 2009)

Managing credit reporting:

Fair Credit Reporting Act (FCRA, 1970) and amendments to this Act in
The Consumer Credit Reporting Reform Act (CCRA, 1996)
Fair and Accurate Credit Transactions Act (FACT Act, 2003)
Consumer Financial Protection Act (CFPA, 2010)
in Dodd–Frank Wall Street Reform and Consumer Protection ACT (2010)
Economic Growth, Regulatory Relief, and Consumer Protection Act
(Dodd–Frank Partial Repeal, 2018)

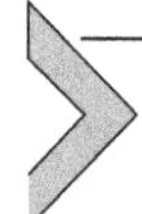

Data privacy and security:

Gramm–Leach–Bliley Act (GLB, 1999)
California Consumer Privacy Act (CCPA, 2018)

TILA

The Truth in Lending Act (TILA) was originally passed on May 29, 1968. Many of the titles that still govern how loans are made predate the internet—literally by decades. This Act supposedly helps customers know what they are agreeing to in a credit transaction, but creditors constantly improvise to keep borrowers confused. TILA created the APR (annual percentage rate) calculation, which requires businesses to disclose their exact credit terms, including monthly finance charges, annual interest rates, payment due dates, total sale prices, and how late charges are assessed and how much they are, and regulates how credit providers can advertise. This is intended to represent the *real* interest rate, assuming that all those fees are just disguised versions of the interest rate (which many are in fact). The APR was well-meaning, a single number that would somehow capture all the fees that particularly came with auto and home loans, but on many other sorts of loans as well.

Auto companies have long since found a way around it entirely, by offering what they call zero interest financing. Of course, there is really no such thing as zero interest financing. What they do is have two prices: one for people that finance at *zero* interest and a lower one, full of so-called discounts, for people who do not want (or need) this cheap financing. The discounts lost are the real interest cost of the loans, plus a risk cost because some loans will not get paid back. Home loan APRs are also deceptive because they assume a thirty-year mortgage when the average holding period is seven or less due to resales and refinances. I believe TILA meant well, but all it seems to have done was to force the profit-seeking financier to use some ingenuity when outsmarting that innocent, the consumer.

ECOA

The Equal Credit Opportunity Act (ECOA), 1974, requires that Credit companies not discriminate against an applicant based on race, color, religion, national origin, age, sex, or marital status—the so-called protected groups. The only justifiable basis for declining to extend credit are things like the applicant's financial status (earnings and savings) and credit record. Basically, a score or scorecard cannot have a factor based on membership in a protected group, nor can it even cause a "disparate [adverse] impact," on any of these groups unless there is a "business necessity" for it.

ECOA is implemented by something called Regulation B, which comes up in a few places relevant to credit data, models, and scores. When originally enacted, ECOA gave the Federal Reserve Board responsibility for Regulation B, but Dodd–Frank gave Regulation B and most consumer regulation to the Consumer Financial Protection Bureau (CFPB). What these regulations do mostly is create *model language*, paragraphs with some blanks in them to write corporate names or time periods, that corporations can include with other long boring language to get safe harbor from the law. In other words, regulations create bureaucracy that does not violate the spirit of the law but sometimes does not further it either: it is the stuff of lawyers. Each of our time is limited and who knows if this or that is important or what can we get away with ignoring. For firms in the businesses regulated, they gravitate to model language to avoid getting sued. Studying for this book, I learned that the reason we always strain to find four credit-related problems, some of which are completely minor and just ridiculous, like saying that the borrower has not borrowed enough money, is because at some time there was a model denial letter, which listed exactly four problems—now everybody copies that for safe harbor purposes.

It happens that ECOA affects us a good deal, affected me a good deal in my work life making models. That is because one thing we have to do is Fair Lending testing to make sure our models do not discriminate. Of course, we never discriminate on purpose, but many of the variables that predict delinquency and default also rise and fall for race, age, and sex. As far as I can see, it is a fairly nebulous where to draw the line. In the end, to have a predictive model means that the model will score one group a little higher on average because that group has lower down payments, higher incomes for the homes it buys, fewer missed payments on debts, and that is likely to correlate with demographics. Life is complicated.

FCBA

The Fair Credit Billing Act (FCBA) was passed originally in 1974 and is the companion of the Truth in Lending Act in that it tries to promise truth in billing. The customer is supposed to notify the credit provider within 60 days of an incorrect charge, and the credit company must respond within 30 days. It sounds good but is incredibly slow for the internet age. Failure of a creditor to comply will result in a $50 credit toward the disputed amount—that is just not a serious sum.

CARD Act

Makes credit cards a little bit simpler and less complex.

FCRA

The Fair Debt Collection Practices Act was originally passed in 1970 and amended by the Consumer Credit Reporting Reform Act of 1996 (which filled in numerous details); the Fair and Accurate Credit Transactions Act of 2003, which also tried to address new internet issues such as fraud and identify theft; and a host of smaller-effect bills. The FCRA defined the landscape of credit in the United States, collecting it, selling it for almost anything where someone would want to know the consumer is likely to pay them, sending credit reports to anyone with permissible purpose (read on) as well as the consumer, allowing credit scores to be estimated and sent with the credit report, helping credit card companies to send mailings, and to be there for hackers to take a crack at. The law in 1970 had much of the flavor it does now, but it has been amended numerous times. It is by far the most important single law for this book, though also toothless and ignored in many details. The preamble of the FCRA begins (paragraph 602):

> *The banking system is dependent upon fair and accurate credit reporting... An elaborate mechanism has been developed for investigating and evaluating the credit worthiness, credit standing, credit capacity, character, and general reputation of consumers... Consumer reporting agencies have assumed a vital role in assembling and evaluating consumer credit and other information on consumers.*

According to the preamble, Congress is entering an issue already in place. I think the FCRA may have frozen that world. In 1970, some companies were already reporting voluntarily to what would become the national CRAs (Consumer Reporting Agencies) because they had the resources and motivation to report. At the time, there were relatively few and small computers, there was no internet, and there was no simple way to do peer to peer communications. Computerization was just beginning. It was the Bureau Age. Consumers certainly had little to no say over it: how would you even consult them? Landlords did not report (and still rarely do). Utility companies rarely reported (and still rarely report). Thus, people who bought services with their own money were very infrequently able to build a reputation for honesty or self-sufficiency (and still are). It is understandable that this was true then: what is odd is that data collecting has changed so little, and the law around it has changed so little, while technology has evolved enormously.

The last sentence of the preamble: "The Fair Credit Reporting Act (FCRA) is designed to help ensure that CRAs (including credit bureaus and credit reporting companies) furnish correct and complete information to businesses to use when evaluating your application for credit, or insurance, or to employers or prospective employers." What complete meant at the time, basically that what was reported was reported correctly, is far from what I think we ought to mean by complete now. The credit and contract history available through the national CRAs are decidedly *incomplete*, in that they mostly only tell us about money-renting. However, there are lots of things people buy and do today that show steady promise-keeping. Additionally, as I point out in several chapters, there is deliberate suppression of the payment data. Last, there is credit score: by being confusing, it demotivates anyone from trying to get their data correct: what should they change?

The FCRA is implemented by Regulation V, originally written by the Federal Reserve but put in the hands of the CFPB as part of Dodd—Frank. It happens that I know some of the economists at CFPB who work on credit. Well-meaning people, but I am not impressed with their insight or independence: they are just trying to keep their jobs.

In general, credit scoring is a wicked curve ball for the disclosure front. It is impossible to know what in all that is disclosed is causing the consumer to get an insufficient score: as one who has made credit scores I can tell you it is a terrible lot of trouble even for the modelers who worked on a score to figure it out for any particular case.

Prospective creditors have few responsibilities, but they do need a "permissible purpose" to see a credit report; but this is pretty broad. If the consumer initiates a potential business transaction with almost any party, that party can get the consumer's credit report. Except for employment purposes, there is no requirement that the other company or person gets the consumer's permission. However, most companies will let the consumer know they are seeking the credit report, and whether they let the consumer know or not, it will appear on the credit report and be available for the consumer to see assuming he or she exercises his or her disclosure rights. If the prospective credit can get the credit report, they can get a credit score to interpret it.

Here is a small part of the sections on permissible purpose [which are unreadable by normal people, but here they are, in part]:

LII U.S. Code Title 15. COMMERCE AND TRADE Chapter1. CONSUMER CREDIT PROTECTION Subchapter III. CREDIT REPORTING AGENCIES Section 1681b. Permissible purposes of consumer reports

15 U.S. Code § 1681b. Permissible purposes of consumer reports

(a) In general Subject to subsection (c), any consumer reporting agency may furnish a consumer report under the following circumstances and no other:
    (1) In response to the order of a court having jurisdiction to issue such an order, or a subpoena issued in connection with proceedings before a Federal grand jury.
    (2) In accordance with the written instructions of the consumer to whom it relates.
    (3) To a person which it has reason to believe—
        (A) Intends to use the information in connection with a credit transaction involving the consumer on whom the information is to be furnished and involving the extension of credit to, or review or collection of an account of, the consumer; or

(B) Intends to use the information for employment purposes; or
(C) Intends to use the information in connection with the underwriting of insurance involving the consumer; or
(D) Intends to use the information in connection with a determination of the consumer's eligibility for a license or other benefit granted by a governmental instrumentality required by law to consider an applicant's financial responsibility or status; or
(E) Intends to use the information, as a potential investor or servicer, or current insurer, in connection with a valuation of, or an assessment of the credit or prepayment risks associated with, an existing credit obligation; or
(F) otherwise has a legitimate business need for the information—
(i) In connection with a business transaction that is initiated by the consumer; or
(ii) to review an account to determine whether the consumer continues to meet the terms of the account.
(G) executive departments and agencies in connection with the issuance of government-sponsored individually-billed travel charge cards.
(4) In response to a request by the head of a State or local child support enforcement agency (or a State or local government official authorized by the head of such an agency), if the person making the request certifies to the consumer reporting agency that—
(A) the consumer report is needed for the purpose of establishing an individual's capacity to make child support payments, determining the appropriate level of such payments, or enforcing a child support order, award, agreement, or judgment;
(B) the parentage of the consumer for the child to which the obligation relates has been established or acknowledged by the consumer in accordance with State laws under which the obligation arises (if required by those laws); ...
(b) Conditions for furnishing and using consumer reports for employment purposes
(1) Certification from user: A consumer reporting agency may furnish a consumer report for employment purposes only if—
(A) the person who obtains such report from the agency certifies to the agency that—
(i) the person has complied with paragraph (2) with respect to the consumer report, and the person will comply with paragraph (3) with respect to the consumer report if paragraph (3) becomes applicable; and
(ii) Information from the consumer report will not be used in violation of any applicable Federal or State equal employment opportunity law or regulation; and

(B) the consumer reporting agency provides with the report, or has previously provided, a summary of the consumer's rights under this subchapter, as prescribed by the Bureau under section 1681g(c)(3) [1] of this title.

(2) Disclosure to consumer

(A) In general

Except as provided in subparagraph (B), a person may not procure a consumer report, or cause a consumer report to be procured, for employment purposes with respect to any consumer, unless—

(i) a clear and conspicuous disclosure has been made in writing to the consumer at any time before the report is procured or caused to be procured, in a document that consists solely of the disclosure, that a consumer report may be obtained for employment purposes; and

(ii) the consumer has authorized in writing (which authorization may be made on the document referred to in clause (i)) the procurement of the report by that person. ...

(1) In general A consumer reporting agency may furnish a consumer report relating to any consumer pursuant to subparagraph (A) or (C) of subsection (a)(3) in connection with any credit or insurance transaction that is not initiated by the consumer only if—

(A) the consumer authorizes the agency to provide such report to such person; or

(B) (i) the transaction consists of a firm offer of credit or insurance;

(ii) the consumer reporting agency has complied with subsection (e);

(iii) there is not in effect an election by the consumer, made in accordance with subsection (e), to have the consumer's name and address excluded from lists of names provided by the agency pursuant to this paragraph; and

(iv) the consumer report does not contain a date of birth that shows that the consumer has not attained the age of 21, or, if the date of birth on the consumer report shows that the consumer has not attained the age of 21, such consumer consents to the consumer reporting agency to such furnishing. ...

(e) Election of consumer to be excluded from lists

(1) In general

A consumer may elect to have the consumer's name and address excluded from any list provided by a consumer reporting agency under subsection (c)(1)(B) in connection with a credit or insurance transaction that is not initiated by the consumer, by notifying the agency in accordance with paragraph (2) that the consumer does not consent to any use of a consumer report relating to the consumer in connection with any credit or insurance transaction that is not initiated by the consumer....

(A) In general

Each consumer reporting agency that, under subsection (c)(1)(B), furnishes a consumer report in connection with a credit or insurance transaction that is not initiated by a consumer, shall—

(i) establish and maintain a notification system, including a toll-free telephone number, which permits any consumer whose consumer report is maintained by the agency to notify the agency, with appropriate identification, of the consumer's election to have the consumer's name and address excluded from any such list of names and addresses provided by the agency for such a transaction;...

(2) Limitation on creditors

Except as permitted pursuant to paragraph (3)(C) or regulations prescribed under paragraph (5)(A), a creditor shall not obtain or use medical information (other than medical information treated in the manner required under section 1681c(a)(6) of this title) pertaining to a consumer in connection with any determination of the consumer's eligibility, or continued eligibility, for credit....

(4) Limitation on redisclosure of medical information

Any person that receives medical information pursuant to paragraph (1) or (3) shall not disclose such information to any other person, except as necessary to carry out the purpose for which the information was initially disclosed, or as otherwise permitted by statute, regulation, or order.

Besides all this, there is still another way that creditors can get at consumer credit reports. For credit and insurance transactions, an anonymized CRA request can be made without permission of the borrower, for making a "firm offer of credit or insurance." A firm offer of credit or insurance may well not be anything you wish to receive. Additionally, there are no limits beyond those that pertain to all cards and insurance what it costs to accept this offer, what the credit limits are, what the delinquency costs are, what taking the credit will do to your credit score, and so. Companies can just vacuum up your data, credit score it, and send you ads, without asking your permission. Now there is a way to stop it, which is supposed to work. Borrowers can "be excluded from the [anonymized marketing] lists" 64 (e) "by notifying the agency...through the notification system maintained by the agency" or with "a signed notice of election." This rarely happens though, probably because it means consumers will not get ads for credit cards that lower their rates, raise their limits, or give points or money back for use. As much as we complain, we apparently want to see the offers. If I am wrong, please opt out.

Gramm–Leach–Bliley Act (GLB, 1999)

GLB has a section dealing with privacy that I think is relevant. It seems to only concern "financial institutions," which is pretty broadly defined, but does not cover Facebook, Google, Amazon, and countless smaller web sites. GLB requires every financial institution to have a policy in place to protect nonpublic information from foreseeable threats in security and data integrity. That is, these companies are supposed to prevent breaches of data held about consumers that identifies them. Did this work? I am afraid I think breaches are inevitable.

Per *Wikipedia*[1]:

> *The Financial Privacy Rule [also] requires* financial institutions *to provide each consumer with a privacy notice at the time the consumer relationship is established and annually thereafter. The privacy notice must explain the information collected about the consumer, where that information is shared, how that information is used, and how that information is protected. The notice must also identify the consumer's right to opt out of the information being shared with unaffiliated parties pursuant to the provisions of the Fair Credit Reporting Act [which you cannot opt out of]. Should the privacy policy change at any point in time, the consumer must be notified again for acceptance. Each time the privacy notice is reestablished, the consumer has the right to opt out again….*

It does not work.

California Consumer Privacy Act (CCPA, 2018)

The CCPA, passed in 2018, extends California's reach into privacy law. CCPA grants consumers the right to know what information companies are collecting about them, why they are collecting that data and with whom they are sharing it. It gives consumers the right to tell companies to delete their information as well as to not sell or share their data. Businesses must still give consumers who opt out the same quality of service. The California Consumer Privacy Act is certainly influenced by Europe's General Data Protection law, though weaker than that. Will it work? Can it work? I doubt it.

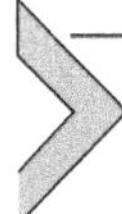

General Data Protection Regulation, European Union, effective May 2018

Why mention a law that is not even in this country? One reason is that the multi-national internet companies, and financial companies, will probably want to minimize the number of ways they do business, and so will have a tendency to conform to this law in the United States as well. That is, it will have an effect on the United States similar to California's effect. However, the second reason is that the United States, led by California, seems headed that way anyway.

The GDPR is described by *Wikipedia*[2] as follows:

Business processes that handle personal data must be built with *data protection by design and by default*, meaning that personal data must be stored using pseudonymization or full anonymization, and use the highest-possible using privacy settings by default, so that the data is not available publicly without explicit, informed consent, and cannot be used to identify a subject without additional information stored separately. No personal data may be processed unless it is done under a lawful basis specified by the regulation, or if the data controller or processor has received an unambiguous and individualized affirmation of consent from the data subject. The data subject has the right to revoke this consent at any time.

A processor of personal data must clearly disclose any data collection, declare the lawful basis and purpose for data processing, how long data is being retained, and if it is being shared with any third-parties or outside of the EU. Data subjects have the right to request a copy of the data collected by a processor in a common format, and the right to have their data erased under certain circumstances. Public authorities, and businesses whose core activities center around regular or systematic processing of personal data, are required to employ a *data protection officer* (DPO), who is responsible for managing compliance with the GDPR. Businesses must report any data breaches within 72 hours if they have an adverse effect on user privacy.

This is in general moving to put the consumer in charge of their data. But I would not underestimate the power of corporations to get consumers to see things their way and share their private data—largely by confusing and overwhelming consumers. I think general data policy is a lot like credit scores—too much to deal with. However, the wrestling match over rights is at least well underway with the GDPR.

Endnotes

[1] The *Wikipedia* entry for the Gramm—Leach—Bliley Act, last edited on July 22, 2019 and reviewed by me on July 27 2019, is at www.en.Wikipedia.org/wiki/Gramm%E2%80%93Leach%E2%80%93Bliley_Act.

[2] The *Wikipedia* entry on Europe's General Data Protection Regulation was last edited on July 27, 2019 and reviewed by me on that same date. Its URL is www.en.Wikipedia.org/wiki/General_Data_Protection_Regulation.

APPENDIX 2

Final rule on credit scores from FHFA

PART 1254—Validation and approval of credit score models

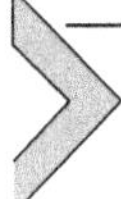

§ 1254.1 Purpose and scope

(a) *The purpose of this part is to set forth standards and criteria for the process an Enterprise must establish to validate and approve any credit score model that produces any credit score that the Enterprise requires in its mortgage purchase procedures and systems.*

(b) *The validation and approval process for a credit score model includes the following phases: Solicitation of Applications, Submission of Applications and Initial Review, Credit Score Assessment, and Enterprise Business Assessment....*

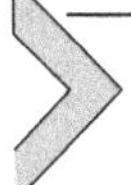

§ 1254.4 Requirements for use of a credit score

(a) *Enterprise use of a credit score. An Enterprise is not required to use a credit score for any business purpose. However, if an Enterprise conditions its purchase of a mortgage on the provision of a credit score for the borrower:*
   (1) *The credit score must be derived from a credit score model that has been approved by the Enterprise in accordance with this part and*
   (2) *The Enterprise must provide for the use of the credit score by any automated underwriting system that uses a credit score and any other procedures and systems used by the Enterprise that use a credit score for mortgage purchases.*

(b) *Replacement of credit score model. An Enterprise may replace any credit score model then in use after a new credit score model has been approved in accordance with this part.*
(c) *No right to continuing use. Enterprise use of a particular credit score model does not create any right to or expectation of continuing, future, or permanent use of that credit score model by an Enterprise.*

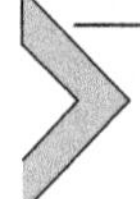

§ 1254.5 Solicitation of applications

(a) *Required solicitations. FHFA periodically will require the Enterprises to solicit applications from credit score model developers. FHFA will determine whether a solicitation should be initiated. FHFA will establish the solicitation requirement by notice to the Enterprises, which will include:*
 (1) *The requirement to submit a Credit Score Solicitation to FHFA for review;*
 (2) *A deadline for submission of the Credit Score Solicitation; and*
 (3) *A timeframe for the solicitation period.*
(b) *Credit Score Solicitation. In connection with each required solicitation, an Enterprise must submit to FHFA a Credit Score Solicitation including:*
 (1) *The opening and closing dates of the solicitation time period during which the Enterprise will accept applications from credit score model developers;*
 (2) *A description of the information that must be submitted with an application;*
 (3) *A description of the process by which the Enterprise will obtain data for the assessment of the credit score model;*
 (4) *A description of the process for the Credit Score Assessment and the Enterprise Business Assessment; and*
 (5) *Any other requirements as determined by the Enterprise.*
(c) *Review by FHFA. Within 45 days of an Enterprise submission of its Credit Score Solicitation to FHFA, FHFA will either approve or disapprove the Enterprise's Credit Score Solicitation. FHFA may extend the time period for its review as needed.*

FHFA may impose such terms, conditions, or limitations on the approval of a Credit Score Solicitation as FHFA determines to be appropriate.

(d) *Publication. Upon approval by FHFA, the Enterprise must publish the Credit Score Solicitation on its website for at least 90 days prior to the start of the solicitation time period.*
(e) *Initial solicitation. Each Enterprise must submit its initial Credit Score Solicitation to FHFA within 60 days of the effective date of this regulation. The initial solicitation time period will begin on a date determined by FHFA and will extend for 120 days.*

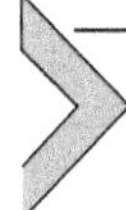

§ 1254.6 Submission and initial review of applications

(a) *Application requirements. Each application submitted in response to a Credit Score Solicitation must meet the requirements set forth in the Credit Score Solicitation to which it responds. Each application must include the following elements, and any additional requirements that may be set forth in the Credit Score Solicitation:*
   (1) *Application fee. Each application must include an application fee established by the Enterprise. An Enterprise may address conditions for refunding a portion of a fee in the Credit Score Solicitation. The application fee is intended to cover the direct costs to the Enterprise of conducting the Credit Score Assessment.*
   (2) *Fair lending certification and compliance. Each application must address compliance of the credit score model and credit scores produced by it with federal fair lending requirements, including information on any fair lending testing and evaluation of the model conducted. Each application must include a certification that no characteristic that is based directly on or is highly correlated solely with a classification prohibited under the Equal Credit Opportunity Act (15 U.S.C. 1691(a) (1)), the Fair Housing Act (42 U.S.C. 3605(a)), or the Safety and Soundness Act (12 U.S.C. 4545(1)) was used in the development of the credit score model or is used as a factor in the credit score model to produce credit scores.*
   (3) *Use of model by industry. Each application must demonstrate use of the credit score by creditors to make a decision whether to extend credit to a prospective borrower. An Enterprise may address criteria for such demonstration in the Credit Score Solicitation. An Enterprise may permit such demonstration of use to include submission of testimonials by creditors (mortgage or non-mortgage) who use the applicant's credit score when making a determination to approve the extension of credit.*
   (4) *Qualification of credit score model developer. Each application must include any information that an Enterprise may require to evaluate the credit score model developer (i.e., relevant experience and financial capacity). Such information must include a detailed description of the credit score model developer's:*
      (i) *Corporate structure, including any business relationship to any other person through any degree of common ownership or control;*
      (ii) *Governance structure; and*
      (iii) *Past financial performance.*
   (5) *Other requirements. Each application must include any other information an Enterprise may require.*

(b) *Historical consumer credit data. An Enterprise may obtain any historical consumer credit data necessary for the Enterprise to test a credit score model's historical record of measuring and predicting default rates and other credit behaviors. An Enterprise may assess the applicant for any costs associated with obtaining or receiving such data unless such costs were included in the up-front application fee.*

(c) *Acceptance of applications. Each application submitted in response to a Credit Score Solicitation within the solicitation time period must be reviewed for acceptance by the Enterprise.*

(1) *Notice of status. Within 60 days of an applicant's submission, the Enterprise must provide the applicant with an Application Status Notice, which will indicate whether the application requires additional information to be provided by the applicant. An applicant may submit additional information through the end of the solicitation period.*

(2) *Complete application. Completeness of an application will be determined by the Enterprise. An application is complete when an Enterprise determines that required information has been received by the Enterprise from the applicant and from any third party. Information from a third party for a specific application may be received by the Enterprise after the solicitation period closes. The Enterprise must notify the applicant upon determining that the application is complete with a Complete Application Notice.*

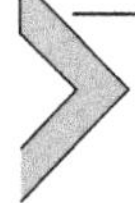

§ 1254.7 Credit Score Assessment

(a) *Requirement for Credit Score Assessment. An Enterprise will undertake a Credit Score Assessment of each application that the Enterprise determines to be complete. An Enterprise must determine whether an application passes the Credit Score Assessment.*

(b) *Testing for Credit Score Assessment. An Enterprise must conduct statistical tests for accuracy and reliability that use one or more industry standard statistical tests for demonstrating divergence among borrowers' propensity to repay using the industry standard definition of default, applied to mortgages purchased by an Enterprise (including subgroups), as identified by the Enterprise.*

(c) *Criteria for Credit Score Assessment. The Credit Score Assessment is based on the following criteria:*

(1) *Testing for accuracy. A credit score model is accurate if it produces a credit score that appropriately reflects a borrower's propensity to repay a mortgage loan in accordance with its terms, permitting a credit score user to rank order the risk that the borrower will not repay the obligation in accordance with its terms relative to other borrowers.*

(i) *Initial Credit Score Assessment. For the Credit Score Assessment of applications submitted in response to the initial solicitation under § 1254.5(e), a credit score model meets the test for accuracy if it produces credit scores that meet a benchmark established by the Enterprise in the initial Credit Score Solicitation, as demonstrated by appropriate testing.*

(ii) *Subsequent Credit Score Assessments. For the Credit Score Assessment of applications submitted in response to any later solicitation under this part, a credit score model meets the test for accuracy if it produces credit scores that are more accurate than the credit scores produced by any credit score model that is required by the Enterprise at the time the test is conducted, as demonstrated by appropriate testing.*

(2) *Testing for reliability. A credit score model is reliable if it produces credit scores that maintain accuracy through the economic cycle. The Credit Score Assessment must evaluate whether a new credit score model produces credit scores that are at least as reliable as the credit scores produced by any credit score model that is required by the Enterprise at the time the test is conducted, as demonstrated by appropriate testing.*

Testing for reliability must demonstrate accuracy at a minimum of two points in the economic cycle when applied to mortgages purchased by an Enterprise (including subgroups), as identified by the Enterprise.

(3) *Testing for integrity. A credit score model has integrity if, when producing a credit score, it uses relevant data that reasonably encompasses the borrower's credit history and financial performance. The Credit Score Assessment must evaluate whether a credit score model applicant has demonstrated that the model has integrity, based on appropriate testing or requirements identified by the Enterprise (which may address, for example, the level of aggregation of data or whether observable data has been omitted or discounted when producing a credit score).*

(4) *Other requirements. An Enterprise may establish requirements for the Credit Score Assessment in addition to the criteria established by FHFA.*

(c) *Third-party testing. Testing required for the Credit Score Assessment may be conducted by:*

(1) *An Enterprise or*

(2) *An independent third party selected or approved by an Enterprise.*

(d) *Timing of Credit Score Assessment. (1) An Enterprise must notify the applicant when the Enterprise begins the Credit Score Assessment. The Credit Score Assessment will begin no earlier than the close of the solicitation time period, unless FHFA has determined that an Enterprise should begin a Credit Score Assessment sooner.*

The Credit Score Assessment will extend for 180 days. FHFA may authorize not more than two extensions of time for the Credit Score Assessment, which shall not exceed 30 days each, upon a written request and showing of good cause by the Enterprise.

(2) *An Enterprise must provide notice to the applicant within 30 days of a determination that the application has passed the Credit Score Assessment.*

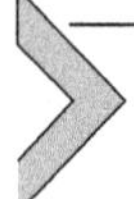

§ 1254.8 Enterprise Business Assessment

(a) *Requirement for Enterprise Business Assessment. An Enterprise will undertake an Enterprise Business Assessment of each application that the Enterprise determines to have passed the Credit Score Assessment. An Enterprise must determine whether an application passes the Enterprise Business Assessment.*

(b) *Criteria for Enterprise Business Assessment. The Enterprise Business Assessment is based on the following criteria:*

  (1) *Accuracy; reliability. The Enterprise Business Assessment must evaluate whether a new credit score model produces credit scores that are more accurate than and at least as reliable as credit scores produced by any credit score model currently in use by the Enterprise. This evaluation must consider credit scores as used by the Enterprise within its systems or processes that use a credit score for mortgage purchases.*

  (2) *Fair lending assessment. The Enterprise Business Assessment must evaluate the fair lending risk and fair lending impact of the credit score model in accordance with standards and requirements related to the Equal Credit Opportunity Act (15 U.S.C. 1691(a) (1)), the Fair Housing Act (42 U.S.C. 3605(a)), and the Safety and Soundness Act (12 U.S.C. 4545(1)) (including identification of potential impact, comparison of the new credit score model with any credit score model currently in use, and consideration of potential methods of using the new credit score model). This evaluation must consider credit scores as used by the Enterprise within its systems or processes that use a credit score for mortgage purchases. The fair lending assessment must also consider any impact on access to credit related to the use of a particular credit score model.*

  (3) *Impact on Enterprise operations and risk management, and impact on industry. The Enterprise Business Assessment must evaluate the impact using the credit score model would have on Enterprise operations (including any impact on purchase eligibility criteria and loan pricing) and risk management (including counterparty risk management) in accordance with standards and requirements related to prudential management and operations and governance set forth at parts 1236 and 1239 of this chapter. This evaluation must consider whether the benefits of using credit scores produced by that model can reasonably be expected to exceed the adoption and ongoing costs of using such credit scores, considering projected benefits and costs to the Enterprises. The Enterprise Business Assessment must evaluate the impact of using the credit score model on industry operations and mortgage market liquidity, including costs associated with implementation of a newly approved credit score. This evaluation must consider whether the benefits of using credit scores produced by that model can reasonably be expected to exceed the adoption and ongoing costs of using such credit scores, considering projected benefits and costs to the Enterprises and borrowers, including market liquidity and cost and availability of credit.*

(4) *Competitive effects. The Enterprise Business Assessment must evaluate whether using the credit score model could have an impact on competition in the industry. This evaluation must consider whether use of a credit score model could have an impact on competition due to any ownership or other business relationship between the credit score model developer and any other institution.*

(5) *Third-Party Provider Review. The Enterprise Business Assessment must evaluate the credit score model developer under the Enterprise standards for approval of third-party providers.*

(6) *Other requirements. An Enterprise may establish requirements for the Enterprise Business Assessment in addition to the criteria established by FHFA.*

(c) *Timing of Enterprise Business Assessment. The Enterprise Business Assessment must be completed within 240 days.*

(d) *FHFA Evaluation. FHFA will conduct an independent analysis of the potential impacts of any change to an Enterprise's credit score model. FHFA will initiate its analysis no later than the beginning of the Enterprise Business Assessment. Based on its analysis, FHFA may:*

(1) *Require an Enterprise to undertake additional analysis, monitoring, or reporting to further the purposes of this part;*

(2) *Require an Enterprise to permit the use of a single credit score model or multiple credit score models; or*

(3) *Require any other change to an Enterprise program, policy, or practice related to the Enterprise's use of credit scores.*

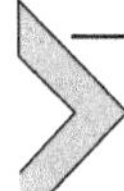

§ 1254.9 Determinations on applications

(a) *Enterprise determinations subject to prior review and approval by FHFA. An Enterprise must submit to FHFA a proposed determination of approval or disapproval for each application. Within 45 days of an Enterprise submission, FHFA must approve or disapprove the Enterprise's proposed determination. FHFA may extend the time period for its review as needed. FHFA may impose such terms, conditions, or limitations on the approval or disapproval of the Enterprise's proposed determination as FHFA determines to be appropriate.*

(b) *Approval of a credit score model. If an Enterprise approves an application for a credit score model following FHFA review of its proposed determination, the Enterprise must implement the credit score model in its mortgage purchase systems that use a credit score for mortgage purchases. The Enterprise must provide written notice to the applicant and the public within 30 days after the FHFA decision on the proposed determination.*

(c) *Disapproval of a credit score model. If an Enterprise disapproves an application for a credit score model following FHFA review of its proposed determination, the Enterprise must provide written notice to the applicant within 30 days after the FHFA decision on the proposed determination. An application may be disapproved under this section at any time during the validation and approval process based on any of the criteria identified in the Credit Score Solicitation. The notice to the applicant must provide a description of the reasons for disapproval.*

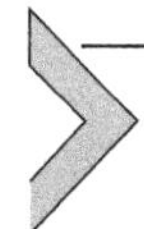

§ 1254.10 Withdrawal of application

At any time during the validation and approval process, an applicant may withdraw its application by notifying an Enterprise. The Enterprise may, in its sole discretion, determine whether to return any portion of the application fee paid by the applicant.

§ 1254.11 Pilot programs

(a) *Pilots permitted; duration of pilots. An Enterprise may undertake pilot programs to evaluate credit score models. If a pilot program involves a credit score model not in current use by an Enterprise, the credit score model is not required to be approved under this part.*
(b) *Prior notice to FHFA. Before commencing a pilot program, an Enterprise must submit the proposed pilot program to FHFA for review and approval. The Enterprise's submission to FHFA must include a complete and specific description of the pilot program, including its purpose, duration, and scope. FHFA may impose such terms, conditions, or limitations on the pilot program as FHFA determines to be appropriate.*

Date: August 13, 2019

Mark A. Calabria,

Director, Federal Housing Finance Agency.

As I understand it, this could only apply to large companies that have already established themselves in the businesses of large creditors. There are two companies that have done so, FICO and Vantage. FICO has been in the United States for decades and holds sway in the mortgage market, though rather old versions of FICO are used, ones that differ a good deal from CRA to CRA on the same person. Vantage does not have the same degree of variability but is wholly owned by the three CRAs together, another example of how the three work together, though they are presumably separate companies.

APPENDIX 3

Attachment: My credit report

EQUIFAX

CREDIT REPORT
ERIC ROSENBLATT
Report Confirmation
7796594480

Summary

Review this summary for a quick view of key information contained in your Equifax Credit Report.

Report Date	Oct 23, 2017
Credit File Status	No fraud indicator on file
Alert Contacts	0 Records Found
Average Account Age	10 Years, 9 Months
Length of Credit History	17 Years
Accounts with Negative Information	0
Oldest Account	CITICARDS CBNA (Opened Oct 01, 2000)
Most Recent Account	BANK OF AMERICA (Opened Nov 15, 2014)

Credit accounts

Your credit report includes information about activity on your credit accounts that may affect your credit score and rating.

Account Type	Open	With balance	Total balance	Available	Credit limit	Debt-to-credit	Payment
Revolving	2	1	$47	$36,953	$37,000	0.0%	$27
Mortgage	1	0	$0	$70,000	$70,000	0.0%	$0
Installment	0	0					
Other							
Total	3	1	$47	$106,953	$107,000	0.0%	$27

Summary > Revolving > Mortgage > Installment > Other > Statements > Personal Info > Inquiries > Public Records > Collections

Other items

Your credit report includes your Personal Information and, if applicable, Consumer Statements and could include other items that may affect your credit score and rating.

Consumer Statements	0 Statements Found
Personal Information	8 Items Found
Inquiries	1 Inquiries Found
Public Records	0 Records Found
Collections	0 Collections Found

Summary Revolving Mortgage Installment Other Statements Personal Info Inquiries Public Records Collections

Revolving accounts

Revolving accounts are those that generally include a credit limit and require a minimum monthly payment, such as credit cards.

Chase card

Summary

Your debt-to-credit ratio represents the amount of credit you're using and generally makes up a percentage of your credit score. It's calculated by dividing an account's reported balance by its credit limit.

Account number		Reported balance	$0
Account Status	PAYS_AS_AGREED	Debt-to-Credit Ratio	0%
Available Credit	$27,000		

Account history

The tables below show up to 2 years of the monthly balance, available credit, scheduled payment, date of last payment, high credit, credit limit, amount past due, activity designator, and comments.

Balance

Year	Jan	Feb	Mar	Apr	May	Jun	Jul	Aug	Sep	Oct	Nov	Dec
2015										$3,985	$2,051	
2016	$4,074	$2,172	$3,614	$4,295	$4,449	$6,532	$1,441	$6,125	$329	$4,768		$610
2017	$2,837	$3,529	$3,025		$4,750	$1,890	$3,514	$4,769	$8,722			
Available Credit												
2015												
2016												
2017												
Scheduled Payment												
2015										$39		
										$25		
2016										$40		
										$25		
										$36		
										$42		
										$44		
										$65		
										$25		
										$61		
										$25		
										$47		
										$25		

2017										$28 $35 $30 $47 $25 $35 $47 $87		

Actual payment

Year	Jan	Feb	Mar	Apr	May	Jun	Jul	Aug	Sep	Oct	Nov	Dec
2015												
2016												
2017												
High Credit												
2015										$14,792	$14,792	
2016	$14,792	$14,792	$14,792	$14,792	$14,792	$14,792	$14,792	$14,792	$14,792	$14,792		$14,792
2017	$14,792	$14,792	$14,792		$14,792	$14,792	$14,792	$14,792	$14,792			
Credit Limit												
2015										$20,000	$20,000	
2016	$20,000	$20,000	$20,000	$20,000	$20,000	$20,000	$20,000	$20,000	$20,000	$20,000		$27,000
2017	$27,000	$27,000	$27,000		$27,000	$27,000	$27,000	$27,000	$27,000			
Amount Past Due												
2015												
2016												
2017												

Activity designator

Year	Jan	Feb	Mar	Apr	May	Jun	Jul	Aug	Sep	Oct	Nov	Dec
2015												
2016												
2017												

Payment history

View up to 7 years of monthly payment history on this account. The numbers indicated in each month represent the number of days a payment was past due; the letters indicate other account events, such as bankruptcy or collections.

EQUIFAX

Summary Revolving Mortgage Installment Other Statements Personal Info Inquiries Public Records Collections

Year	Jan	Feb	Mar	Apr	May	Jun	Jul	Aug	Sep	Oct	Nov	Dec
2017	✓	✓	✓	✓	✓	✓	✓	✓	✓			
2016	✓	✓	✓	✓	✓	✓	✓	✓	✓	✓	✓	✓
2015	✓	✓	✓	✓	✓	✓	✓	✓	✓	✓	✓	✓
2014	✓	✓	✓	✓	✓	✓	✓	✓	✓	✓	✓	✓
2013										✓	✓	✓

✓ Paid on Time | 30 30 Days Past Due | 60 60 Days Past Due | 90 90 Days Past Due | 120 120 Days Past Due

150 150 Days Past Due | 180 180 Days Past Due | V Voluntary Surrender | F Foreclosure | C Collection Account

CO Charge-Off | B Included in Bankruptcy | R Repossession | TN Too New to Rate | No Data Available

Account details

View detailed information about this account. Contact the creditor or lender if you have any questions about it.

High Credit	$20,100	**Owner**	INDIVIDUAL
Credit Limit	$27,000	**Account Type**	REVOLVING
Terms Frequency	MONTHLY	**Term Duration**	0
Balance	$0	**Date Opened**	Nov 18, 2011
Amount Past Due		**Date Reported**	Oct 18, 2017
Actual Payment Amount		**Date of Last Payment**	Oct 01, 2017
Date of Last Activity		**Scheduled Payment Amount**	
Months Reviewed	70	**Delinquency First Reported**	
Activity Designator		**Creditor Classification**	UNKNOWN
Deferred Payment Start Date		**Charge Off Amount**	
Balloon Payment Date		**Balloon Payment Amount**	
Loan Type	Flexible Spending Credit Card	**Date Closed**	
Date of First Delinquency			

EQUIFAX

Summary | Revolving | Mortgage | Installment | Other | Statements | Personal Info | Inquiries | Public Records | Collections

Comments

Contact
CHASE CARD
PO Box 15298
Wilmington, DE 19850-5298
1-800-432-3117

Barclays bank delaware

Summary

Your debt-to-credit ratio represents the amount of credit you're using and generally makes up a percentage of your credit score. It's calculated by dividing an account's reported balance by its credit limit.

Account Number		**Reported Balance**	$47
Account Status	PAYS_AS_AGREED	**Debt-to-Credit Ratio**	0%
Available Credit	$10,000		

Account history

The tables below show up to 2 years of the monthly balance, available credit, scheduled payment, date of last payment, high credit, credit limit, amount past due, activity designator, and comments.

Balance

Year	Jan	Feb	Mar	Apr	May	Jun	Jul	Aug	Sep	Oct	Nov	Dec
2015										$37	$22	
2016			$139	$278		$25	$2					$110
2017		$893				$136	$200	$2	$0			
Available Credit												
2015												
2016												
2017												
Scheduled Payment												
2015										$27	$22	
2016			$27	$27		$25	$2					$27
2017		$27				$27	$27	$2				
Actual Payment												
2015										$916		
2016			$22		$278							
2017					$893	$136	$200	$2				

High Credit

2015								$5,728	$5,728	
2016		$5,728	$5,728	$5,728	$5,728					$5,728
2017	$5,728			$5,728	$5,728	$5,728	$5,728			

Credit Limit

2015								$10,000	$10,000	
2016		$10,000	$10,000	$10,000	$10,000					$10,000
2017	$10,000			$10,000	$10,000	$10,000	$10,000			

Amount Past Due

2015	
2016	
2017	

Activity designator

Year	Jan	Feb	Mar	Apr	May	Jun	Jul	Aug	Sep	Oct	Nov	Dec
2015												
2016												
2017												

Payment history

View up to 7 years of monthly payment history on this account. The numbers indicated in each month represent the number of days a payment was past due; the letters indicate other account events, such as bankruptcy or collections.

Year	Jan	Feb	Mar	Apr	May	Jun	Jul	Aug	Sep	Oct	Nov	Dec
2017	✓	✓	✓	✓	✓	✓	✓	✓	✓			
2016	✓	✓	✓	✓	✓	✓	✓	✓	✓	✓	✓	✓
2015	✓	✓	✓	✓	✓	✓	✓	✓	✓	✓	✓	✓
2014	✓	✓	✓	✓	✓	✓	✓	✓	✓	✓	✓	✓
2013										✓	✓	✓

✓ Paid on Time 30 30 Days Past Due 60 60 Days Past Due 90 90 Days Past Due 120 120 Days Past Due

150 150 Days Past Due 180 180 Days Past Due V Voluntary Surrender F Foreclosure C Collection Account

CO Charge-Off B Included in Bankruptcy R Repossession TN Too New to Rate No Data Available

EQUIFAX

Summary › Revolving › Mortgage › Installment › Other › Statements › Personal Info › Inquiries › Public Records › Collections

Account details

View detailed information about this account. Contact the creditor or lender if you have any questions about it.

High Credit	$5,728	**Owner**	INDIVIDUAL
Credit Limit	$10,000	**Account Type**	REVOLVING
Terms Frequency	MONTHLY	**Term Duration**	0
Balance	$47	**Date Opened**	Apr 21, 2010
Amount Past Due		**Date Reported**	Oct 12, 2017
Actual Payment Amount		**Date of Last Payment**	Sep 01, 2017
Date of Last Activity		**Scheduled Payment Amount**	$27
Months Reviewed	90	**Delinquency First Reported**	
Activity Designator		**Creditor Classification**	UNKNOWN
Deferred Payment Start Date		**Charge Off Amount**	
Balloon Payment Date		**Balloon Payment Amount**	
Loan Type	Credit Card	**Date Closed**	
Date of First Delinquency			

Comments

Contact
BARCLAYS BANK DELAWARE
PO Box 8803
Wilmington, DE 19899-8803
1-866-370-5931

Citicards CBNA (Closed)

Summary

Your debt-to-credit ratio represents the amount of credit you're using and generally makes up a percentage of your credit score. It's calculated by dividing an account's reported balance by its credit limit.

EQUIFAX
Summary | Revolving | Mortgage | Installment | Other | Statements | Personal Info | Inquiries | Public Records | Collections

Account Number		**Reported Balance**	$0
Account Status	PAYS_AS_AGREED	**Debt-to-Credit Ratio**	N/A
Available Credit			

The tables below show up to 2 years of the monthly balance, available credit, scheduled payment, date of last payment, high credit, credit limit, amount past due, activity designator, and comments.

Payment history

You currently do not have any Payment History in your file.

Account details

View detailed information about this account. Contact the creditor or lender if you have any questions about it.

High Credit	$0	**Owner**	INDIVIDUAL
Credit Limit		**Account Type**	REVOLVING
Terms Frequency	MONTHLY	**Term Duration**	0
Balance	$0	**Date Opened**	Oct 01, 2000
Amount Past Due		**Date Reported**	Dec 01, 2009
Actual Payment Amount		**Date of Last Payment**	
Date of Last Activity		**Scheduled Payment Amount**	
Months Reviewed	99	**Delinquency First Reported**	
Activity Designator	PAID_AND_CLOSED	**Creditor Classification**	UNKNOWN
Deferred Payment Start Date		**Charge Off Amount**	
Balloon Payment Date		**Balloon Payment Amount**	
Loan Type	Credit Card	**Date Closed**	Apr 01, 2009
Date of First Delinquency			

Comments
Account closed at consumer's request.

Contact
CITICARDS CBNA
PO Box 6241
Ibs Cdv Disputes
Sioux Falls, SD 57117-6241
1-800-950-5114

Bank of America (CLOSED)

Summary

Your debt-to-credit ratio represents the amount of credit you're using and generally makes up a percentage of your credit score. It's calculated by dividing an account's reported balance by its credit limit.

Account Number		**Reported Balance**	$0
Account Status	PAYS_AS_AGREED	**Debt-to-Credit Ratio**	0%
Available Credit	$13,500		

The tables below show up to 2 years of the monthly balance, available credit, scheduled payment, date of last payment, high credit, credit limit, amount past due, activity designator, and comments.

Payment history

You currently do not have any Payment History in your file.

Account details

View detailed information about this account. Contact the creditor or lender if you have any questions about it.

High Credit	$0	**Owner**	INDIVIDUAL
Credit Limit	$13,500	**Account Type**	REVOLVING
Terms Frequency	MONTHLY	**Term Duration**	0
Balance	$0	**Date Opened**	Dec 01, 2007
Amount Past Due		**Date Reported**	Oct 01, 2009
Actual Payment Amount		**Date of Last Payment**	

EQUIFAX
Summary › Revolving › Mortgage › Installment › Other › Statements › Personal Info › Inquiries › Public Records › Collections

Date of Last Activity		**Scheduled Payment Amount**	
Months Reviewed	22	**Delinquency First Reported**	
Activity Designator	CLOSED	**Creditor Classification**	UNKNOWN
Deferred Payment Start Date		**Charge Off Amount**	
Balloon Payment Date		**Balloon Payment Amount**	
Loan Type	Credit Card	**Date Closed**	Dec 01, 2007
Date of First Delinquency			

Comments

Account closed at consumer's request

Contact

Bank of America
PO Box 982238
El Paso, TX 79998-2238
1-800-421-2110

Mortgage accounts

Mortgage accounts are real estate loans that require payment on a monthly basis until the loan is paid off.

Bank of America

Summary

Your debt-to-credit ratio represents the amount of credit you're using and generally makes up a percentage of your credit score. It's calculated by dividing an account's reported balance by its credit limit.

Account Number		**Reported Balance**	$0
Account Status	PAYS_AS_AGREED	**Debt-to-Credit Ratio**	0%
Available Credit	$250,000		

The tables below show up to 2 years of the monthly balance, available credit, scheduled payment, date of last payment, high credit, credit limit, amount past due, activity designator, and comments.

Payment history

View up to 7 years of monthly payment history on this account. The numbers indicated in each month represent the number of days a payment was past due; the letters indicate other account events, such as bankruptcy or collections.

Year	Jan	Feb	Mar	Apr	May	Jun	Jul	Aug	Sep	Oct	Nov	Dec
2017	✓	✓	✓	✓	✓	✓	✓	✓	░	░	░	░
2016	✓	✓	✓	✓	✓	✓	✓	✓	✓	✓	✓	✓
2015	✓	✓	✓	✓	✓	✓	✓	✓	✓	✓	✓	✓
2014	░	░	░	░	░	░	░	░	░	░	✓	✓

✓ Paid on Time	30 30 Days Past Due	60 60 Days Past Due	90 90 Days Past Due	120 120 Days Past Due
150 150 Days Past Due	180 180 Days Past Due	V Voluntary Surrender	F Foreclosure	C Collection Account
CO Charge-Off	B Included in Bankruptcy	R Repossession	TN Too New to Rate	░ No Data Available

Account details

View detailed information about this account. Contact the creditor or lender if you have any questions about it.

EQUIFAX

Summary › Revolving › Mortgage › Installment › Other › Statements › Personal Info › Inquiries › Public Records › Collections

High Credit	$70,000	**Owner**	JOINT_ CONTRACTUAL_ LIABILITY
Credit Limit	$250,000	**Account Type**	MORTGAGE
Terms Frequency	MONTHLY	**Term Duration**	0
Balance	$0	**Date Opened**	Nov 15, 2014
Amount Past Due		**Date Reported**	Sep 30, 2017
Actual Payment Amount		**Date of Last Payment**	Jul 01, 2016
Date of Last Activity		**Scheduled Payment Amount**	
Months Reviewed	34	**Delinquency First Reported**	
Activity Designator		**Creditor Classification**	UNKNOWN
Deferred Payment Start Date		**Charge Off Amount**	
Balloon Payment Date		**Balloon Payment Amount**	
Loan Type		**Date Closed**	
Date of First Delinquency			

Comments

Contact
BANK OF AMERICA
4909 Savarese Cir Fl
19080147
Tampa, FL 33634-2413
1-800-669-6607

EQUIFAX
Summary Revolving Mortgage Installment Other Statements Personal Info Inquiries Public Records Collections

First Tennessee Bank (Closed)

Summary

Calculated by dividing an account's reported balance by its credit limit.

Account Number	xxxxxxxxx 3449	**Reported Balance**	$0
Account Status	PAYS_AS_AGREED	**Debt-to-Credit Ratio**	0%
Available Credit			

The tables below show up to 2 years of the monthly balance, available credit, scheduled payment, date of last payment, high credit, credit limit, amount past due, activity designator, and comments.

Payment history

You currently do not have any Payment History in your file.

Account details

View detailed information about this account. Contact the creditor or lender if you have any questions about it.

High Credit	$210,000	**Owner**	JOINT_ CONTRACTU LIABILITY
Credit Limit		**Account Type**	MORTGAGE
Terms Frequency	MONTHLY	**Term Duration**	360
Balance	$0	**Date Opened**	Nov 01, 2002
Amount Past Due		**Date Reported**	Feb 01, 2008
Actual Payment Amount		**Date of Last Payment**	Jan 01, 2008
Date of Last Activity		**Scheduled Payment Amount**	$1,529
Months Reviewed	61	**Delinquency First Reported**	
Activity Designator	TRANSFER_ OR_SOLD	**Creditor Classification**	UNKNOWN
Deferred Payment Start Date		**Charge Off Amount**	
Balloon Payment Date		**Balloon Payment Amount**	
Loan Type	Conventional Real Estate Mortgage	**Date Closed**	Feb 01, 2008
Date of First Delinquency			

EQUIFAX

Summary | Revolving | Mortgage | Installment | Other | Statements | Personal Info | Inquiries | Public Records | Collections

Comments
Fannie mae account

Contact
FIRST TENNESSEE BANK
Credit Inquiry Dept
Knoxville, TN 37995-1501

Wells Fargo Home Mortgage (Closed)

Summary

Calculated by dividing an account's reported balance by its credit limit.

Account Number	xxxxxxxxx 2661	**Reported Balance**	$0
Account Status	PAYS_AS_AGREED	**Debt-to-Credit Ratio**	0%
Available Credit			

The tables below show up to 2 years of the monthly balance, available credit, scheduled payment, date of last payment, high credit, credit limit, amount past due, activity designator, and comments.

Payment history

View up to 7 years of monthly payment history on this account. The numbers indicated in each month represent the number of days a payment was past due; the letters indicate other account events, such as bankruptcy or collections.

Year	Jan	Feb	Mar	Apr	May	Jun	Jul	Aug	Sep	Oct	Nov	Dec
2015	✓	✓										
2014	✓	✓	✓	✓	✓	✓	✓	✓	✓	✓	✓	✓
2013										✓	✓	✓
2012												
2011												

✓ Paid on Time | 30 30 Days Past Due | 60 60 Days Past Due | 90 90 Days Past Due | 120 120 Days Past Due
150 150 Days Past Due | 180 180 Days Past Due | V Voluntary Surrender | F Foreclosure | C Collection Account
CO Charge-Off | B Included in Bankruptcy | R Repossession | TN Too New to Rate | No Data Available

Account details

View detailed information about this account. Contact the creditor or lender if you have any questions about it.

High Credit	$210,000	**Owner**	JOINT_ CONTRACTUAL_ LIABILITY
Credit Limit		**Account Type**	MORTGAGE
Terms Frequency	MONTHLY	**Term Duration**	360
Balance	$0	**Date Opened**	Nov 06, 2002
Amount Past Due		**Date Reported**	Mar 09, 2015
Actual Payment Amount	$34,624	**Date of Last Payment**	Mar 01, 2015
Date of Last Activity		**Scheduled Payment Amount**	$1,624
Months Reviewed	83	**Delinquency First Reported**	
Activity Designator	PAID_AND_ CLOSED	**Creditor Classification**	UNKNOWN
Deferred Payment Start Date		**Charge Off Amount**	
Balloon Payment Date		**Balloon Payment Amount**	
Loan Type	Conventional Real Estate Mortgage	**Date Closed**	Mar 01, 2015
Date of First Delinquency			

Comments
Fannie mae account
Fixed rate

Contact
WELLS FARGO HOME MORTGAGE
PO Box 10335
Des Moines, IA 50306-0335
1-800-288-3212

EQUIFAX

Summary | Revolving | Mortgage | Installment | Other | Statements | Personal Info | Inquiries | Public Records | Collections

Bank of America (Closed)

Summary

Calculated by dividing an account's reported balance by its credit limit.

Account Number		**Reported Balance**	$0
Account Status	PAYS_AS_AGREED	**Debt-to-Credit Ratio**	0%
Available Credit	$115,600		

The tables below show up to 2 years of the monthly balance, available credit, scheduled payment, date of last payment, high credit, credit limit, amount past due, activity designator, and comments.

Payment history

View up to 7 years of monthly payment history on this account. The numbers indicated in each month represent the number of days a payment was past due; the letters indicate other account events, such as bankruptcy or collections.

Year	Jan	Feb	Mar	Apr	May	Jun	Jul	Aug	Sep	Oct	Nov	Dec
2014	✔	✔	✔	✔	✔	✔	✔	✔	✔	✔	✔	
2013										✔	✔	✔
2012												
2011												

✔ Paid on Time 30 30 Days Past Due 60 60 Days Past Due 90 90 Days Past Due 120 120 Days Past Due
150 150 Days Past Due 180 180 Days Past Due V Voluntary Surrender F Foreclosure C Collection Account
CO Charge-Off B Included in Bankruptcy R Repossession TN Too New to Rate No Data Available

Account details

View detailed information about this account. Contact the creditor or lender if you have any questions about it.

High Credit	$108,313	**Owner**	JOINT_ CONTRACTUAL_ LIABILITY
Credit Limit	$115,600	**Account Type**	MORTGAGE
Terms Frequency	MONTHLY	**Term Duration**	0

(Continued)

EQUIFAX

Balance	$0	**Date Opened**	Sep 01, 2005
Amount Past Due		**Date Reported**	Dec 31, 2014
Actual Payment Amount		**Date of Last Payment**	Nov 01, 2014
Date of Last Activity		**Scheduled Payment Amount**	
Months Reviewed	99	**Delinquency First Reported**	
Activity Designator	PAID_AND_CLOSED	**Creditor Classification**	UNKNOWN
Deferred Payment Start Date		**Charge Off Amount**	
Balloon Payment Date		**Balloon Payment Amount**	
Loan Type		**Date Closed**	Nov 01, 2014
Date of First Delinquency			

Comments
Account closed at consumer's request
Contact
BANK OF AMERICA

4909 Savarese Cir Fl 19080147
Tampa, FL 33634-2413
1-800-669-6607

Huntington Mortgage (Closed)

Summary

Calculated by dividing an account's reported balance by its credit limit.

Account Number	xxxxxxxxx 7353	**Reported Balance**	$0
Account Status	PAYS_AS_AGREED	**Debt-to-Credit Ratio**	0%
Available Credit			

The tables below show up to 2 years of the monthly balance, available credit, scheduled payment, date of last payment, high credit, credit limit, amount past due, activity designator, and comments.

EQUIFAX
Summary Revolving Mortgage Installment Other Statements Personal info Inquiries Public Records Collections

Payment history

You currently do not have any Payment History in your file.

Account details

View detailed information about this account. Contact the creditor or lender if you have any questions about it.

High Credit	$140,000	**Owner**	INDIVIDUAL
Credit Limit		**Account Type**	MORTGAGE
Terms Frequency	MONTHLY	**Term Duration**	360
Balance	$0	**Date Opened**	Jun 01, 2003
Amount Past Due		**Date Reported**	Apr 01, 2008
Actual Payment Amount		**Date of Last Payment**	Apr 01, 2008
Date of Last Activity		**Scheduled Payment Amount**	$795
Months Reviewed	56	**Delinquency First Reported**	
Activity Designator	PAID_AND_CLOSED	**Creditor Classification**	UNKNOWN
Deferred Payment Start Date		**Charge Off Amount**	
Balloon Payment Date		**Balloon Payment Amount**	
Loan Type	Conventional Real Estate Mortgage	**Date Closed**	
Date of First Delinquency			

Comments

Contact
HUNTINGTON MORTGATE
PO Box 1558
Dept EA4W25
Columbus, OH 43216-1558
1-800-480-2265

EQUIFAX
Summary Revolving Mortgage Installment Other Statements Personal Info Inquiries Public Records Collections

Installment accounts

Installment accounts are loans that require payment on a monthly basis until the loan is paid off, such as auto or student loans.

Ford Motor Credit Co. (Closed)

Summary

Your debt-to-credit ratio represents the amount of credit you're using and generally makes up a percentage of your credit score. It's calculated by dividing an account's reported balance by its credit limit.

Account Number	xxxxxx 06	**Reported Balance**	$0
Account Status	PAYS_AS_AGREED	**Debt-to-Credit Ratio**	0%
Available Credit			

The tables below show up to 2 years of the monthly balance, available credit, scheduled payment, date of last payment, high credit, credit limit, amount past due, activity designator, and comments.

Payment history

You currently do not have any Payment History in your file.

Account details

View detailed information about this account. Contact the creditor or lender if you have any questions about it.

High Credit	$7,500	**Owner**	JOINT_ CONTRACTUAL_ LIABILITY
Credit Limit		**Account Type**	INSTALLMENT
Terms Frequency	MONTHLY	**Term Duration**	36
Balance	$0	**Date Opened**	Jun 01, 2009
Amount Past Due		**Date Reported**	Mar 01, 2010
Actual Payment Amount	$6,273	**Date of Last Payment**	Mar 01, 2010

Date of Last Activity		**Scheduled Payment Amount**	$236
Months Reviewed	9	**Delinquency First Reported**	
Activity Designator	PAID_AND_CLOSED	**Creditor Classification**	UNKNOWN
Deferred Payment Start Date		**Charge Off Amount**	
Balloon Payment Date		**Balloon Payment Amount**	
Loan Type	Auto	**Date Closed**	Mar 01, 2010
Date of First Delinquency			

Comments	Contact
	FORD MOTOR CREDIT CO. PO Box 542000 Omaha, NE 68154-8000 1-800-727-7000

Summary Revolving Mortgage Installment Other Statements Personal Info Inquiries Public Records Collections

Other accounts

Other accounts are those that are not already identified as Revolving, Mortgage or Installment Accounts such as child support obligations or rental agreements.

You currently do not have any Other Accounts in your file.

Summary Revolving Mortgage Installment Other Statements Personal Info Inquiries Public Records Collections

Consumer statements

Consumer Statements are explanations of up to 100 words (200 words if you live in Maine) you can attach to your credit file to provide more information on an item you may disagree with or would like to provide details on. Consumer statements are voluntary and have no impact on your credit score.

You currently do not have any Consumer Statements in your file.

Personal information

Creditors use your personal information primarily to identify you. This information has no impact on your credit score.

Identification

Identification is the information in your credit file that indicates your current identification as reported to Equifax. It does not affect your credit score or rating.

Name	ERIC L ROSENBLATT
Formerly known as	
Social Security Number	xxxxx 4712
Age or Date of Birth	May 13, 1956

Other identification

You currently do not have any Other Identifications in your file.

Alert contact information

You currently do not have any Alert Contacts in your file.

Contact information

Contact information is the information in your credit file that indicates your former and current addresses as reported to Equifax. It does not affect your credit score or rating.

Address	Status	Date Reported
16517 KEATS TER DERWOOD, MD 20855	Current	Oct 23, 2017
10945 BUCKNELL DR WHEATON, MD 20902	Former	Jul 14, 2015
8040 NEEDWOOD RD APT 102 DERWOOD, MD 20855	Former	Jan 08, 2015
4250 CONNECTICUT AVE NW WASHINGTON, DC 20008	Former	Oct 01, 2009

Employment history

Employment history is the information in your credit file that indicates your current and former employment as reported to Equifax. It does not affect your credit score or rating.

Company	Occupation	Start Date	Status	Address
			Current	
	ECONOMIST		Previous	
CITY FEDERAL SAVINGS			Previous	PARSPPNY, NJ

Summary Revolving Mortgage Installment Other Statements Personal Info Inquiries Public Records Collections

Inquiries

A request for your credit history is called an inquiry. There are two types of inquiries - those that may impact your credit rating/score and those that do not.

Hard inquiries

Inquiries that may impact your credit rating/score

These are inquiries made by companies with whom you have applied for a loan or credit. They may remain on your file up to 2 years.

You currently do not have any Hard Inquiries in your file.

Soft inquiries

Inquiries that do not impact your credit rating/score

These are inquiries, for example, from companies making promotional offers of credit, periodic account reviews by an existing creditor or your own requests to check your credit file. They may remain on your file for up to 2 years.

Date	Company	Description
Apr 03, 2016	EQUIFAX	Credit Report

Public records

This section includes public record items Equifax obtained from local, state and federal courts through a third party vendor, LexisNexis. They can be contacted at: www.equifaxconsumers.lexisnexis.com

LexisNexis Consumer Center

P.O. Box 105615 Atlanta, GA 30348-5108

Bankruptcies

Bankruptcies are a legal status granted by a federal court that indicates you are unable to pay off outstanding debt. Bankruptcies stay on your credit report for up to 10 years, depending on the chapter of bankruptcy you file for. They generally have a negative impact on your credit score.

You currently do not have any Bankruptcies in your file.

Judgments

Judgments are a legal status granted by a court that indicates you must pay back an outstanding debt. Judgments stay on your credit report up to 7 years from the date filed and generally have a negative impact on your credit score.

You currently do not have any Judgments in your file.

Liens

A lien is a legal claim on an asset, and Equifax only collects tax related liens. Liens stay on your credit report up to 10 years and generally have a negative impact on your credit score.

You currently do not have any Liens in your file.

Summary > Revolving > Mortgage > Installment > Other > Statements > Personal Info > Inquiries > Public Records > Collections

Collections

Collections are accounts with outstanding debt that have been placed by a creditor with a collection agency. Collections stay on your credit report for up to 7 years from the date the account first became past due. They generally have a negative impact on your credit score.

You currently do not have any Collections in your file.

Summary Revolving Mortgage Installment Other Statements Personal Info Inquiries Public Records Collections

Dispute file information

If you believe that any of the information found on this report is incorrect, there are 3 ways to launch an investigation about the information in this report.

When you file a dispute, the credit bureau you contact is required to investigate your dispute within 30 days. They will not remove accurate data unless it is outdated or cannot be verified.

To initiate a dispute online please visit www.ai.equifax.com

To check the status or view the results of your dispute please visit www.ai.equifax.com

APPENDIX 4

A summary of your rights under the Fair Credit Reporting Act

The federal Fair Credit Reporting Act (FCRA) promotes the accuracy, fairness, and privacy of information in the files of consumer reporting agencies. There are many types of consumer reporting agencies, including credit bureaus and specialty agencies (such as agencies that sell information about check writing histories, medical records, and rental history records). Here is a summary of your major rights under the FCRA.

For more information, including information about additional rights, go to www.consumerfinance.gov/learnmore **or write to: Consumer Financial Protection Bureau, 1700 G Street N.W., Washington, DC 20552.**

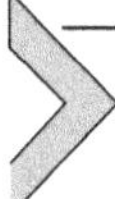

You must be told if information in your file has been used against you

Anyone who uses a Credit Report or another type of Consumer Report to deny your application for credit, insurance, or employment - or to take another adverse action against you - must tell you, and must give you the name, address, and phone number of the agency that provided the information.

You have the right to know what is in your file

You may request and obtain all the information about you in the files of a consumer reporting agency (your "file disclosure"). You will be required to provide proper identification, which may include your Social Security number. In many cases, the disclosure will be free. You are entitled to a free file disclosure if:

- a person has taken adverse action against you because of information in your credit file; - you are the victim of identity theft and place a fraud alert in your file;
- your file contains inaccurate information as aresult of fraud;
- you are on public assistance;
- you are unemployed but expect to apply foremployment within 60 days.

In addition, all consumers are entitled to one free disclosure every 12 months upon request from each nationwide credit bureau and from nationwide specialty consumer reporting agencies. See www.consumerfinance.gov/learnmore for additional information.

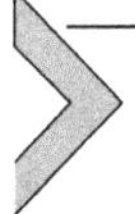

You have the right to ask for a credit score

Credit scores are numerical summaries of your credit-worthiness based on information from credit bureaus. You may request a credit score from consumer reporting agencies that create scores or distribute scores used in residential real property loans, but you will have to pay for it. In some mortgage transactions, you will receive credit score information for free from the mortgage lender.

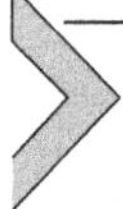

You have the right to dispute incomplete or inaccurate information

If you identify information in your file that is incomplete or inaccurate, and file it to the consumer reporting agency, the agency must investigate unless your dispute is frivolous. See www.consumerfinance.gov/learnmore for an explanation of dispute procedures.

Consumer reporting agencies must correct or delete inaccurate, incomplete, or unverifiable information

Inaccurate, incomplete or unverifiable information must be removed or corrected, usually within 30 days. However, a consumer reporting agency may continue to file information it has verified as accurate.

Consumer reporting agencies may not report outdated negative information

In most cases, a consumer reporting agency may not report negative information that is more than seven years old, or bankruptcies that are more than 10 years old.

Access to your file is limited

A consumer reporting agency may provide information about you only to people with a valid need – usually to consider an application with a creditor, insurer, employer, landlord, or other business. The FCRA specifies those with a valid need for access.

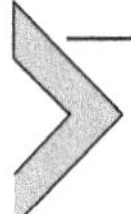

You must give your consent for reports to be provided to employers

A consumer reporting agency may not give out information about you to your employer, or a potential employer, without your written consent given to the employer. Written consent generally is not required in the trucking industry. For more information, go to www.consumerfinance.gov/learnmore.

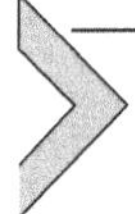

You may limit "prescreened" offers of credit and insurance you get based on information in your credit file

Unsolicited "prescreened" offers for credit and insurance must include a toll-free phone number you can call if you choose to remove your name and address from the lists these offers are based on. You may opt-out with the nationwide credit bureaus at 1-888-5OPTOUT (1-888-567-8688).

You may seek damages from violators

If a consumer reporting agency, or, in some cases, a user of consumer reports or a furnisher of information to a consumer reporting agency violates the FCRA, you may be able to sue in state or federal court. Identity theft victims and active duty military personnel have additional rights. For more information, visit www.consumerfinance.gov/learnmore.

States may enforce the FCRA, and many states have their own consumer reporting laws. In some cases, you may have more rights under state law. For more information, contact your state or local consumer protection agency or your state Attorney General. Federal enforcers are:

1a. Banks, savings associations, and credit unions with total assets of over $10 billion and their affiliates.
Contact
Bureau of Consumer Financial Protection
1700 G Street NW
Washington, DC 20552

1b. Such affiliates that are not banks, savings associations, or credit unions also should list, in addition to the CFPB
Contact
Federal Trade Commission: Consumer Response Center - FCRA
Washington, DC 20580 (877) 382-4357

2a. To the extent not included in item 1 above: a. National banks, federal savings associations, and federal branches and federal agencies of foreign bank
Contact
Office of the Comptroller of the Currency Customer Assistance Group
1301 McKinney Street, Suite 3450
Houston, TX 77010-9050

2b. State member banks, branches and agencies of foreign banks (other than federal branches, federal agencies, and insured state branches of foreign banks), commercial lending companies owned or controlled by foreign banks, and organizations operating under section 25 or 25A of the Federal Reserve Act
Contact
Federal Reserve Consumer Help Center
P.O. Box 1200
Minneapolis, MN 55480

2c. Nonmember Insured Banks, Insured State Branches of Foreign Banks, and insured state savings associations
Contact
FDIC Consumer Response Center
1100 Walnut Street, Box #11
Kansas City, MO 64106

2d. Federal Credit Unions
Contact
National Credit Union Administration Office of Consumer Protection (OCP) Division of Consumer Compliance and Outreach (DCCO) 1775 Duke Street
Alexandria, VA 22314

---

3. Air carriers
Contact
Asst. General Counsel for Aviation Enforcement & Proceedings
Aviation Consumer Protection Division Department of Transportation
1200 New Jersey Avenue, SE
Washington, DC 20590

4. Creditors Subject to Surface Transportation Board
Contact
Office of Proceedings, Surface Transportation Board Department of Transportation 395 E Street, SW
Washington, DC 20423

5. Creditors Subject to Packers and Stockyards Act, 1921
Contact
Nearest Packers and Stockyards Administration area supervisor

6. Small Business Investment Companies
Contact
Associate Deputy Administrator for Capital Access United States Small Business Administration 409 Third Street, SW, 8th Floor
Washington, DC 20416

7. Brokers and Dealers
Contact
Securities and Exchange Commission
100 F Street NE
Washington, DC 20549

8a. Federal Land Banks, Federal Land Bank Associations, Federal Intermediate Credit Banks, and Production Credit Associations
Contact
Farm Credit Administration
1501 Farm Credit Drive
McLean, VA 22102-5090

8b. Retailers, Finance Companies, and All Other Creditors Not Listed Above Contact
FTC Regional Office for region in which the creditor operates or Federal Trade Commission: Consumer Response Center - FCRA Washington, DC 20580 (877) 382-4357

APPENDIX 5

Your rights under State law

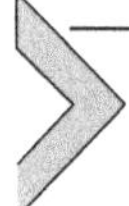

Statement of Rights of the Consumer - Annotated Code of Maryland Commercial Law Article (141201, et seq.)

As a resident of the State of Maryland, you have the following rights as a consumer under the laws of the State of Maryland relating to consumer credit information.

You have the right to request, in writing, that a consumer reporting agency restrict the sale or other transfer of information in your credit file to:

1. A mail-service organization;
2. A marketing firm; or
3. Any other similar organization that obtains information about a consumer for marketing purposes.

You have a right, upon request and proper identification, to receive from a consumer reporting agency an exact copy of any credit file on you, including a written explanation of codes or trade language used in the report.

You have a right to receive disclosure of information in your credit file during normal business hours:

- In person, upon furnishing proper identification.
- By telephone, if you make written request with proper identification, and toll charges, if any, are charged to you.
- In writing, if you make written request and furnish proper identification.

You may be accompanied by one other person of your choosing, who must furnish reasonable identification, and the consumer reporting agency may require a written statement from you granting permission to discuss your credit information in this person's presence.

You have a right to dispute the completeness or accuracy of any item of information contained in your credit file, and if you convey the dispute in writing, the consumer reporting agency will, within 30 days, reinvestigate and record the current status of that information, unless it has reasonable grounds to believe that the dispute is frivolous or irrelevant.

If, after reinvestigation, the information you disputed is found to be inaccurate or cannot be verified, the consumer reporting agency will delete the information and mail to you a written notice of the correction and will also mail to each person to whom the erroneous information was furnished written notice of the correction. You will also be sent a written notice if the information you disputed is found to be accurate or is verified.

You will not be charged for our handling of the information you dispute, nor for the corrected reports resulting from our handling.

You have 60 days after receiving notice of correction or other findings to request in writing that the consumer reporting agency furnish you with the name, address, telephone number of each creditor contacted during its reinvestigation, and it will provide this information to you within 30 days after receiving your request.

If the reinvestigation does not resolve your dispute, you may file with the consumer reporting agency a brief statement of not more that 100 words, setting forth the nature of your dispute. This statement will be placed on your credit file, and in any subsequent report containing the information you dispute, it will be clearly noted that the information has been disputed by you, and your statement or a clear and accurate summary of it will be provided with that report.

Following deletion of any information you disputed that is found to be inaccurate or could not be verified, at your request, the consumer reporting agency will furnish notification of the information deleted or your statement, or statement summary, to any person you designate who has received your report within the past two years for employment purposes, or within the past one year for any other purpose.

Your Commissioner of Financial Regulation is Sarah Bloom Raskin. In the event you wish to file a complaint, please write or call the Office of the Commissioner of Financial Regulation, Complaint Unit, 500 N. Calvert Street, Suite 402, Baltimore, MD 21202; telephone number is (410) 230–6097. In addition to the rights above, you are entitled to request a copy of your file free of charge, one time within a twelve month period, and thereafter for a $5.00 charge each time.

State Of Maryland - Notice to Consumers

You have a right, under Section 14-1212.1 of the Commercial Law Article of the Annotated Code of Maryland, to place a security freeze on your credit report. The security freeze will prohibit a consumer reporting agency from releasing your credit report or any information derived from your credit report without your express authorization. The purpose of a security freeze is to prevent credit, loans, and services from being approved in your name without your consent.

You may elect to have a consumer reporting agency place a security freeze on your credit report by written request sent by certified mail or by electronic mail or the internet if the consumer reporting agency provides a secure electronic connection. The consumer reporting agency must place a security freeze on your credit report within 3 business days after your request is received. Within 5 business days after a security freeze is placed on your credit report, you will be provided with a unique personal identification number or password to use if you want to remove the security freeze or temporarily lift the security freeze to release your credit report to a specific person or for a specific period of time. You also will receive information on the procedures for removing or temporarily lifting a security freeze.

If you want to temporarily lift the security freeze on your credit report, you must contact the consumer reporting agency and provide all of the following:

A consumer reporting agency must comply with a request to temporarily lift a security freeze on a credit report within 3 business days after the request is received or within 15 minutes for certain requests. A consumer reporting agency must comply with a request to remove a security freeze on a credit report within 3 business days after the request is received.

If you are actively seeking credit, you should be aware that the procedures involved in lifting a security freeze may slow your own applications for credit. You should plan ahead and lift a security freeze, either completely if you are seeking credit from a number of sources, or just for a specific creditor if you are applying only to that creditor, a few days before actually applying for new credit.

A consumer reporting agency may charge a reasonable fee not exceeding $5 for each placement, temporary lift, or removal of a security freeze. However, a consumer reporting agency may not charge any fee to a consumer who, at the time of a request to place, temporary lift, or remove a security freeze, presents to the consumer reporting agency a police report of alleged identity fraud against the consumer or an identity theft passport.

A security freeze does not apply if you have an existing account relationship and a copy of your credit report is requested by your existing creditor or its agents or affiliates for certain types of account review, collection, fraud control, or similar activities.

Note: In accordance with Maryland law, temporary lifting of a security freeze on a minor's or protected person's credit report is not permitted.

To place a security freeze on your Equifax credit report, send your request via certified mail to:

Equifax Security Freeze
P.O. Box 105788
Atlanta, GA 30348

Or, you may contact us on the web at equifax.com or call 800-685-1111.

The fee to place a security freeze is $5.00. If you are a victim of identity theft and you submit a copy of a valid police report of alleged identity fraud or an identity theft passport, no fee will be charged. Include your complete name, complete address, social security number, date of birth and payment, if applicable.

Written confirmation of the security freeze will be sent within 5 business days of receipt of the request via first class mail. It will include your unique personal identification number and instructions for removing the security freeze or authorizing the release of your credit report for a specific party or period of time.

Index

Note: 'Page numbers followed by "*f*" indicate figures and "*t*" indicate tables'.

E

F

G

O

P

R

S

Printed in the United States
By Bookmasters